VIKING
CANADA

Harperland

Also by Lawrence Martin

Iron Man: The Defiant Reign of Jean Chrétien
Chrétien: The Will to Win
Harry Thode (co-author)
The Antagonist: Lucien Bouchard and the Politics of Delusion
Mario: A Biography of Mario Lemieux
The Red Machine: The Soviet Quest to Dominate Canada's Game
Behind the Red Line: An American Hockey Player in Russia
(co-author)
Breaking with History: The Gorbachev Revolution
Pledge of Allegiance
The Presidents and the Prime Ministers

LAWRENCE
MARTIN

Harperland

*The Politics
of Control*

VIKING
CANADA

VIKING CANADA

Published by the Penguin Group

Penguin Group (Canada), 90 Eglinton Avenue East, Suite 700,
Toronto, Ontario, Canada M4P 2Y3
(a division of Pearson Canada Inc.)

Penguin Group (USA) Inc., 375 Hudson Street, New York, New York 10014, U.S.A.
Penguin Books Ltd, 80 Strand, London WC2R 0RL, England
Penguin Ireland, 25 St Stephen's Green, Dublin 2, Ireland (a division of Penguin Books Ltd)
Penguin Group (Australia), 250 Camberwell Road, Camberwell, Victoria 3124, Australia
(a division of Pearson Australia Group Pty Ltd)
Penguin Books India Pvt Ltd, 11 Community Centre, Panchsheel Park,
New Delhi – 110 017, India
Penguin Group (NZ), 67 Apollo Drive, Rosedale, North Shore 0745, Auckland, New Zealand
(a division of Pearson New Zealand Ltd)
Penguin Books (South Africa) (Pty) Ltd, 24 Sturdee Avenue, Rosebank,
Johannesburg 2196, South Africa

Penguin Books Ltd, Registered Offices: 80 Strand, London WC2R 0RL, England

First published 2010

1 2 3 4 5 6 7 8 9 10

Manufactured in the U.S.A.

LIBRARY AND ARCHIVES CANADA CATALOGUING IN PUBLICATION

Martin, Lawrence, 1947–
Harperland : the politics of control / Lawrence Martin.

ISBN 978-0-670-06517-2

1. Harper, Stephen, 1959-. 2. Executive power--Canada.
3. Canada--Politics and government--2006-. I. Title.

FC640.M27 2010   971.07'3   C2010-903065-

Visit the Penguin Group (Canada) website at **www.penguin.ca**

Special and corporate bulk purchase rates available; please see
www.penguin.ca/corporatesales or call 1-800-810-3104, ext. 2477 or 2474

In memory of Alfred Martin
The father of the team
1914–2004

CONTENTS

AUTHOR'S NOTE

Stephen Harper could be gone in a few months or he could be prime minister for another ten or fifteen years. While it's obviously better to view the record when his stewardship is completed, he is too important a force to await the final reckoning before putting pen to book. In four and a half years his impact on the country has been profound.

With *Harperland* I wanted to chronicle the events of these years—to bring the story together so as to provide readers with a better overview than they might get from the episodic renderings of the daily press. A major focus of the book is on the exercise of power—the politics of control, as the subtitle says. In just a few years, Stephen Harper came to amass executive power and dominate Ottawa in a way few, if any, other prime ministers have. Much of my research has concentrated on the work of the prime minister's office, the lead players there, because this, not cabinet, is where the critical decisions were and are made.

The PMO players are largely unknown to the public because most of them are off limits to the media. For this book, many who worked in the PMO in Harper's first two or three years gave on-the-record interviews while some spoke on background.

While the book delves into policy developments, exploring the thinking behind initiatives, any comprehensive policy analysis for the Harper years must await further studies. Issues like the economy,

Afghanistan, the environment, and foreign policy merit books on their own.

One of the most controversial aspects of the Harper story involves his authoritarian methods. As a journalist during Jean Chrétien's years in power, I spent a good deal of time—much to the delight of conservatives—exploring abuse of power under the Liberals. That experience has helped shape my perspective in assessing what the Harper Conservatives have done in this regard.

I wish to thank all those who provided their time for interviews and any other assistance for this book. My thanks also to the staff at Penguin, in particular non-fiction editor Diane Turbide and editors Karen Alliston and Janice Weaver. Huge thanks to my wife Maureen for her unflagging good cheer in abiding the twelve-hour work days and to our spectacular daughters Katie and Kristina for their support from afar. My time spent covering Parliament Hill as a *Globe and Mail* columnist was obviously very helpful in writing the book and I am grateful to the editors of the paper for their toleration of my labours.

Mistakes, authors like to say, are inevitable. They shouldn't be, but it's a convenient rationale. I hope I wasn't taken for a ride too many times and that in pulling together some of the strands of the story of the last four years, the public will have a better idea of how our democracy is evolving and devolving.

Lawrence Martin
Ottawa, August 2010

CHAPTER ONE

A Different Conservative

"Tonight, my friends, our great country has voted for change." The first words from Stephen Harper on election night 2006 were spoken with an exuberance not common to him. His customary blank look, which hid a resourceful intellect, was gone. His melancholy eyes turned luminous for the moment. Never one for lofty rhetoric, he stuck to a banal message, the cliché frequently trotted out by election victors: Change, my friends, it's all about change. In this case however they were words that Canadians would have been well advised to heed.

On this day, while there was no palpable sense of a dramatic turn, voters had conferred power on a decidedly different party, a substantively different man, a long-excluded region. In making Stephen Harper Canada's twenty-second prime minister, they had ventured—arguably for the first time in their history—outside the mainstream, beyond the broad middle of the political spectrum where the country's consensus resided.

They were gambling on a leader from the conservative hardlands, one who had been a founding member of a party, Reform, that not so long before was seen as a threat to the Canadian way. Third parties, whether on the left or the right, had been around through most of the nation's history, but Canadians, a cautious lot in selecting their governments, had always kept them on the periphery of power.

Harper had been made well aware of this during his time at Reform and as leader of its successor formation, the Alliance Party. These parties had the image—an image that stirred the wrath of Harper—of being home to counterclockwise thinkers who could use some central Canadian sophistication. Voters east of Manitoba flatly rejected them.

But he found a way around the barrier. In December 2003, his Alliance Party amalgamated with the more traditional Progressive Conservatives, giving it credibility as part of a big-tent political formation.

The merger was a ruse of sorts. This was no equal partnership. The merged party had five times as many Alliance MPs as old Tory ones. In the election before this merger, the Alliance Party had won sixty-six seats, the Tories only twelve. Before long, Harper won the leadership of the new party, making the domination of the Reform–Alliance wing even more pronounced. This wasn't so much a merger as the Alliance Party's annexing of an auxiliary group.

Viewing what was transpiring, members of the old Tory Party—members like Scott Brison—could see that the deck was stacked against them. Shortly before the merger was signed, Harper had invited Brison to his Stornoway residence, where he told him he liked his thinking on economics and wanted him to play an important role in the new party. When Brison raised the issue of gay rights, it became clear to him which of the two parties would be running things. Harper told him that social conservatism was a large part of his support base and was here to stay. A short time later, Brison, who appreciated Harper's frankness, crossed the floor to the Liberals.

He knew that the days of the old Tories were numbered, and that the choice for Canadian voters was no longer the same. The country's political culture was shifting. Some were comfortable calling these new Conservatives by the old Tory name, but this was hardly the party of John A. Macdonald, Robert Borden, John Diefenbaker, or Brian Mulroney. This Prairie-driven breed was more hard-edged on questions of law and order, a strong military, social conservatism. They believed more in survival of the fittest than they did in big government and they saw the world in the context of a clash of civilizations.

These were orthodoxies that could be altered by Harper, a politician capable of pragmatic compromise to fit the political climate. But the instincts were in place, and if given the opportunity, they would be exhibited.

In place also among this breed of new conservative was a different temperament. It was an attitude not readily found in the traditional Canadian middle-of-the-road parties, but more common to a strain of American Republicans. It was a current of bitterness, an anger born of a sense of exclusion.

David Emerson, the former British Columbia MP, had the rare opportunity of serving in the cabinets of both Paul Martin and Stephen Harper, and was thus well positioned to see the contrasts. He found the Harper operation so efficient, so disciplined compared to the scattershot Liberals of Paul Martin. But he couldn't fathom the intense level of acrimony. He had never seen this kind of thing with the Liberals. But with Harper and his men, it was woven deep. Emerson spoke of them as "viscerally hating their political opposition. Sometimes it was just startling to me."

Liberal MP Keith Martin, who also served in both parties, standing as a candidate for the Alliance leadership in 2000, found the same as Emerson—politicians who had been in an environment "that has bred a hatred" towards the traditional Liberal way. Because of the pronounced influence of religion in the party, he found it strange. He understood that Liberals had positions that ran counter to their own. "But why do they hate them?"

Ian Brodie, the former academic who served as Harper's chief of staff, believed the malice had its roots in decades of Liberal condescension towards Westerners: "Jean Chrétien consistently treated conservatives as if we were un-Canadian." Harper, said Brodie, took clear note of this, and the anger deepened. "Does he hate Liberals?" Brodie asked. "Some of them." He referenced an occasion in the 2000 federal election campaign when Chrétien intimated that Westerners were not his type of people. "Chrétien repeatedly said he didn't like dealing with people from Alberta. I think that stung [Harper] pretty badly."

There were scores that had to be settled. And although Harper was actually, Brodie contended, more of a unifier than a divider, he was well capable of settling scores. He could be, his top aide said, a "sonofabitch."

Harper cut his teeth in the hothouse of the Reform movement, recalled Rod Love, the Tory political strategist and long-time adviser to Ralph Klein. The branding of Reformers by Liberals as "unbalanced populist crazy men" was something Harper just couldn't get over. "Others got over it," said Love. "Harper? It was just burned in his psyche. So when he came to power, it was payback time. This wasn't just about going after someone in the Commons in the day, then going out for a beer at night. This was about destruction."

The degree of resentment gave Harper a motivation, a relentless single-minded passion to succeed and a willingness to go places where other leaders would fear to tread. Jean Chrétien also used a sense of belittlement to fuel his drive from the streets of Shawinigan to the top. In his case, it was his sense that he was viewed by the Quebec intelligentsia as a small-town peasant. He was desperate to prove them wrong—and he did so. But now things had taken a strange turn. The perceived condescension by Chrétien and by his own party set the basis for the rise of the right and the rise of Stephen Harper.

Since the late 1950s, for an entire half century, the Liberals' attitude to the West had been one of benign and not so benign neglect. The Grits decided after the Diefenbaker sweep in the election of 1958 to basically write off that region of the country, to bank on the big tides in Ontario and Quebec to sustain them. "We suffer from what I would call a lack of sympathy for the Prairie approach to life, a lack of identification," observed Allan MacEachen, a Maritime Liberal and cabinet minister under Pierre Trudeau. "In our efforts to rebuild the party after the 1958 defeat, we concentrated on Quebec and Ontario. The West became an afterthought." MacEachen made that statement in a speech he gave in Winnipeg in 1966. At that time, the story of the neglect had barely begun. The National Energy Program and other manifestations of that condescension were still to come.

In his election victory speech Harper noted the shift in the geographic dynamic, announcing with delight that the West was finally in. But more than the West was in. The hard right of the Conservative Party, for the first time in the country's history, was in. An ideological man bearing an unusual depth of animosity—"hatred," as colleagues described it—towards the Canadian liberal tradition was in.

This was a leader who came with an extraordinary political skill set as well. Harper combined the traits of two Liberal leaders he had watched with aversion. He combined Pierre Trudeau's imperious intellectual strengths with Jean Chrétien's bare-knuckled toughness, but had neither man's charms. He was single-minded and, as anyone who ever worked near Harper could attest, he had a ravenous hunger for control. He was methodical, deliberate, and puritanically disciplined. Gerry Nicholls, who spent several years with Harper at the National Citizens Coalition, described him as "an emotionless robot," the dispassion leavened occasionally by a crisp sense of humour.

During the election campaign a sense of apprehension set in. Harper feared Canadians were catching on, becoming worried that there were radicals at the gate, that the country was at a parting of the

ways. It prompted him to speak out in an unusual fashion. He tried
to reassure voters that he was not a threat, that the system could not
be radically altered. "The reality is that we will have for some time to
come," Harper said, "a Liberal Senate, a Liberal civil service … and
courts that have been appointed by the Liberals. So these are obviously checks on the power of a Conservative government."

Instead of having a calming effect, his statement did the opposite,
vaulting the subject into the headlines. But it was fitting that it was
highlighted because, as those in his camp knew, Harper's purpose
was indeed to change the Canadian way. Keith Beardsley, one of his
senior advisers, had been around long enough to understand his
warlord's battle plan. "He hates the Liberal Party," Beardsley said,
"and I would say his aim from day one—and I don't think anyone
would disagree—was to break the brand. The long-term strategy, that
was it."

The plan was to turn the juggernaut into a tugboat. The Harper
challenge, as Beardsley put it, was to the Liberal order. But it was
no small task the new prime minister had set for himself. Given that
party's domination of the power structure through time, the Liberal
order and the Canadian order were almost one and the same. To take
down one was to take down the other.

CHAPTER TWO

The Luck of the Draw

Sometimes the gods smile on a politician, sometimes they turn away. More so than the best-made plans, it is often the bends of fortune that change the history of man and country.

How improbable was it that after retiring from political life in 1979 with no historic achievement, Pierre Trudeau would be ushered back to power to give the country the Charter of Rights and Freedoms? Only an intervention of the gods—*deus ex machina*—could do it. In this case, the Tories of Joe Clark miraculously squandered their minority government because they couldn't count votes. The Northern Magus was back in business.

How many fewer majorities would Jean Chrétien have won if the Tory Party in 1993 had not dissolved itself into a dew, staging the biggest collapse of any party in the country's history? A decade-long division of the right into two warring factions ensued. The little warrior from Shawinigan breezed into the history books.

By age forty, Stephen Harper was heading up a small right-wing lobby group of no particular consequence called the National Citizens Coalition. Harper had quit as an MP, had burned bridges, had little in the way of a political support network, peanuts for financial resources, and if he had anything resembling personal allure, few had noticed. "People believe Harper's cold," observed the old Tory,

John Crosbie. "And he is cold. He doesn't have human warmth. He's not able to even work a room." Work a room? said Rod Love. "You've got to be kidding. Harper could never work a room. Trying to watch him work a room was just painful. The guy was hopeless."

The thought of this brainy, sunless figure of the hard right becoming prime minister within a few years, barring some unimaginable developments—*a deus ex machina* or several of them— was not to be taken seriously.

The unlikely developments, a striking run of fortune, would begin in 2002. Before that time, Harper demonstrated character traits that showed him more inclined to receding than leading. Not many politicians make their way by acts of disengagement. But such was the penchant of the young and suspicious man.

In 1978, he graduated at the top of his class from a suburban Toronto high school and enrolled at the University of Toronto, where he was expected to excel. That's when he made his first surprise retreat. He had hardly got there before he dropped out and moved to Alberta to take a low-level job, courtesy of his uncle's help, in the mailroom at Imperial Oil.

After three years with that company, he left and returned to school at the University of Calgary. Goldy Hyder, a long-time Tory strategist and lobbyist, was a student there at the same time. He found Harper brilliant but aloof. "If there was a social event going on, he'd be the guy in the corner, pen and paper in pocket, looking at us in a kind of condescending way," Hyder recalled. "It was like 'Those kids! There they are, drinking again.'"

Once he'd earned his economics degree, the young Harper, enthused by Brian Mulroney's mountainous majority win in 1984, set off for Ottawa to work for Jim Hawkes, a Progressive Conservative MP from Calgary. He spent a year there—a year during which, Hawkes noted, he did not appear to make a single friend.

Dismayed with the Mulroney Tories, Harper retreated again. Back in Calgary, he got in on the ground floor with the ascendant Reform Party, becoming the author of its policy book. He decided in the 1988 election to challenge for a seat in the House of Commons—the very one owned by Jim Hawkes. The chutzpah displayed by that decision raised eyebrows, but Hawkes easily retained his seat.

Harper then dug in with Reform. He became a close associate of a University of Calgary professor of political science, Tom Flanagan, who was fast becoming one of the party's superior strategic voices. Flanagan saw something special in Harper right away. "I found him persuasive, almost mesmerizing," he recalled. "For one so young—thirty-three at the time—he combined a remarkably wide knowledge of politics with a keen strategic mind."

In 1993, Harper ran for Reform against Hawkes again—this time defeating him. In the Commons, he quickly impressed. He had a rigorous intellect and a way of crystallizing thoughts that marked him as a player to watch. But he soon collided with Preston Manning, the party leader, publicly accusing him of expense account abuses. The party had internal mechanisms for handling such infractions, and Manning was stung by Harper's effrontery in making his accusations public. Though his charges were credible, it was not something a team player was supposed to do. Harper had taken on Hawkes and now Manning, both of whom had helped him in the past. Some saw unbridled ambition, but others, like his friend John Weissenberger, saw a commitment to principle. Reform Party members were supposed to be different. No feathering of nests. Harper, said Weissenberger, "knew about this situation with Preston for quite a while. And it wasn't an easy thing for him to have to do that ... He didn't try to do it to gain a position for himself."

During this time, Tom Flanagan was writing a book on Manning called *Waiting for the Wave*. Little did Manning know that Harper, who had worked in his office, was a quiet collaborator, feeding

Flanagan everything he could about his leader. "Stephen was virtu-ally a silent co-author of that book," recalled Flanagan. "He made extremely valuable contributions, and he also furnished documents to me."

Harper was willing to leak information about the leader of his party. But a strange thing happened years later when Flanagan was writing a book about Harper called *Harper's Team*. The American-born Flanagan served as Harper's chief of staff at the Alliance Party. After helping Harper become prime minister he returned to Calgary but remained an important Harper strategist. He informed him about the book in advance, a fine book that reflected positively but frankly on the leader and that provided insights into the Alliance operation. Flanagan sent out advance copies of the manuscript to colleagues and friends for their comments. He was soon surprised to receive a call from Harper's chief of staff, Brodie. He wanted the book killed.

"I said it was too late for that," Flanagan recalled. Failing that, Brodie wanted extensive revisions, the great majority of which Flanagan agreed to: "I cut out a lot of anecdotes they considered too revealing." But Harper was still angry—and his close and important relationship with Flanagan ended on account of it. Flanagan had little sympathy for Harper's thin-skinned attitude: "The problem wasn't that I revealed anything that was harmful," he said, "just that I had written the book at all."

He found it interesting that it was okay for Harper to provide insider information for a book on Manning, but when it came to a positive book on himself written by a close colleague, he would react with such hostility. Still, Flanagan might have known beforehand from his experiences with Harper that he could react this way. Harper, Flanagan had noticed, was very unusual in respect to secrecy and information control. He was practically manic.

After his election in 1993, Harper served as an MP for a little over three years, until 1997. Not pleased with Manning's management of the party, he then staged another exit—one that perplexed colleagues—and resigned his seat. He would have easily been re-elected in his riding. What's more, he needed only two more years in the House to qualify for a fat MP's pension. "How many other members of Parliament," asked Goldy Hyder, speaking of Harper's principles, "would pass up that opportunity?"

The principles did not extend, however, to the grassroots approach of the Reform Party. From day one Harper had favoured something closer to the opposite approach, while Manning, at least ostensibly, wanted considerable input from below. "Harper was the policy guy," recalled Hyder, "and it was like, 'Here I am coming up with all these policies and you want me to take them to some freaking assembly in Moose Jaw and have people there vote on supply side economics!?'" Manning noticed that Harper was inclined to withdraw when he didn't get his own way. Of his attitude, Manning wrote, "Stephen has difficulty accepting that there might be a few other people—not many, but perhaps a few—who were as smart as he was with respect to policy and strategy."

Although Harper was admired for his intellect and his analytical powers, his readiness to retreat was becoming noticed. He watched from the sidelines as Jean Chrétien trounced Stockwell Day, the new Alliance Party leader, in the 2000 election. Incensed by what he saw as the Liberals' redneck-baiting campaign against the West, Harper now wanted his retreat to extend to his adopted province. He advocated that Alberta rebel against Ottawa control. In January 2001, he and several other conservatives recommended in a newspaper article that a firewall be built around the province against interference from the federal Liberals.

This was while Harper was serving as the head of the National Citizens Coalition. Formed in 1967, the NCC campaigned over the years in favour of privatized health care and against budget deficits, taxes, and so-called gag laws (laws that limit spending by non-party organizations during election campaigns). Harper spent four years at the NCC, where, recalled its vice-president, Gerry Nicholls, he was methodical and hard-edged. He worked long hours and kept tabs on others to make sure they did the same. A little Friday afternoon drinks party, an NCC tradition, was terminated. Purse strings were tightened, and Christmas bonuses dropped. One of Harper's few excesses was food. He was a junk food addict, which prompted NCC staffers to refer to him behind the scenes as Fatboy—or FB, for short.

His presence gave the little lobby group added visibility and prestige. Unlike previous leaders, who had put the emphasis on publicity campaigns, Harper believed legal challenges were the way to bring about change. Under him, the NCC helped mount cases against election gag laws and Quebec language laws as they applied to commercial signs and schooling. The legal challenges were expensive and usually unsuccessful, but they were clearly Harper's strategic preference and would remain so in the future.

Never one to cozy up to the media, Harper told NCC staff that the one thing he admired about Pierre Trudeau was his disdain for journalists, adding that it never seemed to hurt him. But to keep his name in political circulation, he lobbied Don Newman to get on his *CBC News: Politics* show, even phoning him to ask for a regular panel spot. Newman gave him a try and he passed the test.

At the NCC, Harper's style was domineering. Nicholls recalled one day when he was preparing a billboard advertisement on forced unionism and decided he should run it by Harper for approval. The boss suggested that the wording be changed, but Nicholls thought his suggestions made the ad somewhat confusing. "So I called him up," he recalled. "'Hi Stephen,' I said. 'We were going over your billboard idea, and we think it needs to be changed.'" Not wanting to hear this, Harper responded icily, "I don't give a fuck what you think."

Nicholls was taken aback: "That sort of stunned me." Despite such moments, Nicholls, who would later have a falling-out with

Harper, found him generally good to work for. "He was tough ... but if you did your job, you got along well with him." The staff admired his breadth of knowledge and the surgeon-like clarity of his thinking. Yet there was a frightening side to him, a vindictive streak, as Nicholls saw it, a pressing need to confront and destroy adversaries. His goal, he made clear, was to have the Liberals disappear as they had in Britain; the approach was withering, what Nicholls termed "Genghis Khan politics." Harper wanted to "wipe out the city completely."

While at the organization, Harper gave serious consideration to making a bid for the Tory Party leadership, which became vacant in 1998. That he showed interest in heading up the moderate Tories was as an indicator of his willingness to compromise ideology for the attainment of power. Not surprisingly, this flirtation prompted ire in the Reform Party camp. Stories were leaked condemning him, and he grew suspicious that Manning was behind them. He tried to get Nicholls to write a memo with embarrassing information about Manning and leak it to the media. Nicholls refused, but he was struck by the intensity of Harper's pursuit, noting in his journal that it was "like Captain Ahab hunting the white whale."

IN THE YEARS since stepping down as an MP, Harper had hardly prepared the track for a run for high office. With his flirtation with the Tories, his tussles with the Manning crowd, his firewall letter, he had alienated potential support. But he wanted to get back on the political frontlines, and it was now that the stars would begin to align for him.

So much would have to fall into place. Not just one or two turns of happenstance. More like six or seven.

The first turn came after Stockwell Day captured the Alliance Party leadership in July 2000. Although it looked for all intents and purposes as if the position would be occupied for years to come, Day's leadership quickly unravelled, and just eighteen months later, the prize became available again. In another unlikely development, no one of magnitude stepped forward to claim it. Apart from Harper, the leadership race featured only Grant Hill and Diane Ablonczy, two caucus members with little support, as well as the largely discredited Day. In the campaign's initial stages, Harper had problems raising funds and assembling an effective team. He was highly tempted, even with the lack of competition, to stage another retreat. But in the end he stayed on, recharged his campaign, and rolled over his opponents to an easy triumph.

In the wake of the leadership convention, he was effective in healing the internal divisions that Day's chaotic stewardship had fostered. Yet the party remained low in the polls. There was no bounce and—with Harper's flat image—not much hope for growth. But just two months after he took over came news of a scandal that would eat away at Grit popularity for years to come. Commonly known as the sponsorship scandal, the scam involved public servants awarding millions in government funding to Liberal-friendly ad agencies in Quebec for little or no work in return. For a leader like Harper whose dream was to cripple the Liberal Party, this was a precious gift. Harper hammered away at the issue, expressing frustration over the government's stonewalling and secrecy. "We expect open and honest information here," he complained, "not to have to make fifty-eight thousand access-to-information requests."

His relentless attacks didn't resonate with voters, however, and his party lagged in the polls with the first big test of his leadership, a May 2003 by-election in the Ontario riding of Perth–Middlesex, looming. Determined to show that he could make up ground, Harper put all his resources into the battle, including a wealth of party funds and every available body to help out in the campaign. The result was an embarrassment. The Tories, who by this time had no active leader, won the riding, and the Alliance finished a dismal third. The poor showing cast a pall on Harper's leadership, but as fortune would have it, the defeat was just what the party needed.

When Harper took over as Alliance leader in March 2002, he announced with conviction that the party was here to stay. For years, he had been a leading opponent of a merger between the Progressive Conservative Party and Reform–Alliance. One day over lunch with Rick Anderson, a key Manning strategist, and Rod Love, he asked why they were wasting their time on a unity drive. It wasn't necessary, he said. The PCs would die of their own accord. But the embarrassing by-election loss was what served to finally convince him he was wrong. Combining forces with the Tories, he realized, was the only way forward.

He needed a wholly unforeseeable turn, however, for that to be possible. The Tories were revving up for their leadership convention, hoping to use it as a springboard to a new day for the party so that amalgamation would be unnecessary. But the convention turned into a fiasco. Peter MacKay won it by making a secret pact with David Orchard, a left-leaning candidate who controlled a big chunk of convention votes. The backroom deal between the two, in which MacKay pledged to make no agreement with the Alliance Party, was exposed, and MacKay looked underhanded as a result. His victory was Pyrrhic. The party limped out of the convention, its new leader's credibility severely diminished. Its most realistic option was now a merger.

Remarkably, the convention's big winner was Harper. "The impact of that Orchard deal," recalled Scott Brison, one of the Tory leadership candidates, "was to allow Harper to move in for the kill."

Harper had only stood and watched as his two big rivals, the Tory Party and the Liberal Party, stabbed themselves in the gut, the Grits with a crippling scandal, the Tories with a leadership convention from hell. Harper now took advantage of the opportunity to bring conservatives together, displaying strategic moxie along the way. He once had told a friend, "I think about strategy twenty-four hours a day," and it was only a small exaggeration. His Alliance caucus made it easy for him, however, as it was prepared to do virtually anything to get a deal. MacKay had the more difficult task of dissolving a party that dated to the days before Confederation.

Given the albatross of the convention, MacKay was in no position to seek the leadership of the newly unified party. One possible contender was Bernard Lord, the New Brunswick premier. More than anyone else, Harper feared Lord, who was young, bilingual, and a clear-cut favourite in Quebec.

In making the merger, Harper had agreed to give equal representation to every riding in the leadership vote. He realized, recalled Ian Brodie, that this was giving "a massive leg-up to Lord," but he was prepared to take the risk anyway. "The histories so far claim that he was a shoo-in to lead the combined party," said Brodie, "but that wasn't his assessment when he decided to do the deal."

The decision here reflected Harper's go-for-broke management style, said Brodie. "The PM's critical moves actually come in the rare instances where he can put a lot into play in anticipation of a decisive win, or a catastrophic loss. He won't bet the house, or anything actually, on the prospects of a marginal advance."

In the case of Lord, however, it turned out that Harper didn't have to worry. Fortune was on his side again. A New Brunswick election had left Lord's provincial Tories with a majority of just a single seat. If he left for a federal bid, the party's hold on power in his province would be tenuous at best. To the relief of Harper, he backed away from a leadership run.

With the conservatives united and a new party in place, the leadership prize was one worth pursuing. But remarkably, once again no strong candidates other than Harper came forward. The only challengers were the wealthy and glamorous Belinda Stronach, who had no political experience and was unilingual, and the competent but underwhelming Tony Clement, a former Ontario cabinet minister who had suffered a series of electoral setbacks. The lacklustre field was a woeful comment on the state of Canadian politics. The Tory leadership races of 1968, 1976, and 1983 had all produced impressive slates of candidates.

As expected, Harper won the leadership easily, taking it on the first ballot with more than 50 percent of the vote. In his victory speech on March 20, 2004, he noted that the party needed "the democratic reform vision of a government that is responsible to the people," not to the Prime Minister's Office. His timing again turned out to be heavenly. When he first took over the Alliance leadership in 2002, the sponsorship debacle had just landed on the Liberals. Now the scandal detonated even more explosively. Auditor General Sheila Fraser released a report with allegations of Liberal hacks stealing from the national coffers. The party was left reeling, and Paul Martin then made a decision that played right into Harper's hands. Instead of turning the charges over to the police and moving on, he appointed the Gomery Commission to investigate them, giving the unseemly saga legs for years to come.

In January 2004, polls had shown the Martin Liberals at about 45 percent support, a lead of about 25 percent over the newly amalgamated Conservatives. Harper's hopes were scant. But in the wake of Fraser's sponsorship report, Liberal support plummeted to 36 percent, while the Conservatives moved up to 27 percent. Suddenly, the game was on.

In the 2004 election in June, Harper came up short, but he did manage to bring the Liberals' standing down to a minority. It was a good showing, but he went away depressed and came close to resigning the leadership. In the following year, Belinda Stronach deserted the party and Harper struggled to increase his popularity. The summer of 2005, his team members recall, was one of the low points. The party was losing confidence that it could win with Harper, but it need not have been concerned. The fates were again about to inter-vene on his behalf.

The Liberal minority government fell in November 2005, trig-gering another election. Harper battled effectively in the ensuing campaign, running a highly tuned operation. But at the midway point, his Conservatives still trailed the Liberals by a healthy margin. He needed another gift. Then—stunningly—the RCMP made public the news that it was investigating the Liberals over alleged leaks on the income-trust file. The Mounties had never done anything like this in the course of an election. It looked very much as if they were trying to have a hand in the outcome. If so, it worked. The momentum of the campaign swung to the Conservatives overnight, and it remained there right through to their January 23 victory and the coronation of Stephen Harper as Canada's twenty-second prime minister.

With that came yet more welcome news. The Liberals would be leaderless for the rest of the year. Instead of fighting on, as Lester Pearson, John Turner, Mackenzie King, and Wilfrid Laurier had after election defeats, Paul Martin announced that he was stepping down. Harper's minority had been given a free pass until a convention almost a year away. The Liberals were not about to force an election under their interim leader, Bill Graham.

In assessing the ways of fortune, some like to resort to the old cliché that you make your own luck. In the case of Stephen Harper, whose run of luck was far from over, the old cliché was twaddle. Most of the breaks that catapulted him to power were from out of the blue. Before him it was Liberal leaders who seemed to profit from Providence. Now it looked to be the turn of his party. With all that had happened in the previous four years he could perhaps be forgiven, as he took office in February 2006, for thinking destiny was on his side.

CHAPTER THREE

Enemies Everywhere

When they finally took power after so long in opposition they were a wary bunch. They knew how to oppose, how to attack, how to pull triggers. But they didn't know how to govern. They had a rookie prime minister, all rookie cabinet ministers except one, and rookie staff. Everything was new and they were in a minority situation. To say the level of anxiety was high was to underestimate the degree of tension.

"You know what it was like," recalled Bruce Carson, Harper's senior policy adviser. "It was like every day could be the last day." Carson, a sixtyish former Ottawa lawyer who had spent two decades working for federal and provincial conservatives, felt the government would be lucky to last a year. Though he was the policy man, he didn't see policy as the top priority. The top priority was discipline, not screwing up: "We had only one chance to get this thing right."

Another veteran on the team was Keith Beardsley, a deputy chief of staff. A heavy-set man with a genial yet assertive way about him, Beardsley had served Harper for three years in opposition and knew his way around Toryland. He had worked for two former leaders, Joe Clark and Jean Charest, and was the chief of staff to a minister in the Mulroney government.

During the election campaign, Harper had put Beardsley through some tough stretches, hollering at him on several occasions. After the victory, he held a reception to thank everyone for their contribution to the campaign. When he saw Beardsley standing in the corner with his wife, he came over to him. "I want to apologize," said the new prime minister. Beardsley asked why. "Well, all those times during the morning briefs when I yelled at you. I wasn't really mad at you." He explained that he was just releasing stress.

That was good for Beardsley to hear, but he wasn't worried about Harper's moods. Like Carson, he was worried about whether the Conservatives were ready to govern. He had been with Harper during the losing campaign in 2004 and had told him afterwards, "We were probably lucky we lost." The Conservatives, Beardsley explained, weren't ready to take power at that time. They didn't have the political staff, the hundreds of experienced professionals who could move in and run the government. It would have been close to chaos.

By 2006 things had improved, but in Beardsley's view, the party still didn't have the necessary resources. There could still be chaos. "We had brand-new ministers and we were dealing with ministerial staff who knew nothing, communications people who in some cases were right out of college," he said. "We were probably 90 percent inexperienced at that level." Given the situation, they had to ensure that things didn't get out of hand. This would require extraordinary measures of oversight and control.

While in opposition, Harper had seen how easy it was for the governing Liberals—even their veteran ministers—to get mauled. The Grits were made available to the media after cabinet meetings where they were often blindsided by questions. Harper's rapid-response unit, headed by Beardsley, watched it all on the TV monitors, gleefully preparing attack lines. The new prime minister told his advisers he didn't want a repeat of this with his cast of greenhorns.

He had to find a way to keep them out of the spotlight, safe from the braying journalistic pack.

Harper knew that in politics, loose lips were death. He had only to look at the fractious Tory history to see that a lack of discipline and unity had crippled the party almost every step of the way. Every Tory prime minister going back to R.B. Bennett in the 1930s had faced an internal revolt of some kind. In Bennett's reign, Harry Stevens, a maverick minister, broke ranks and formed his own party, hurting Bennett's prospects for re-election. The Diefenbaker years were bloodied by internal uprisings, and during Joe Clark's time in office, there were multiple rebellions. Of course, Harper knew all about how his own Reform Party had ripped the heart out of the Mulroney coalition in the West. The split between Tories and Reformers helped keep the Grits in power through the 1990s and beyond. And when the Conservatives did finally unite in 2003, they still had too many members speaking out of turn, scaring off voters with ideological blasts.

Harper vowed then to silence them. He was well positioned to exert his authority because he had come to power without a suitcase full of IOUs. He had made it on his own terms without having to pawn himself. He owed nothing to special interests—not to Bay Street, not to the establishment. There was no party kingmaker to whom he was beholden. He had no friends in West Palm Beach, having never ingratiated himself with that crowd. His suspicious nature never allowed him to get close to many people.

To understand Harper, said his close friend John Weissenberger, it was necessary to understand that he's an outsider: "He is by nature an introvert and an intellectual." Flanagan, who worked with Harper on and off for fifteen years, painted a similar portrait: "He doesn't repose trust easily. He's always got his antennae up. His first reaction to anything new is almost always negative. It's a personality trait."

But the paradox was that, as introverted as he was, Harper, as Flanagan found and as Nicholls discovered at the NCC, was consumed with the need for ironclad, dictatorial control of communications. It bothered Flanagan and he tried to get an explanation. But it was a frustrating exercise, and he ultimately decided there was no use pushing. It was something psychological. "I think these things are deeply seeded personally," said Flanagan. "I concluded there was a package there that wasn't in my power to change." It was part of what the professor described as Harper's "drive to dominate."

That drive was about to be put to the test. Moving in to the prime minister's office, Harper was surrounded by his public enemy number one. Ottawa was a Liberals' sanctuary. If not in reality, then in his own mind, during the thirteen-year reign of Chrétien and Martin they had come to dominate the bureaucracy, the foreign policy establishment, the fourth estate, agencies, the NGOs, the watchdog groups, and the courts. Turning an opposition team into a governing team was only one problem confronting Harper. The most daunting challenge was going to be turning a capital awash in Grit red into shades of Tory blue.

The sprawling and powerful bureaucracy was high up on his list of threats to good Conservative governance. It was what made the government function and it teemed with Liberal sympathizers. Unelected deputy ministers ran the cabinet departments, and most had been chosen by Liberal prime ministers. Moreover, the senior layers of the bureaucracy were stocked with administrators who had been on the personal staffs of Liberal cabinet ministers. Many had taken advantage of a rule stipulating that once someone had worked on a minister's staff for three years, he or she could move to the top of the queue for appointments to permanent public service jobs. There was a fear, recalled Keith Beardsley, "that any agenda we put forward would be delayed or killed." You could call it paranoia, he said, but the Conservatives had reason to worry that these politicized bureaucrats would slip secrets to their old Liberal friends.

Previous Conservative prime ministers had confronted this same problem after coming to power following a long Liberal run. Diefenbaker had railed about the Liberal-stained mandarinate, seeing plots and conspiracies everywhere. His solution was to freeze the deputy ministers out of policy formation and his governance, it was widely believed, suffered for it. When Brian Mulroney came to power, he warned that he wouldn't be putting up with any Liberal-biased public service. On the campaign trail, he declared that he would be bearing gifts for the bureaucrats: "Pink slips and running shoes." He changed his mind before long, however, and when he met Gordon Osbaldeston, the Clerk of the Privy Council, he extended his hand and, with his classic capacity for ingratiating himself, declared, "Gordon, I want you to know I trust you completely."

But Harper, coming from further on the right than either Diefenbaker or Mulroney, had even a deeper, Alberta-driven animosity towards the existing order. His mistrustfulness extended to the members of the fourth estate. They were also, in his mind, Liberally tainted and would have to be dealt with accordingly. According to his advisers, the 2004 campaign was the turning point in his media relations. He was apprehensive about the scribes going in, but aides had convinced him to open up and he tried to do so. He held long scrums, taking questions until reporters had no more. He thought, his friend John Weissenberger observed, that there would be a bit of a trade-off—that he'd get good treatment in return. But it didn't happen.

Late in the campaign, Harper's strategists over-reached. They put out the unsupportable charge that Paul Martin was soft on child pornography. An avalanche of criticism followed, but Harper was hesitant to issue an apology. At one point, the media surrounded his campaign bus, stalking him like jackals. Inside, Harper stewed. He couldn't get out without facing them. After the campaign, still bitter about the incident, he told a visiting newspaper editor, "They surrounded my goddamn bus. I couldn't get off my goddamn bus." Then, in a screw-them tone of voice, he vowed never to allow journalists to treat him like that again.

After the campaign, he kept his distance from reporters, getting less coverage as a result than opposition leaders normally do. He insisted that the media were out to get him and was soon provided with evidence. In the summer of 2005, he attended the Calgary Stampede. Doing the usual political thing, he donned cowboy gear—the big hat, the jeans, the leather vest. But he didn't appear comfortable in the get-up, and a photographer caught Harper in a most unflattering pose, looking like a dolt. Usually, the media wouldn't run such pictures. This one appeared everywhere.

So when he won the election, how could anyone, Weissenberger asked, expect him to be open to the media pack? It wasn't just their treatment of him, said his friend, but their treatment of the whole Conservative caucus. If Harper's members were given a chance to speak their minds, it backfired. "If there was one millimetre of light between what one of our MPs said and the leader," said Weissenberger, "the media would just pounce on it." During the 2006 election, many observers were of the view that the Liberals received worse press than the Conservatives. But the new prime minister didn't see it that way.

His adversary list extended to the Senate and the Supreme Court. The Senate had an imposing Liberal majority that could stall and block his legislation. Harper had been a non-stop critic of the Senate; he favoured an elected chamber and wanted to make that change. As for the Court, it had long been a target of the Reform movement. Harper came out of a region and a political formation that opposed judicial activism. He held firmly to the view that, as he once said, judges are there to apply the law, not make it. Harper and colleagues saw the chief justices as soft on crime, soft on sentencing, excessively liberal.

What made his attempts to overturn the existing order even more daunting was his government's minority status. The Conservatives were an isolated minority, having no other parties of similar ideological persuasion to team up with. This made them more vulnerable. Although Lester Pearson had accomplished a lot with his minority governments in the 1960s, he was able to partner with the New Democratic Party on the left. The same was true of Pierre Trudeau, who allied with the NDP to sustain his minority from 1972 to 1974. But in Harper's case, there were no natural allies. All the other parties were on the centre-left, ready to join hands and pull him down at the moment of their pleasing.

No natural allies. In a sense that was just right for Stephen Harper. It had always been his way. Tim Powers, a lobbyist and Tory spokesman from Newfoundland, saw Harper's situation as comparable to that of a proprietor of a family business. The business was the Conservative government, and the prime minister "was going to exercise as good a control over that as he could. He really was like that store owner. It is my store and I am the proprietor." Running a minority Parliament was like facing constant hostile takeover bids. Therefore, Harper had to run a permanent campaign to stay alive. "Like it or not," said Powers, "in a minority Parliament it is battlefield war on a daily basis." One thing the new PM admired about Jean Chrétien, the analyst added, was his combativeness. "Harper understood that to be successful, you can never take your foot off the throat of your opponent."

Harper had fought two leadership campaigns and two general elections. In his mind, there was always a war on, whether it was between East and West, left and right, Liberals and Conservatives. He always had to be armed, on the attack, wary of attack. And now more than ever. In his new and besieged circumstances, politics would take priority over policy. There would be no long-range strategic planning because there was little likelihood the minority would be in power for long.

Mark Cameron, a young, self-effacing policy team member who had worked with Stockwell Day, recalled that talk around the Harper table in the initial days centred on three possible scenarios. One was to follow the "big vision" path of a Mulroney or a Trudeau. The second, he said, was to pursue a Reagan or Thatcher kind of model, with the intent of radically reducing the size of government. Both of these options, however, required more time and more political capital than these Conservatives had. The third scenario was the political goal, "a sort of Mackenzie King path of building an enduring coalition and nurturing it," said Cameron. "And I think that's the role he chose." His plan was to identify potential Conservative growth areas and target them, while undermining the Liberal Party at every opportunity.

That Harper wasn't ready to break open big cartons of right-wing ideology was reflected in his allegiance to Bruce Carson, who hailed from the moderate Red Tory centre. When, as opposition leader, Harper brought Carson aboard as his policy man, he told him there were two reasons for his decision. "One is that you are older than I am and have a lot more experience. The second, Bruce, is that I know you are to the left of me." When the Conservatives formed the government, Carson noted that there weren't many Red Tories left in the neighbourhood. "People from the Progressive Conservative side were leaving to do other things. So I was there as sort of a guardian of the left. It was like 'Let's see how it washes with Carson because he has that odd point of view of the way the world works.'" With his input he felt he could prevent the Harper image from getting overly heated. He felt he could prevent him from putting anything too scary in the window.

Carson wasn't the only holdover from the opposition. In fact, the team that started governing was essentially the same one that had run the Opposition Leader's Office (OLO). The conventional wisdom had always been that it was the opposition's role to oppose and the government's to propose. But nothing was written in stone. No one said the government couldn't function like an opposition.

Basically, the plan, recalled Keith Beardsley, was to clamp down on everything. With everyone so new and inexperienced, with survival at stake, putting the party and the government in a straitjacket would provide some security against what had befallen previous Tory prime ministers. But the clampdown strategy was supposed to be a short-term thing. "The idea," as Beardsley remembered, "was to have it last for six months until everybody got into their jobs, got trained, and staff got trained." That, at least, was the idea. But what happened, said the Harper adviser, was that the six months came and the six months went and nothing seemed to change. The straitjacket strategy remained in effect: "I never saw it really let up."

CHAPTER FOUR

Promises of Openness

"People didn't leave the Liberals because of their ideas," observed Matt Brown, a British analyst of progressive governance. "They left them because of the way they were doing politics." Years of Liberal malfeasance, most notably on the sponsorship scandal, had helped bring the Conservatives to power, and they were acutely aware of that fact. In the run-up to the election, Stephen Harper had rolled out the rhetoric on the need for clean and transparent government, expressing frustration with Paul Martin's Liberals over their alleged secrecy and obstructionism. "When a government starts trying to cancel dissent or avoid dissent," Harper declared in a statement to be later viewed as notable for ironic content, "is frankly when it is rapidly losing its moral authority to govern."

But Harper was facing a dilemma. On the one hand, he had to sell the public on the idea that his government would be refreshingly open and democratic. On the other, he was instinctively inclined in the opposite direction, particularly in a town so Liberal.

During the campaign, he pitched his tent on the moral high ground, and he did it with more than just rhetoric. Well before the election call, Harper gave Mark Cameron, an adviser who had witnessed Liberal abuses close up, the assignment of creating one of the most far-reaching ethics-reform packages the country had ever seen.

Cameron knew just who to go to for help. He had an old friend from his university days, Duff Conacher, who now headed Democracy Watch, a group that monitored governments on a range of accountability questions and issued forensic reports on their performance. Conacher had been trained in the ethical arts by the Ralph Nader group in Washington. He then toured Canadian universities to organize Public Interest Research Groups. At McGill he met Cameron, who was the vice-president of the student council.

Cameron was a Liberal then, and he worked for a period in Jean Chrétien's government. He became frustrated with the direction the party was taking, though, and switched over to the Alliance Party under Stockwell Day and then Harper. In the spring of 2005, he sat down with Conacher at Ottawa's Sparks Street Mall and told him of his mission—an accountability package like no other. Conacher was only too glad to hear it. Within days, he presented his old friend with a list of no less than fifty-two reform proposals.

Conacher didn't hear anything back at first, but in early November, Cameron called to tell him Harper would be unveiling something the next day that he might find interesting. The prime minister met his caucus that morning, then gave a speech setting out a sixty-point accountability platform. It was an extensive overhaul, and the critics were impressed. Harper clearly meant business. The platform included the creation of a public appointments commissioner to reduce patronage, stringent measures to curb lobbying, an increase in the number of departments and agencies subject to access-to-information laws, the appointment of a parliamentary budget officer to monitor spending, whistle-blower protection, election-spending reform, enhanced powers for the auditor general, and a host of other measures.

"We are going to change the way government works in Ottawa," the Conservative leader pledged. The sponsorship scandal, he said, happened "because of a culture of entitlement in the Liberal Party.

And it happened because that party allowed the veils of secrecy to close around its actions."

Duff Conacher was pleased. Of the fifty-two measures he'd recommended, forty were in the package. He felt that change was coming to the capital. During the election campaign that followed the announcement, Harper continued to score points on accountability because the Martin team, puzzlingly, failed to put forward a reform package of its own. But the integrity issue really began to resonate when the RCMP made public its investigation of the Liberals on the income-trust file, it being an emphatic reminder to voters of past Liberal transgressions.

The Mountie intrusion into the election campaign led to accusations that the force was biased against the Martin Liberals. This was a telling piece of irony for the Conservatives, who had long suspected the Mounties of being too close to Jean Chrétien. During the uproar over alleged conflicts of interest in the Shawinigate controversy, Conservatives had howled in protest at how the Mounties appeared to be backing Chrétien at every turn. Giuliano Zaccardelli, then the RCMP commissioner, enjoyed a close working relationship with Chrétien. One time at an American embassy reception he told a journalist just how that relationship had benefited him. He described how he was now a celebrated figure in his Italian home town because of his status as commissioner. What had helped him succeed, he explained, was that he had backed the right Liberal horse. His fellow Italian, Liberal MP Maurizio Bevilacqua, didn't enjoy the same status in his home country, Zaccardelli said, because he had sided with the wrong guy—Paul Martin.

Zaccardelli declined to look into the Shawinigate affair, claiming there was no basis for an investigation. When Joe Clark, then the leader of the Progressive Conservatives, met with him to outline conflict-of-interest breaches and suggest avenues of inquiry, Zaccardelli was unmoved.

At the centre of the Shawinigate storm was François Beaudoin, the former president of the Business Development Bank of Canada. Beaudoin complained of political interference after Chrétien tried to get him to give a loan to an acquaintance in his constituency. In what many suspected was a vendetta campaign by Chrétien, the bank president was later subjected to an RCMP investigation, which included repeated raids at his home, cottage, and golf club, and was forced out of his job. The Mountie probe was prompted by allegations that a Quebec Superior Court judge later called "completely vexatious and without foundation."

But if the RCMP had done the Liberals' bidding under Chrétien, it certainly wasn't doing it under Martin. Conservatives saw the mid-campaign intrusion as poetic justice.

Unbeknownst to the public—it wouldn't be revealed until much later—the Conservative campaign featured some questionable activity for a party running on a platform of openness and accountability. The Conservatives were quietly operating an election-financing scheme that drew the ire of Elections Canada and later prompted a police raid on party headquarters. The Conservatives had a national election-spending limit of $18.3 million. But they were able to exceed that amount by adjusting the books so as to shift the costs of radio and TV ads to some candidates' local campaigns.

The manoeuvring was so questionable that some local Conservatives, worried about the propriety of the plan, complained to party headquarters. In one case, the campaign manager for the Conservative candidate in the Ontario riding of Oxford wrote to a regional director of the party, John Bracken, to express his concerns. Bracken passed on the complaint to the party's national director, Michael Donison, who was furious that anyone would protest. "What a bunch of turds," he wrote back to Bracken. "This is not going to cost them a cent nor give them a moment of cash-flow problem." He wrote that "the fear of God needs to be put in these Oxford people," to which

Bracken suggested having "heavies from Ottawa come down like a ton of bricks" on them. For party rank and file the excessive reaction was a sign of things to come. Under Stephen Harper, they would be expected to march in single file.

Donison had come up with the money-shuffle scheme, which came to be known as the "in-and-out affair." A lawyer by profession, he had found a loophole in the election-financing laws that he felt made the scheme permissible. In Harper's office, Keith Beardsley recalled, there wasn't much concern over the ploy. "We had a legal opinion saying it was legitimate to do it." By early 2010, the courts still had not determined whether the scheme was legal. But the Conservatives had won an important case on the matter to begin the year and were confident of full exoneration.

Duff Conacher saw the case as an example of shrewd but dubious Tory tactics, the type of thing practised by their Republican brethren in the United States. Until Donison, no one had been cynical enough to use money transfers to get around spending caps. "So without checking with Elections Canada to get permission, they go ahead anyway," said Conacher, "and reap the benefits of the extra spending and dare to be called on it." The litigation route was something the Harper Conservatives were prepared to exploit far more than other governments. They realized, as Conacher put it, that if they bent or broke the rules, they could litigate through the appeals process for years, diminishing the negative political fallout.

FOLLOWING THE ELECTION VICTORY, Harper made a bold move that put his promise of high ethical standards under a cloud before his stewardship had barely begun. The investiture of the cabinet takes place at Rideau Hall, the official residence of the governor general. On the day of the swearing-in, journalists were a bit startled to find a former Liberal industry minister, David Emerson, on the grounds. Bruce Carson and other Tory strategists, wanting to keep the reason for Emerson's presence under wraps until the swearing-in, started a rumour that they'd needed someone from the previous government to bring in the Great Seal of Canada. "It was the funniest thing," recalled Carson. But he knew the humour wouldn't last long when the real reason was revealed: Emerson was being appointed Harper's minister of trade. Only two weeks earlier, the same man had been elected under the Liberal banner in the riding of Vancouver Kingsway. He had been one of Paul Martin's prominent ministers. When the Tories picked up rumblings that he was prepared to cross the floor, they convinced him to do so by offering him a cabinet post.

Floor-crossings were common enough in the Canadian Parliament. They had happened in most every session. Among the more noteworthy crossings was one by Léon Balcer, a minister in the Diefenbaker government who had a major falling-out with the Chief. As recounted in Peter C. Newman's *Distemper of Our Times*, as the unpopular Balcer crossed the floor "several Tory backbenchers banged their desks in approval. One Saskatchewan M.P. said to his seat mate, 'I feel as if our party has just had a bowel movement.'"

Just seven months before Emerson changed parties, the Liberals had poached Belinda Stronach from the Tories, saving the Martin government from losing a confidence vote. Her desertion had rankled Harper, and he seized this chance for some revenge, even if it came at a cost.

The cost was substantial. A member who crosses the floor after serving the riding for a couple of years is one thing. One who crosses immediately after being elected is practically unheard of. Where, critics wondered, was the democratic principle in that? Liberal voters in Emerson's riding were enraged. He was pilloried by the press and the people for weeks to come, as was Harper. Accountability? This was the very opposite. Elect a Liberal—be represented by a Conservative.

Harper and Emerson, while expecting criticism, were taken back by the extent of the backlash. "I think it's fair to say that neither of us saw it coming to the degree that it did," recalled Emerson, who said that despite all the uproar, he would do the same thing over again. The PM's strategists later conceded that they might have been better off waiting a few months before naming Emerson to cabinet. But though the timing was bad, there were dividends to be had. Harper had no representation in Canada's three largest cities, and Emerson gave him that. He had a cabinet of no experience, and Emerson gave him experience. And he was out to slay the Liberals, and Emerson helped with that goal.

Harper's chutzpah didn't end there. Although he had long derided the appointed Senate, he now turned against the spirit of his word by elevating a senator to his cabinet. In an attempt to court Quebec and gain representation in Montreal, he promoted Michael Fortier, a long-time Tory and party fundraiser, to his executive. Now the critics had another appointment to condemn.

The Emerson appointment prompted a clash between the PM and his communications director, William Stairs. A former staffer for Peter MacKay, Stairs was a conscientious, respected adviser who had good relations with the media. He sometimes tried to convince Harper to take a more open approach and show a warmer side to the public. During the election, one of Stairs's more challenging assignments was to get Harper to smile. The Tories were well aware that the leader's typically frozen countenance was hardly a big seller, so just before each public appearance, Stairs was given the task of approaching Harper and giving him a hand signal, an upward motion at his cheeks, in the hope that he would take the hint.

When the Emerson story hit, Stairs wanted to meet the media criticism openly by having Emerson and perhaps the PM as well give press interviews. Harper thought differently, his preferred option being to hunker down. As the coverage on the story worsened, there was no getting Harper to smile. He took it out on Stairs, displaying blazing anger and deciding to dump him outright.

The abrupt dismissal sent a chill through the office, as staffers thought it was brutally unfair. Stairs had barely settled into the communications director's job and was gone. The job was one of the toughest under Harper. Before Stairs, he had lost talented communications men, the witty and calm Jim Armour and Geoff Norquay, a consummate professional. Stairs's leaving had a lasting impact. He was replaced by the lobbyist and sometimes commentator Sandra Buckler, who took a more hostile approach, prompting unnecessary acrimony between the PMO and the press.

The Emerson shocker claimed other victims as well. Garth Turner got caught up in everyone's crosshairs. The Toronto MP was first elected under Brian Mulroney and then served briefly, as did everyone else, in Kim Campbell's cabinet. He didn't cause much trouble in those days, one reason being that Tories had more liberty to speak their minds. But over time he came to be seen as a loose cannon. He had an independent streak that, serving in the Harper government, was not to be recommended.

Turner tested the new era of accountability right off the top when he decided to start a blog and a webcast. What a way, he thought, to enhance participatory democracy! The day following his January election victory, he boastfully blogged about breaking down the walls between voters and politicians. "By connecting people intimately with what the federal government does, and letting them access that which it's supposed to offer," he wrote, "maybe we can change the very image of government."

When news of the Emerson appointment surfaced, Turner saw his electronic message board light up with constituents venting their anger. New government! Same old politics! This prompted the Halton MP to pause for a media scrum at which he expressed his dismay, pointing out that while his colleagues had been up in arms over the Belinda Stronach floor-crossing, they didn't seem to mind the Emerson one at all.

The party hierarchy reacted swiftly. When she saw Turner, Senator Marjory LeBreton issued a full-throated reprimand that could be heard in adjacent corridors. Jay Hill, the government House leader, and other MPs confronted him, and then it was the turn of the prime minister himself. Usually, PMs left such matters to their underlings. In such cases as this one—a member straying from the party hymn book—the standard line of defence was to put out a statement to the effect that of course there will be differences of opinion in the party, and these differences should be welcomed because this is what democracy is all about.

But Harper was not inclined to this kind of approach. The PM wanted to make an example of Turner, to make it clear that if you stepped out of line, you stepped into the grave. At a meeting in the PMO, Turner recalled, "my bottom was barely in the chair when Harper let it fly." In a tone that the MP found "condescending, belittling, and menacing," Harper explained that he had intended to offer Turner an important caucus assignment, but there would be nothing for him now.

Turner dug in, telling Harper that he still thought the Emerson appointment was unprincipled. That same evening, he blogged constituents to inform them of the trouble he was in and to reiterate his belief that if Emerson wanted to be a Conservative, he should run in an election as a Conservative. Newspapers reprinted the blog, which further enraged the PM's team. Now Harper's chief of staff, Ian Brodie, weighed in. On the phone, Turner recalled, he said, "Let me make this clear: I am telling you, you will not give any more media interviews. I am telling you, you will stop writing the blog. And I'm telling you that you will issue a press release today praising the prime minister's appointment of Emerson. Are you clear?"

What was clear, Turner would later say, was that an unelected political staffer had tried to gag an MP, threatening to throw him out of the party and ordering him to make a false statement. Brodie said he couldn't remember what he'd told Turner. But whatever it was, he wasn't bothered by it. "I am prepared to say, for the record, that Turner certainly brings out the worst in everyone." Turner continued to disregard orders and to incur the wrath of the brass. Before long, the online bad boy was thrown out of the party and had made his way to the Liberals.

There were other signals of the type of approach the Harper team was taking. When Peter MacKay, named foreign affairs minister, began looking for some new advisers, he thought he had found an excellent chief of staff in the young Graham Fox. Graham was the son of Bill Fox, who had been Brian Mulroney's director of communications, and like his father, he was sharp and focused. MacKay, who knew how hard it was to find good people, was pleased and didn't think there would be a problem hiring him. After all, MacKay had been a leading force in the amalgamation of the Tories and the Alliance and was no small player in the party. But if he thought that meant he had the freedom to choose his own chief of staff, he soon realized he was mistaken. He received an order from the PMO telling him to drop Graham Fox.

Most were perplexed by the move, but a few remembered an analysis the young Fox had written for the *Toronto Star* the previous summer. It questioned aspects of Harper's strategy in running the Conservative Party. That was enough to bar him from working for the Tories. Friends of MacKay's thought that he should have held his ground, that his response should have been "I'll appoint my own staff, thank you very much." By caving into Harper, they reasoned, he diminished his stature.

WHILE THE CONTROVERSY over the Emerson and Fortier appointments continued, the prime minister prepared to formally announce the party's accountability package. Since many of the measures had originated with Democracy Watch, Duff Conacher was watching closely—and becoming increasingly disappointed. Though the prime minister had introduced new conflict-of-interest and post-employment codes for holders of public office a couple of weeks after the election, Conacher couldn't help noticing that several loopholes in these codes had been left open. A measure requiring ministers to enter into fully blind trusts in regard to their business interests was softened, and a plan to allow the public to file complaints with the ethics commissioner was watered down.

When the Conservatives introduced their accountability bill in early April, it had only thirty-four measures, little more than half the number originally promised. Among the eliminated items was the section requiring ministers or senior government officials to record contacts with lobbyists. The promise to publish all government public opinion research within six months was diluted, as was the whistle-blower protection.

Despite the changes, the legislation still contained many advances over what had gone on before. If the included changes were held to, Conacher felt there would still be an improvement overall. But given some of the other signals Harper and his team were sending, he was beginning to have doubts.

In February 2006, Justice John Gomery tabled a much-anticipated report on how to improve openness and accountability in govern-ment. It offered nineteen recommendations, including one that the role of the Clerk of the Privy Council be reviewed because of doubts concerning his or her independence. It also recommended ways to reduce the powers of the prime minister. But the vast majority of the recommendations were ignored. Gomery, whose inquiry into the sponsorship scandal had facilitated the decline in Liberal support, was once a godsend to the Tories. But now that they were in office, they had little interest in what he had to say about reforming the system.

CHAPTER FIVE

A Day in a Life

O n a normal day Stephen Harper would arrive at the office at around 8:30 a.m., after dropping the kids off at school. A bit later, the prime minister, a man, said David Emerson, "who could say no better than anyone I'd ever met," stepped into a boardroom next to his office for the meeting that set the marching orders for the day.

At that instant, his staff got a clue of his mood. Was he weighed down by one of his deep and brooding resentments? Was he eager, his hard gaze focused on a challege to surmount? Or was there something else that stirred him? "Sometimes," recalled Mark Cameron, "there would be a really bad story happening, and he would be invigorated by the challenge and be quite optimistic. Other days there would be nothing that really happened, but there would be some very minor gossipy story which he got all agitated about."

Seldom did Harper make introductory remarks. An adviser handed him a report, the issues report, and he'd say go ahead. This report, which also contained the daily press briefing, was prepared in a pre-meeting chaired by either Ian Brodie or Bruce Carson which reviewed major developments of the past twenty-four hours and sorted out which points to put to the boss. The key, said Carson, was to nail things down. If you were all over the map, the PM could turn ugly.

At the main meeting, Keith Beardsley gave the issues report, summarizing, among other things, recent media coverage, a sometimes delicate task. On bad-news days, some staffers argued in the pre-meeting to keep the worst of it hidden from Harper. Why put him in one of his funks? But most often the decision was made to give him the straight goods. "In some cases he'd blow a gasket," Beardsley recalled. "And others it would be like 'Well, same old critics. They're never going to change.'"

Occasionally Harper had a plan he wanted to talk about right off the top. He would sit down and just look around the room and say "I'm thinking of doing this" and await reaction. If it was negative, he sometimes put his foot down and advisers would back off: "Well fine prime minister, your call." Often, though, he'd show flexibility and come back later and say, "What about if we change it and do it this way?" The prime minister liked to be challenged, but only with specific counterpoints, not generalities. During a staff purge in his opposition days, he kept Beardsley because he was one of the few who would take him on.

At the morning meeting the press briefing was a central focus. But it did not get into media personalities. There was no slamming of the fist on the table or shouts of "That son of bitch nailed us again." It was a report on what was said, not who said it. "Very antiseptic" said Carson. Surprisingly so, he added, because knowing what Harper thought of some journalists "you'd think it would have been like, 'Well hell, look who wrote it! Who the fuck cares!?'"

The media rundown started with the most watched television programs, with CFTO in Toronto often getting top billing, and proceeded in descending order of importance, with Harper posing questions on the way. Local newscasts collectively had a much larger reach than national ones, so they usually came first. The print journalists were typically last.

Although the prime minister maintained that he didn't pay much attention to the media, staff didn't believe it. They could often tell by

Harper's responses that he'd read the article or seen the TV report they were discussing. In more informal moments with staffers, he sometimes gave his views on media pundits. His pointed jibes were reserved not just for the liberally inclined but also for some conservative commentators like Terence Corcoran and Lorne Gunter.

Around the meeting table there weren't many who were eager to butt heads with Harper. Usually the task was left to senior advisers like Carson, who would start in softly by saying, "Geez, Prime Minister, I'm not sure ..." When it was most tense was when the advisers were all agreed on one strategy and the PM wanted to go another way. He could be loud and foul-mouthed, but to Carson, that was no different from other leaders with whom he had worked. "If he got pissed off, he got pissed off and he would certainly let you know he was pissed off. But this is not the guy in the *Li'l Abner* cartoon with the cloud hanging over his head."

Carson once made the mistake of trying to say something positive about the CBC, not one of the PM's favourite media outlets. Carson suggested that the government intervene to prevent the network from losing its broadcast rights to the *Hockey Night in Canada* theme song. He argued that since the song was kind of like a second national anthem, something should be done. "Well," recalled the senior adviser, "to say I got my ass handed to me is a mild way of putting it."

Unlike some presidents or prime ministers, who liked issues to be boiled down to a one-page memo, Harper wanted details. He did his homework, reading studies and briefing papers thoroughly. Participants at meetings of the Priorities and Planning Committee, which sets the agenda for the government and most cabinet departments, were amazed at the amount of detail Harper absorbed. Senator Marjory LeBreton approached Carson after one of the meetings and exclaimed, "Jesus, Bruce. He even reads the annex items!" On a daily basis, Harper received several reports from the Privy Council Office. Staffers there, not used to this from other PMs, got them sent back with specific comments and instructions, signed "SH." Sometimes he was blunt. On one PCO report on the income-trust file, he wrote "This is bullshit!," underlined it, and provided marching orders.

After the senior staff meeting, the PM usually met with the Clerk of the Privy Council, the country's top civil servant. While the staff meeting had handled political matters, this meeting was Harper's opportunity to delve into the meat of the issues. For the first few months, Alex Himelfarb, the clerk under Paul Martin, remained in the post before being replaced by Kevin Lynch. Having worked for Liberal prime ministers, Himelfarb was initially viewed with suspicion. Many thought he and Harper wouldn't get along. They were mistaken. The two men worked comfortably together, and neither Harper nor his advisers asked Himelfarb for information about life under Paul Martin. But the clerk, according to colleagues, noticed the stark changes coming to the operations. Everything was being centralized, regimented. It was "the new Prussia," one co-worker said.

Meetings between Harper and the clerk were marathon affairs. When the House wasn't sitting, they regularly went on for three or four hours at a stretch. They both had their own list of issues, and Harper had a stack of notes to accompany his list. They would deal with the two or three major concerns first and then move on to maybe fifteen or twenty other items on the agenda.

Harper's specialty was economics, as was Lynch's. Harper wasn't an economist as such, never having practised in the field. "I've got a degree in philosophy," Paul Martin once cracked, "but I don't consider myself a philosopher." But Harper at these meetings and others often went deeply into the intricacies of finance. He wanted detailed explanations of the methodologies involved, for example, in deficit forecasting. "He drove the witches and warlocks of Finance to distraction with his ever more technical questions about their craft," recalled an adviser.

Hugely intricate matters, like the equalization payment structure for the provinces and transfer payment reform, fascinated Harper, and he wanted to gain a complete understanding of them. Said the adviser: "The PM probably spent hundreds of hours—I'm not exaggerating—working out the details of the fiscal balance package."

New in the job, Harper needed a lot of answers from the bureaucrats, and while he got along well with the clerks, the levels below often frustrated him. The answers were too slow in coming. "One of Harper's traits is that he is very impatient," said Beardsley. "And that would come out in a variety of ways. He'd ask for an answer on something that he considered relatively simple and—you know, typical bureaucracy—it would take two weeks to get him an answer. That would drive Harper nuts!"

Following the morning meetings, there was time for a quick lunch. Harper didn't return home, like Chrétien often did, at noon hour. A believer in that old maxim that failing to prepare is preparing to fail, Harper wanted to devote maximum time to getting ready for the afternoon's Question Period. He spent far more time on this than any other prime minister before him. He went to the extent of convening a full cabinet meeting every day beforehand, having already discussed possible questions at the morning staff meeting. As well, he'd already had a separate QP briefing with Beardsley, who gave the prime minister a yellow-paged book with suggested responses to a wide variety of questions.

But the big preparatory session was when the full cabinet met for a dress rehearsal. For other prime ministers, a prep session from the press secretary and a couple of aides had sufficed. But this general wasn't about to send his men onto the battlefield without full armour. As opposition leader, he had gathered his shadow cabinet together before each Question Period and found that it helped. And so, Bruce Carson thought, Why not do it while in government as well? "I was so terrified that we weren't ready for prime time," he recalled. The

PM agreed. As a measure of how secretly he ran things, no one in the media found out about the daily cabinet meetings until well into his tenure.

Initially, it was Beardsley who quarterbacked these meetings. "I had free rein," he said. "They didn't know what the questions would be. I'd throw the question out and the PM would be sitting there watching. And if the minister wasn't prepared, Harper knew it." The ministers had their own briefing books with preset answers. "But the last thing they wanted to do was to be frantically looking through their books with the prime minister staring at them." When an iffy answer was given, Beardsley would look over at Harper with raised eyebrows, as if to say, "What do you think?" And Harper, he recalled, "would just shake his head like 'That's no damn good.'"

For Trade Minister David Emerson, the cabinet member who had crossed the floor, it was eye-opening stuff. "You'd go through a dry run as to what was going to be said," he explained, "and the prime minister himself would intervene regularly to shape someone's response to an issue. And the discipline was amazing." So were the results. The prep session was remarkably accurate in forecasting what would be asked during Question Period. "You'd probably capture 90 percent of what was coming," said Emerson.

The trade minister drew a portrait of a schoolroom, with the prime minister as headmaster assessing the students' responses. It was such a contrast to the environment he had encountered in the Martin government, where the discipline, he said, wasn't half what it was under Harper. Emerson was new to politics when he entered the Martin cabinet and could have used some tutelage. But "it was kind of chaotic ... There really wasn't much guidance and support in terms of Question Period." He liked the new way because it gave him access to Harper every day the House of Commons was in session. At the end of the dress rehearsal, he could catch him for a few minutes to discuss any subject he wished.

On days when he was in a good mood, Harper delighted colleagues at these meetings. He had considerable talent as an impersonator and sometimes mimicked opposition members, doing impressions of them asking the questions. His show eased tensions, producing rounds of laughter. And this pre–Question Period session had other uses. Sometimes issues were hashed out as if it were a regular cabinet meeting. It gave ministers more chance to show their mettle and the prime minister more opportunity to assess the effectiveness of the players on his team. It was clear from the start, however, that all the prepping was not intended to produce candid answers to opposition queries. The strategy was not to reveal information but to shield it and counterattack. The Liberal record gave the Conservatives ample ammunition. Harper's cabinet had documented Liberal failures on every conceivable issue. On some days, the Tories turned almost every opposition question into a counterblast. All governments had used this tactic, but it soon became apparent that this government would exceed all others. The Conservatives didn't mind looking evasive. They didn't mind if it looked intellectually infantile to defend their own inadequacies by pointing to the inadequacies of others. But Harper himself gave more straightforward responses than most of his ministers. Advisers found that he wasn't intimidated by Question Period because he was good at it.

Question Period ended at 3 p.m. Now came the post-game review. PMO staff always monitored the performance on television, and once the session was finished, Harper would come over and huddle with the group, which usually consisted of Bruce Carson, Keith Beardsley, Sandra Buckler, and one other, often Dmitri Soudas, a young aide who had a close relationship with the PM and was capable of being frank with him. The prime minister would ask how it went, how he came across, how the others did. Harper, they found, was one of his own worst critics.

Usually he worked until about 6:30 p.m., but he often liked to linger, reading reports, discussing the day with advisers, while

downing Chinese food by the carton. His junk-food addiction had
slowed somewhat. As prime minister, he couldn't be seen lining up
at Harvey's as he sometimes was as opposition leader. These evening
sessions were the ones Harper's team enjoyed the most. Often issues
were debated at length, leaving staffers bleary-eyed the next morning.
But Harper would get more personal in the evenings. His dry sense
of humour would surface, and aides saw a side of him they wished
the public could see. And there was hockey talk, always hockey talk.
No one, it was said, could challenge Lester Pearson on baseball stats,
and no one could challenge Stephen Harper on hockey stats. Some
nights, it was off to the arena to watch his son Ben, a good player, in
action on the left wing. At the rink, he often ran across Paul Dewar,
the NDP's foreign affairs critic, whose boy Nathaniel played on the
same team on the right side. Dewar was struck, especially at their
initial meetings, by Harper's social shyness, his quiet, restrained way.

The prime minister followed his son intently but would seldom
shout out encouragement, leaving that to the extrovert in the family,
his wife, Laureen. And work was never far from his mind. During
one game at Brewer Park, a small rink with hardly any viewing capacity, he sought out Dewar and presented him with an envelope. It
contained the government's proposal for Senate reform. He wanted
Dewar to have a look.

In the House of Commons one day before QP, Dewar went to his
seat and was told by colleagues that the prime minister had just come
by and left him something in an envelope. It was a picture of Dewar's
son in a game with Ben. For the New Democrat, seeing Stephen
Harper in the hockey environs was to see someone who looked reluctant, almost timid—a quiet hockey dad hoping his son would do well.
Dewar had a difficult time believing that this was the same man who,
in a different arena, had a killer instinct few leaders could match.

CHAPTER SIX

The Incrementalist Approach

To counter Paul Martin's image as the hundred-priority man, Stephen Harper put the focus in the Conservatives' first months in power on five priorities: a GST cut, accountability legislation, a crackdown on crime, reduced health care wait-times, and a cash handout in place of a national daycare plan. All of these initiatives were doable and none was terribly ambitious, which raised more than a few eyebrows. Thirteen years of central Canadian Liberal domination—its anti-West bias, its statist lean, its arrogance—and this was it? Five middling measures? An agenda this mundane from a prime minister who many viewed as a movement politician?

But Stephen Harper had no intention of trying to hit a grand slam. Infield singles would do. Modest measures would diminish Canadians' fear that knuckle-draggers were in command. "Harper and his advisers thought the government was not going to last long," said Bruce Carson. The idea was to simply put "some stuff in the window that could be done in a short period of time."

One of the guiding principles of the government, as described by strategist Tom Flanagan, was incrementalism. His theory was that "small conservative reforms are less likely to scare voters than grand conservative schemes, particularly in a country like Canada, where conservatism is not the dominant public philosophy." Sweeping visions have a place in intellectual discussion, he said, "but they are toxic in practical politics."

That said, the Tories had never hesitated to put forward big ideas, whether it was R.B. Bennett's belated New Deal, John Diefenbaker's ill-defined "northern vision," or Brian Mulroney's Free Trade Agreement and constitutional reforms. But Harper tended to share Flanagan's perception of the dangers of the big-vision approach. In politics, there were realists and romantics. No one ever counted Stephen Harper among the latter.

The intent was to slowly shape the country into something more conservative. Given his government's minority status, however, Harper knew that he had to stabilize its footing. To do that, he had to take firm hold of the machinery of government, and that meant putting the focus more on politics than on policy. This would be amply demonstrated during the government's first six months.

The policy bias in those early days, recalled Mark Cameron, was on small-scale, consumer-oriented issues. In the Harper five-pack, the two economic measures—the GST cuts and the daycare payout—fit conservative framing nicely. Let the people, not the state, decide what to do with their money. And so, Paul Martin and Ken Dryden's national daycare plan was scrapped in favour of a twelve-hundred-dollar taxable yearly allowance for each child under six. The Tory money came with no strings attached. It could be used for lollipops and roses or, as a Liberal strategist infamously declared, Pilseners and popcorn.

For Harper, a national daycare plan bordered on being a socialist scheme, a phrase he had once used to describe the Kyoto Protocol on climate change. For Martin, whose plan would have transferred to the provinces $5 billion over five years, the national program was what Canadianism was all about. "Think about it this way," he said. "What if, decades ago, Tommy Douglas and my father and Lester Pearson had considered the idea of medicare and then said, 'Forget it! Let's just give people twenty-five dollars a week.' You want a fundamental difference between Mr. Harper and myself? Well, this is it."

Opinion studies showed that Canadians leaned to the Liberals on this issue. But on the GST, the Conservatives had a clear political winner with their 2 percent cut, one percent of which was introduced immediately. The policy was politically expedient. Harper's economics background, critics suggested, was surely sufficient for him to understand that personal income tax cuts were preferable to consumption tax cuts. The 7 percent GST, courageously introduced by Brian Mulroney to waves of scorn, had become the federal treasury's cash cow. It was a slayer of deficits in bad times and a surplus provider in good. Trimming it would cripple the revenue base. And once the tax had been trimmed—politics being what they were—it would be next to impossible to get it back up again.

Harper had an election to win, however, and he was not about to pass up an opportunity like this one. Cameron and others argued against the idea, but after the election, the dissenters concluded they were wrong. They noted that the GST cut turned out to be more popular than any other campaign promise. The Conservatives had stared this gift horse in the mouth for a long time. The Grits were terribly vulnerable on the GST because of a promise they made in the 1993 campaign to abolish it. In the 2000 campaign, the Liberals were worried when they heard rumours that Stockwell Day was about to go after the tax. But Day backed away, as did Harper in the 2004 campaign. This time, however, he thought better of it.

With their defeat, the Liberals also left behind the long-running softwood lumber dispute with the United States. Harper assigned the trade portfolio to his newest Tory, David Emerson, who had worked on the file as a Grit, to prove that the Conservatives could get an agreement their opponents could not. The dispute had intensified in 2002, when the U.S., alleging that Canada unfairly subsidized producers, imposed 27 percent duties on the lumber. Under the terms of the Free Trade Agreement, a joint trade panel was to settle the problem. All the rulings went Canada's way, but Washington, to the consternation of Canadian negotiators, was not prepared to let those verdicts stand and insisted instead on a negotiated settlement.

Having run the Canfor Corporation, B.C.'s giant forestry company, Emerson knew the file well. He had come very close to getting a settlement for the Liberals, which may well have helped them do better in B.C. in the 2006 election. "But the problem," recalled Emerson, "was that there was an element in the agreement that would have required higher tariffs on western B.C. producers than on eastern producers." That, he said, would have caused too much discord. Under the Tories, however, he engineered his way around that obstacle and secured the deal. The new bilateral accord required the U.S. to pay back about $4 billion of the more than $5 billion it had collected on lumber imports. The missing billion prompted some complaints, but the consensus was that a flawed deal was better than none at all. Harper was pleased. His much-derided floor-crosser got the job done.

HARPER'S FIVE PRIORITIES did not include a buildup of the country's armed forces. During the election campaign, he hadn't dwelled on the subject because he didn't want to be seen as too close to the hawk-ish Bush–Cheney agenda. But a strong military was a conservative touchstone, and within two months of taking power, the new prime minister was off to visit the Canadian troops in Afghanistan. The visit was a hit. The photos projected a strong leader, and Harper's words did the same. He was taking ownership of the war and setting down stakes for a long fight.

"We don't make a commitment and then run away at the first sign of trouble," Harper told a thousand cheering soldiers. "There will be some who want to cut and run, but cutting and running is not my way, and it's not the Canadian way." Canada, he declared, had spent too long in the bleachers. "I want Canada to be a leader. Your work is about more than just defending Canada's national interests. Your work is about demonstrating an international leadership role for our country."

Canada had twenty-three hundred troops in Afghanistan in 2006. Ten soldiers and a diplomat had been killed since 2002, when the mission quietly began under Jean Chrétien. The former prime minister never sought to dramatize the conflict, nor did Paul Martin, although he had been intending to visit Afghanistan before he lost the election. Martin also appointed Rick Hillier to lead the country's armed forces and laid out plans for a $12-billion increase in defence spending. Harper was only too happy to up the ante—and not just because it was the Conservative thing to do.

His family was steeped in military history. Christopher Harper, the first arrival, came from Yorkshire, England, in 1774, settling near what is now Sackville, New Brunswick. There, he and his fellow Yorkshiremen were caught in the colonial battles of the day. Christopher Harper fought against the New England revolutionaries and was forced to watch as they burned down his farm. Stephen's grandfather, a teacher in New Brunswick, enjoyed putting his students through marching drills. And his father, Joe, was a collector of military insignia and wrote a small book on the subject. It all rubbed off on a young Stephen, who took considerable pride in Canada's war record in the first half of the twentieth century while being less enthused about the lean to soft power in the second half.

His devotion to the war effort and the revitalization of the armed services were part of an effort to shape a Tory patriotism, one predicated on symbols and traditions. This was central to his goal of taking the flag away from the Liberal Party (whose prime minister, Lester Pearson, had given the country its own flag in the 1960s).

But, hailing from Reform country, Harper had a regionalist image to overcome. "I don't think Mr. Harper thinks in terms of great national endeavours," Ken Dryden said in the campaign. "I don't think that's how his mind works. I don't think that's what's in his bones." The famous former goalie wondered if Harper had ever played a team sport, or if he just thought in terms of individuals and their pocketbooks.

Anticipating this current of criticism, Harper had put one of his chief strategists, Patrick Muttart, to work on the patriot strategy, and in the summer of 2005, he and his team came up with the slogan "Stand Up for Canada." It was the backdrop for most every subsequent event in the Tory campaign—and Harper put meat on the motto. In Newfoundland, he pledged to assert control of the fisheries. In the north, he pledged to build three icebreakers to protect Canadian sovereignty. On the West Coast, he decried a U.S. submarine's passage through territorial waters and promised to beef up military outlays to secure sovereignty there. He had progressed since the days of his Alberta-centric regional thinking. Now he was sounding like he wanted to build a firewall around the entire country. In spreading the news, he levelled a broadside at Canada's foreign service. "When a country's national interests are at stake, we won't hesitate to have diplomatic battles," Harper said. "That's what the foreign service is for—not just to clink glasses at cocktail parties."

The "Stand Up for Canada" campaign extended to the Afghanistan mission as well, and Harper wanted everyone to know that he was the commander-in-chief, not Rick Hillier. A brash and folksy Newfoundlander, Hillier liked the cameras. He had a gift for the gab—and the jab. He had riled the Liberals a little with some of his frank commentary about the need to get out there and kill those enemy "scumbags." But Paul Martin didn't intervene, recalled Tim Murphy, his chief of staff, because "at the end of the day, Hillier was fully supportive of the policy that the civilian overseers in the government made the final call. So we let him be."

Harper, however, didn't let him be. In March 2006, Hillier gave a series of interviews to promote the forces and assist recruiting efforts. His words sounded innocent enough, but the PMO was not forewarned and took offence. Defence Minister Gordon O'Connor called the general into his office for a chat. "We want to see less of you," he told him and proceeded to give him new marching orders. From that day, all Hillier's press dealings and speaking engagements, as well as those of other senior military officers, had to be approved in advance by Harper's staff. Although Hillier had heard talk of the demanding ways of the new supreme ruler, this was hard to take.

More conflict arose. Following the death of Captain Nichola Goddard, the first female soldier killed in combat, Hillier was called in to one of the backrooms at the Royal Military College in Kingston. There he found PMO officials awaiting him. They told him to have the plane carrying Goddard's coffin turned away from the cameras, Hillier recalled, "so that people [couldn't] see the bodies coming off." What was obvious, said the general, was that they "didn't want that picture of the flag-draped coffin in the news." Hillier heard them out, then turned to Gordon O'Connor and said, "Minister, we ain't going to do that. It's as simple as that." The fallen, he felt, deserved the recognition the media coverage brought.

Captain Goddard's death occurred just before a pivotal vote in the Commons on whether to extend the Afghanistan mission by two years. Harper angered the opposition by giving only two days' notice of the vote and by threatening to extend the mission by a year no matter what the vote. He won it by a narrow margin of 149 to 145 and walked across the floor to shake hands with Bill Graham, the Liberals' interim leader. Graham had complained bitterly of having to vote "with a gun to our heads," but he supported Harper nonetheless. Michael Ignatieff voted for extending the mission, while Dryden and future leader Stéphane Dion were against.

THE SILENCING OF Hillier and the handling of the war vote offered examples of the type of change Harper was introducing. Tim Murphy, who helped the Tories with the transition, saw the contrast. "The fundamental lesson that Stephen Harper took out of Paul Martin's experience," he said, "is that being open is the worst possible thing to do." With his curious mind, Martin wanted to invite input from everywhere, including the inner ranks of the bureaucracy. "You had assistant deputy ministers and directors of policy who would get calls from the prime minister," recalled Murphy, "and you could imagine the excitement and consternation that would create."

Martin's management style was flat, lacking hierarchical discipline. Brian Mulroney's had been similar in the early years, until he brought in the clear-minded Derek Burney as chief of staff. Harper's was anything but flat. David Emerson said the differences between Martin and Harper were like night and day. One was scattershot, the other an expert marksman. Under Martin, "there was a proliferation of people with ideas but no one who was pulling it all together in what you might call a robust, coherent, social-democratic vision for the country." Cabinet meetings were unproductive. An issue would come up and "you would have one minister raise her or his hand and decide to make a contribution. And when that happened, every single minister around the table felt compelled to offer their view and you almost felt embarrassed if you sat there and didn't say anything." In the chair, Emerson said, Paul Martin was too lenient. He had always been a good listener, but he was sometimes too good. "Paul would just sit there and let this go on," he recalled. "So you could be in the cabinet meeting from nine till noon, no problem at all, and really nothing would happen other than people would download their views."

Occasionally, the atmosphere was so freewheeling that it bordered on the chaotic, and on those days, Martin would try to exercise some authority by pounding the gavel on the table. He sometimes pounded so hard that Emerson thought he was going to break it. But order was still slow in coming.

Harper stood in bold contrast. "In the Harper cabinet, you really did not intervene unless you had something to say. The cabinet meetings were short and succinct, far more disciplined, far more organized." The gavel wasn't necessary because Harper was an intimidating presence. People were uneasy around him, Emerson observed. Though he could be personable in small groups, "it was a very controlled atmosphere in there. You felt you shouldn't open your mouth unless you had something really important to say."

Emerson was "amazed" at how knowledgeable Harper was on the issues and just as amazed at the discipline he imposed on himself. It made it difficult for others to complain when they were expected to do the same. "He was inevitably out there with the teleprompter and staying absolutely true to his script and the message for that day," said Emerson, who liked to freewheel with journalists and caught bad looks from the PM for doing so. "I couldn't operate that way. I'd go crazy."

At cabinet meetings, Martin seldom delved into the politics of an issue, but Harper was again the opposite. Most everything was put under the political microscope. Everything—his political machine, his polling operation, his strategizing—was more sophisticated. One PM was a thinker, the other was a thinker and a political animal. Emerson could not remember a single instance of Martin talking to him about how something should be handled politically. But Harper and his team didn't hesitate, strategizing at cabinet meetings, for example, about how policies might be better contoured to appeal to ethnic groups. Emerson and other ministers were often instructed to be more political by sharpening their message and attacking opponents. "There was always a little bit of grumbling from ministers that they were being controlled too much," Emerson recalled, "and that the young kids around the PMO were driving too much of the business of government." That assessment was echoed by veteran Progressive Conservatives, who could often be found on the Hill, cursing about having been told what to do by, as one put it, "some debutant neo-con in the PMO who knows nothing."

The politicized, all-controlling efficiency of the Harper approach didn't bother Emerson much. After a few months of settling in, he was accepted and felt more comfortable than he had with some Liberals, who looked upon him, he said, as "kind of a chamber-of-commerce guy." But the visceral animosity Conservatives displayed towards their opponents was something he couldn't figure out. He was bothered too by the way they reduced so much of what they were doing to crass political ends.

Politics could be treated as a battlefield war or as a high-minded debating exercise on what was in the public interest. "Paul Martin's calling of an inquiry into the sponsorship scandal was the right thing to do," said Emerson. "But did it do him any good politically?" That was the dilemma. But for the Harper Tories, there was no dilemma. They had chosen their style of politics—and it was not the one Aristotle would have applauded.

CHAPTER SEVEN

The Control Fixation

M ark Tushingham was a scientist with Environment Canada. He had written a book on global warming, a work of fiction called *Hotter Than Hell*, and he was scheduled to speak about it at the National Press Club in the spring of 2006. But a few minutes before the event, word came down from the office of Environment Minister Rona Ambrose that he could not proceed.

The minister's office claimed the problem was that Tushingham was advertised as a government speaker, but the luncheon had only billed him as an Ottawa environmental scientist. He was promoting his book, as all authors do, and the book was a novel, an imaginary account. But it was enough to have him silenced.

At the time, Natural Resources Minister Gary Lunn was charging hard against the Kyoto Protocol, dispensing with fifteen programs from the Martin and Chrétien years. The Tushingham book, even though it was fiction, was off message—hence the gag order. The author's treatment prompted journalists to wonder if, in all the country's history, any other government had censored an author from talking about his or her novel.

Had this been an isolated occurrence, it wouldn't have seemed so significant. But as seen in the case of Tom Flanagan's book, it was far from isolated. The PMO was in the course of putting in place a message-control system, a vetting operation unlike anything ever seen in the capital. No other government had even come close to such a system of oversight.

The new regimen called for all public pronouncements by civil servants, diplomats, the military, cabinet members, and Conservative MPs to be approved by the Prime Minister's Office or its bureaucratic arm, the Privy Council Office (PCO). The vetting was by no means a quick rubber-stamping procedure. If a government official or a caucus member wanted to say something publicly, he or she would first have to fill out a Message Event Proposal (MEP) and submit it to central command. This form had sections with such titles as Desired Headline, Strategic Objective, Desired Sound Bite, and the like. It also had areas for supplying details on the speaking backdrop, the ideal event photograph, and even the speaker's wardrobe.

Once submitted, the MEP was studied by PMO and PCO officials, often bouncing back and forth between apparatchiks before getting final approval. Some MEPs required less vetting than others, but the massive centralization caused logjams, delays, and in some cases, cancellation of planned events because the requester never heard back in time. Keith Beardsley recalled even events for cabinet ministers being derailed. "Every communications director for every minister was trying to get stuff through. Their ministers wanted to do things," he said. But "because of the backlog [sometimes an event] got delayed and delayed and it was cancelled."

In the past, while there was some vetting, departments produced their own news releases and scheduled events for ministers independently. Under Harper, such freedom was not allowed. The surveillance applied even to minor occurrences at departments like Parks Canada. News releases on the state of wildlife in the forests had to get approval from the PMO/PCO. One Parks Canada official noted that he'd written a release on the mating season of the black bears, and even it—"a bombshell if there ever was one," he said—had to be approved by one of Harper's censors.

The idea of controlling the message so completely was first concocted by Phil Murphy, one of Harper's advisers, when the Conservatives were still in opposition. Patrick Muttart, Harper's key strategic planner, developed the idea into the MEP system. Initially, the plan was to apply only to the prime minister's events. So that there would be no mistakes, Muttart arranged every Harper event down to the very last syllable and footstep. When this approach proved to be effective, the government decided to expand it—and kept on expanding it throughout government. It was micromanagement Soviet-style, but it was introduced in such a staggered way that it didn't generate headlines on the curbing of democratic freedoms.

New controls were also being put in place in other communications areas. The PMO was introducing restrictive new policies on relations with the media, for example. And there were signs of a crackdown on the government's handling of access-to-information requests, one of the most important tools available to private citizens.

Control the message and stifle dissent—that was the operating plan. It was risky business, though, especially when the Conservatives were elected on a platform of transparency and accountability. But in the early months, Harper was giving every indication he was prepared to take the risk. There were all those threats to the well-being of his government—a minority government—and he had to overcome them.

Message control, Harper's top advisers said, was the key. When Tom Flanagan was his chief of staff at the Alliance Party, he discovered that Harper had a relaxed attitude to some other areas of the operation. He would try to talk to him about plans for some big new expenditure, for example, but could hardly get Harper's attention. The same was true, he said, for a lot of the party's organizational matters. "If he thought it was being done competently, he didn't worry about it," said Flanagan. But "I just let Stephen be his own chief of staff with respect to messaging. That's where he has taken measures of centralization to new levels." Other officials confirmed that there were exceptions to his control obsessions. "He actually doesn't care about a lot of issues that have preoccupied other prime ministers," recalled a former member of his inner sanctum. He didn't care much about who got big ambassadorships or appointments to Crown corporations or even to the bench. "Didn't give a damn," the official said. An exception was Senate appointments. Those who worked extra hard for the party got their reward with seats in the red chamber.

Chief of Staff Brodie oversaw the MEP system. Brodie, who had an informal manner that was much appreciated by his staff, didn't have the high-powered reputation of a Derek Burney under Mulroney or a Jean Pelletier under Chrétien, but no one doubted his authority. Recruited by Flanagan at the Alliance Party, the former political science professor at Western University in London, Ontario, rose through the ranks, becoming national director of the unified Conservatives before getting the top job under Harper. He was ideologically committed, distressed, as he put it, at how "the Trudeau government deliberately and systematically went about redoing the country," and determined, like Harper, to repair the damage.

He was "100 percent" behind the imposition of the vetting, or, as critics saw it, the censorship system. "No professional organization communicates without planning first," said Brodie. "One five-minute interview can do a lot of good or a lot of bad. A five-minute interview should take an hour or two of planning, especially if someone is planning to speak on behalf of the government of Canada. Before we were elected, I think there was a view that you basically winged it in an interview."

Harper, he said, was acutely aware of the mistakes of past Tory governments. So often, the problem, he and his team concluded, was a lack of discipline. They were especially cognizant of the stumbles that caused the quick fall of Joe Clark's minority government because they had studied a book on Clark, Jeffrey Simpson's *Discipline of Power*. "Our views on this—mine, Muttart's, Buckler's, Harper's—were indelibly formed by one source, *Discipline of Power*," said Brodie. "We all read the book and all resolved never to let our government turn into a gong show." Too many people around Ottawa, Brodie found, "want to talk without thinking first. When you ask them what they plan to say, they're evasive or uncertain. MEPs make them do better." The system, he maintained, worked. "Ask yourself this: is the PM generally regarded as someone who speaks carefully and deliberately? As someone who looks like he's in charge … As an effective leader? Yes on all counts."

There was no doubting, said policy adviser Mark Cameron, that the Harper crackdown rubbed a lot of people the wrong way. Public servants were used to more liberty. "I think there had been, under Chrétien, a kind of coziness between some senior political people and the senior bureaucrats that was no longer in place," he observed.

Cameron and most others in the PMO defended the crackdown as necessary for a government in a minority situation. Caucus and cabinet members weren't overly impressed. One caucus member, Ontario's Dean Del Mastro, not realizing a reporter was within earshot, said the controls were so bad, particularly at the outset, that he and other MPs worried about what colour necktie they put on in the morning.

Cabinet ministers received from Harper, as cabinets did from other prime ministers, what were called mandate letters. The mandate letters listed the general duties the minister was expected to perform and asked that they be faithfully executed. But under Harper the nature of the mandate letters changed. The instructions were something more akin to being handed straitjackets. There was no question, Cameron candidly recalled, that Harper's was a far more directive process. "Under our government the mandate letters tended to list every platform or Throne Speech commitment affecting that department and dictating who you're supposed to work with and whether you were going to get any funding."

The measures did help diminish the propensity of some cabinet ministers to float trial balloons, which was the type of thing that had led to mixed messaging in other governments. Some ministers got a bit more leeway than others. Trade Minister David Emerson did not dispute the "control freak" label that was being pinned on Harper, but he found that the levels of control were different for each minister, depending on his or her rank and the level of trust he or she had gained. After the first few months, Emerson gained some trust and was put on key committees. Although he was instructed to be more political in his dealings, he did not find the atmosphere overly oppressive.

But those who had been around in previous Tory governments noticed the contrast. Keith Beardsley had served as a chief of staff to Immigration Minister Gerry Weiner in the Mulroney government. Mulroney, he said, trusted most of his ministers and left them alone. "If a story broke and shit was flying in the paper, you might get a call saying, 'What the hell's going on?' So we'd give them the background and they'd say, 'Okay, you guys deal with it.'" The odd time, Beardsley said, ministers would be called to a meeting with Deputy Prime Minister Don Mazankowski. "[But] they'd never come out and say, 'Here's your talking points.'"

Under Chrétien, the PMO could be heavy-handed, depending on the circumstances, but senior cabinet ministers like John Manley, Sheila Copps, and Paul Martin still had considerable independence, so much independence in Martin's case that he stirred a caucus rebellion. Chrétien trusted his ministers to carry out their responsibilities and, like Mulroney, would bother them only if they got in trouble. The Franco-Ontarian Don Boudria served in his cabinet as minister of public works and government House leader. He was often seen scurrying down Parliament's halls overloaded with briefing books, and consequently took on the moniker Binder Boy. Chrétien would outline for you your job as minister, Boudria recalled. "He was very clear, but that was the end of it, to the point where you were wondering sometimes, 'Am I doing this right?' He would never tell you anything. You were kind of craving some feedback." As House leader, Binder Boy got a call from the boss every couple of weeks asking about the status of certain bills. "I'd say, 'Well, Prime Minister, it's in second reading and I think we'll finish the debate Tuesday.' He'd say, 'Okay, goodbye,' and hang up. That was it."

Deputy ministers also had more leeway, but Harper's men had only to look at the human resources department—where the structure was so loose it led to the Chrétien-era controversy known as the billion-dollar boondoggle—for proof that excessive liberty could stir trouble in those ranks too.

UNDER HARPER, anyone who stepped out of line ran the risk of encountering—to use the hockey talk favoured by the PM—a member of his goon squad. There were two particular members of this team who spread fear through the ranks and, Tory insiders complained, contributed heavily to the image of Harper as overly authoritarian and undemocratic. One was Doug Finley, a former airline executive who had worked for the Scottish National Party and for the Liberals in Quebec. He was the director of political operations. The other was Jenni Byrne, who did a variety of senior PMO jobs and many political assignments under Finley.

In Watergate parlance, as one wag cracked, Finley and Byrne were the Haldeman and Ehrlichwoman of their time. Finley, whose wife, Diane Finley, was the minister of immigration, was a first-rate political organizer who did yeoman work in bringing Harper to power. But he operated like a tyrant, bullying people left and right,

seeing conspiracy theories everywhere. He cultivated some friends
in the media and in caucus but was generally viewed as someone
who played to Harper's baser instincts. He was tightly connected,
however, so no one wanted to mess with him.

Jenni Byrne kept a low profile, never going near the media, but
inside the tent her profile was anything but low. She had an out-of-
control temper, colleagues said, and would let fly on the slightest of
provocations. One day outside the Sheraton Hotel in Ottawa, a top
official spent five minutes listing off civil servants and party members
she had sought to belittle. Like Finley, she had once worked for Tom
Flanagan, but while Flanagan admired Finley, he was less enthusiastic about Byrne. "I was hoping she would develop more self-control
as she got older," he said. "I don't see any signs of change."

She had her strengths. She was competent and the fiercest loyalist
one could imagine. But the greatest need, most Tories felt, was for
Harper to temper his overly aggressive instincts. Finley and Byrne did
the opposite, and they were joined in that respect by another fierce
combatant, the PMO communications director, Sandra Buckler.

With the abrupt firing of Communications Director William Stairs
after the Emerson affair, Harper had sent a signal that he wanted
more pushback, that Stairs's attitude to the media had been too soft.
In came Buckler. A long-time party activist, lobbyist, and occasional
media pundit, she had worked on the communications teams of
Kim Campbell, Preston Manning, and Tom Long, the former president of the Ontario Progressive Conservative Party and the chair of
Mike Harris's two victorious election campaigns. Once on board,
she immediately started putting Harper's restrictive new policy into
effect.

Harper never liked the tradition of holding media scrums after
cabinet meetings. He started concealing the times of those meetings
to keep his ministers away from the microphones. Cabinet and caucus
members, with few exceptions, were instructed to avoid talking to the

media without prior approval. At press conferences, Harper's office also wanted to control who asked questions. The press conferences were limited to specific issues as Harper did away with the wide-open meetings with the media, which had been a long-time custom, albeit a waning one.

Feeling that the Ottawa press gallery was biased against the Conservatives, Harper vowed to deal more with local and regional media. The Ottawa media's calls to Buckler sometimes went unanswered. A major strike against journalistic access came via Harper's vetting system. With civil servants and caucus silenced to such a degree, the media could no longer access information the way they had been able to in the past.

Flare-ups ensued. In April, Harper caused a flap when he refused to recognize the next questioner in line at a press conference, picking a reporter in the back instead. This prompted the snubbed journalist, the CBC's feisty Julie Van Dusen, to ask, "Why are you ignoring the lineup? We're in a lineup, and I'm next." Harper continued to ignore her, but the reporter he'd called on chose not to ask a question. Van Dusen kept pressing and asked hers instead. The PM gave a terse response and, with a to-hell-with-this look, headed for the exit.

The notion that the prime minister should be allowed to dictate who can ask questions and who can't was formally challenged by media executives. Harper told one of them he didn't need reporters, could do fine without them, and didn't care if they didn't get to ask questions. Tom Flanagan summed up the view of many in Harperland when he said, "The press gallery is a bunch of self-important, preening prima donnas who think they're crucial because they're stationed in Ottawa and they've watched *All the President's Men* too many times."

Harper relished sticking it to the fourth estate. The more difficult Buckler made it for journalists, the more he applauded her. Though her bar-the-door campaigns prompted negative commentary from print and television journalists, she had support from the PM, Ian Brodie, Bruce Carson, and Keith Beardsley. She tried occasionally to persuade Harper to take a more open and friendly approach, Beardsley noted, but she didn't get far. Harper wanted her out there with a horsewhip. Although she was not an ogre by nature, in the view of the assembled Ottawa scribes, Harper turned her into one.

But even some of his aides recognized that the prime minister had a wrongheaded view of the media. His thinking was at least a decade behind the times. Back then, the Liberals held the balance of media power and Conservatives had a right to grouse. But times had changed. The balance had switched to the right side of the spectrum. The arrival of the *National Post* and the conservative Canwest chain, which owned most of the country's big newspapers, had given the Tories an edge. The tabloid *Sun* chain was conservative, as was *Maclean's* magazine, and AM radio was full of right-wing talk jocks. Neither CTV nor Global Television was pro-Liberal. And while Conservatives railed against the CBC, it was no longer the Liberal bastion of old, at least not on the television side. Of its prominent pundits—Rex Murphy, Andrew Coyne, Allan Gregg, Chantal Hébert—not one was on the political left.

The change in the media tilt was of major significance. What could make or break a story was whether it had legs. Negative stories that held the headlines for only a day or two were of marginal consequence. What often determined whether a story had legs was the lean of the media franchises. A Conservatively tilted media was more inclined to give the government the benefit of the doubt and to give smaller display to controversial stories.

But Harper couldn't be persuaded that he had journalistic allies. After the 2004 election, he noticed that a couple of reporters who had given him a particularly rough time during the campaign went straight into the employ of Liberal cabinet ministers. Much later, Harper was still railing about it. When CTV's Craig Oliver tried one day to suggest to him that the media wasn't biased, Harper cited this example. Oliver pointed out in response that reporters had also signed up to work for the Conservatives after some election campaigns. Harper was unconvinced.

Although there were prime ministers who had cultivated reporters—inviting them to Sussex Drive for drinks or calling them up to schmooze—Harper, said his friend John Weissenberger, simply wasn't interested. He was more inclined to do the opposite. His operatives often went directly to media owners and publishers to complain about coverage and single out journalists they didn't like.

In taking on the fourth estate, Harper was hardly without historical company. Citing an obscure section of the criminal code, Prime Minister R.B. Bennett once threatened to have the ink-stained wretches locked up. John Diefenbaker phoned reporters at all hours of the night to berate them. Lester Pearson, like Harper, suspended the post-cabinet scrums. Brian Mulroney was contemptuous of many journalists, as was Pierre Trudeau. And Jean Chrétien's office once lobbied to have a columnist (this writer) dismissed for his coverage of Liberal malfeasance.

But most prime ministers had tried, at least at the outset, to establish good relationships with journalists. Harper's negative attitude, by contrast, was set in stone from day one.

IN ADDITION TO COMMUNICATIONS, Harper was looking to assert more control over other centres of power. One was the Senate, which had a Liberal majority, but which in time he could change. Another was agency heads and tribunals and watchdogs, where Liberal appointees could be moved out. Yet another was broadening Conservative influence over important house committees.

On the latter he moved right away, not seeming to worry that he looked hypocritical in doing so. In opposition, Harper had railed against Chrétien for controlling the appointments of committee

chairpersons. In so doing, he exacerbated tensions in the Liberal
ranks between Martin and Chrétien, who had a row over the issue.
But once in power, Harper realized that these appointments were too
important to be left to others. No matter what he had said in the past,
he was not about to cede such an advantage. He did an about-face. Of
the twenty-two permanent House committees, he put his Conservative members in control of all but three.

His stewardship was only just beginning, but already the authoritarian tendencies were starting to be noticed. In an editorial, *The
Globe and Mail* lamented that ministers were being gagged and that
the PM was reversing himself on many promises in his accountability legislation and other initiatives. "On that fabled British television
show *Yes, Minister*," the editorialist wrote, "the duplicitous senior
bureaucrat bluntly advises an underling that open government is 'a
contradiction in terms: you can be open or you can have government.'
Mr. Harper has converted that wicked satire into his own depressing
catechism."

Before Harper was elected prime minister, William Johnson had
published a biography of him—*Stephen Harper and the Future of
Canada*—which charted many of his strengths but warned of a basic
flaw. "He constantly displays an excess of partisanship. From the
time he was elected to the Commons, his attacks on Chrétien, and
now Martin, have often been over the top. There is harshness, a lack
of humour, humanity and moderation that disregards the traditions
of Parliament where all members have a right to be treated as honour-
able." The author's words were starting to sound prophetic.

The catalogue of heavy-handed acts grew with the controversy
over Harper's planned Public Appointments Commission. Intended
as one of the pillars of his accountability legislation, which was now
working its way through Parliament, the commission was to be
responsible for severely restricting, if not eliminating, the age-old
practice of patronage. It was to take charge of filling more than three

thousand federal appointments through "a fair and open selection process based on merit."

But when Harper appointed Gwyn Morgan to be its chair, the opposition rebelled. Morgan, an Alberta oilman with a first-rate reputation as a company executive, was a friend of Harper's and of the party's. The opposition saw a patronage appointee heading the anti-patronage commission. How could Morgan, they asked, be an objective arbiter of other appointments? "It's the principle that the appointment commission itself be appointed in a way that is non-partisan," said Liberal MP Stephen Owen. "It just gives exactly the wrong message at the very start of a worthy cause to pervert it in that way."

Moreover, the opposition charged that Morgan had made preju-dicial remarks regarding minorities. Earlier in the year, he had questioned the value of multiculturalism and suggested that it divides Canadians. He linked Canada's gang-violence problem to immigration from places like Jamaica and Southeast Asia.

In the end, the operations committee voted down the Morgan appointment. In an apparent fit of pique, Harper refused to nominate a new chair and instead annulled the entire commission. He would revert to the old patronage system. "What this tells us," he angrily stated, is that "we won't be able to clean up the process in this minority Parliament. We'll obviously need a majority government to do that in the future."

The episode showed shades of the old Harper. When not getting his way, he turned away. He could have easily found another nominee with a less partisan background to do the job. The notion that he was truly irritated by the turn of events was scoffed at by opponents. They suggested that he was probably quietly celebrating. The outcome was ugly for the opposition, which wanted the reform, and for a system badly in need of such a reform. Harper's image would have benefited from a well-run commission, but for "the control freak," as he was now being called on a daily basis, maintaining control of patronage had many advantages.

Harper's other appointments at this time were less controversial. He replaced Allan Rock at the United Nations with John McNee, a career diplomat. Michael Wilson, a Mulroney-era Tory, became the ambassador to the United States. He then surprised many with his nomination of Marshall Rotstein, who was not considered ideological, to the Supreme Court. (Given his long-standing opposition to court activism, Harper had been expected to name an ideologue.) He also introduced some accountability to the process of bench selections, allowing an all-party committee of MPs to question nominees in publicly televised hearings.

DESPITE THE INCREASING CRITICISM Harper was facing for his closed style of operating, much had gone well in his first months. Progress had been made on many of his five priorities, he'd gotten a softwood lumber deal and an extension of the Afghan war mission, and Finance Minister Jim Flaherty had brought in a reasonably popular first budget.

Flaherty had been a charter member of Mike Harris's so-called Common Sense Revolution in Ontario. In those days, he was the hardliner of hardliners, banning squeegee kids and promising to hire constables to round up the homeless and remove them from the streets. In Ottawa, he sported a friendlier look. In the budget, he issued many new tax credits, including one for five hundred dollars to parents of children playing sports. He also brought in corporate and small-business tax cuts. Polls showed that Canadians approved of the budget by a two-to-one margin.

Normally, cabinet members filled the Commons foyer after a budget to give their thoughts to reporters, but Harper ordered all his ministers except one or two to stay away from the media. When John Baird, the Treasury Board president, was later spotted in Hy's

Steakhouse, one journalist cracked, "I see Harper let you out for a beer." Joe Fontana, the long-time Liberal MP from London, Ontario, sauntered over. "Ninety percent of that budget was the Liberal budget," he barked, mocking the Tories for all their self-congratulation when it was the Liberals who had left them the big surplus. He launched into a long tirade about Ottawa's new dictatorship. "God, are they arrogant," he complained. "It took us ten years to get as bad as these control freaks."

In the prime minister's office, they heard the criticism but weren't terribly concerned. They expected it. Harper, his party a victim of lack of discipline in the past, was not about to have that past repeated. The discipline and control he was introducing, even if it meant his caucus members were waddling around like trained seals, even if it meant the government had the look of a one-man democracy, appeared to be paying off. "The proof was in the pudding," said his policy director, Bruce Carson. "There weren't many stumbles in the early months."

CHAPTER EIGHT

The Green Games

In April, just a few months after the Harper government was installed, Brian Mulroney came to Ottawa to give his first major address in the capital since 1993. The former prime minister was to receive an award for being Canada's greenest prime minister. While in office, he had won an acid rain treaty with the United States, was the first leader to sign the United Nations Framework Convention on Climate Change, and had promoted many other green initiatives. In this and other areas, his stewardship, while rueful in some respects, was anticipatory.

In his speech to Conservatives, the sixty-seven-year-old baritone underscored the importance of green governance. "Whether the process proves to be Kyoto or something else," he said, "let's acknowledge the urgency of global warming." He sought to link custodianship of the environment to a broader cause. "The future of this country is going north," Mulroney stated, "and it's time for a new northern vision: one of sustainable development that preserves the Arctic wilderness, protects wildlife, and sustains a way of life for our indigenous people."

Harper was already drawing criticism for his reluctance to set a bold national direction, and now here was another Tory prime minister telling him to clear the small potatoes from his plate. The message may have been discomfiting. Earlier in the day, Harper had told reporters that Mulroney was being crowned the greenest of the green because "he didn't pursue grandiose schemes and unworkable arrangements and the kind of problem we got into on Kyoto. Instead he decided to make real progress, concrete progress on particular issues."

The contrasts between the two men had been evident for a long period. The relationship was never going to be easy, not since Harper, as one of Preston Manning's consorts, had blown to pieces the old Tory base in the West. Instead of airing their grievances within the party, the Reformers bombed the bridges. Mulroney felt he had tried to address many of the West's demands. As his defenders pointed out, he sounded the death knell of the National Energy Program, eliminated the Foreign Investment Review Agency, moved the National Energy Board to Calgary, brought in the Free Trade Agreement, and answered most of the West's calls with the Meech Lake Accord proposals.

Harper wasn't impressed. In 1991, with Reform in the ascendancy, he said of Mulroney, "The man has a pettiness and a credibility problem that is so large that it's tough for voters to support him even when he does things that may benefit their region or benefit them personally. He really is an anathema." On becoming Alliance leader in 2002, however, Harper was more conciliatory. With conservatives moving towards a merger, he needed to reach out to the Tory wing. Just prior to the amalgamation, he told his Alliance Party caucus, "We're going to be building a party with people who revere Brian Mulroney. You need to forget everything you've been saying about him for years."

After the two sides joined hands, Mulroney, having helped the process along, backed Belinda Stronach in the leadership race. But with Harper's victory, grudges were put aside and the two made peace. In Quebec, Mulroney and Senator David Angus hosted dinner parties for the socially uncomfortable leader, introducing him to the cultural and political elite. The former prime minister also occasionally conferred behind the scenes with Harper, including once to warn him about Tom Flanagan's book *Harper's Team*. Mulroney had seen an early draft or been briefed about it. "Mulroney called Stephen and told him it was going to create lots of waves," recalled Flanagan. The warning was one of the factors that prompted Harper to try to stop the book being published.

At the dinner to fete Mulroney's environmental award, Harper was gracious, but hardly enthused about being counselled in such a high-profile way to move on global warming and adopt grand visions for the nation. He didn't sense the urgency that Mulroney—or much of the rest of the world—sensed on the environment. Global warming hadn't made it to his list of five priorities. It was an issue that his party base viewed with scepticism and as such served as a reminder that this was a different party from Mulroney's—or Stanfield's or Diefenbaker's. Although the new Conservatives were trying to be more moderate, the party's preponderant Reform–Alliance wing still had sharp edges. Harper knew that climate change was too important an issue to ignore, but he wouldn't be trying to win any green awards.

In his first meeting with Harper after he became prime minister, Jack Layton presented him with a seminal environmental book, *The Weather Makers*, by Tim Flannery. Layton's inscription said climate change was the vital issue for his children and Harper's. At their second meeting, the NDP leader was pleased to see the book still prominently positioned on Harper's desk. But his enthusiasm was not to last.

The new prime minister chose Rona Ambrose to be his first environment minister. She was a petite, raven-haired Edmontonian who grew up in Brazil, read Ayn Rand novels, became a public policy consultant for the Alberta Tories, and first won election to Parliament in 2004. On a Harper team short on female up-and-comers, she had potential. The PMO liked her style. During the debate on national daycare, she told Ken Dryden, "Working women want to make their own choices. We don't need old white guys telling us what to do."

Ambrose's first task was to bury the Kyoto accord, and she did so with relish. "We would have to pull every car and truck off the street and shut down every train and ground every plane to reach the Kyoto target negotiated by the Liberals," she declared. Canada became the first Western government to shelve Kyoto, earning the Harper team an anti-green reputation right out of the gate. While holding to this position, Ambrose had to chair a United Nations conference on climate change. Critics on the left sneered at the hypocrisy, but on Kyoto she had a convincing case to make. Under the Grits, Canada had committed to reducing its greenhouse gases by 6 percent from 1990 levels by 2008 to 2012. Instead, the levels had risen a spectacular 26 percent by 2004. The Kyoto targets were far out of reach, just as Ambrose suggested, but the onus was on her to come up with a viable alternative plan. Here she stumbled.

Environment was a complex portfolio, and Ambrose was both new in it and getting no clear direction from her superiors. She had trouble at her office and with her bureaucracy, losing her chief of staff and her deputy minister. She was criticized for preventing Mark Tushingham from promoting his global-warming novel. Jack Layton, already persuaded that the prime minister wasn't paying any attention to the book he'd left him, had his party table a motion to force Ambrose to resign after only five months on the job.

She survived the vote, and a few days later, the Conservatives held a cabinet retreat in Quebec City. Bruce Carson, the senior policy adviser, was sitting around talking hockey with Harper in a suite at the Château Frontenac when the subject switched to the beleaguered environment minister. Noting that Ambrose was without a chief of staff, Carson suggested he spend his afternoons at her shop, helping to put together a green alternative. The PM gave the go-ahead, and Carson got to work with Ambrose on a plan while she tried to fight off the tree-huggers. On this she didn't help her cause when the issue of the Northern Spotted Owl arose. In British Columbia, only seventeen of these owls remained, but Ambrose claimed the species was in no imminent danger of extinction, occasioning quite a howl over the owl.

In the fall, she introduced the Clean Air Act, a plan to reduce the level of greenhouse emissions starting in 2020 and have them down to about half of 2003 levels by 2050. The plan had some laudable features, such as regulations on motor vehicle emissions, but it was roundly denounced. The Green Party's Elizabeth May, who was an environmental activist and the former director of the Sierra Club of Canada, said that moving the baseline level for emissions to 2003 was foolhardy because reductions from that high a starting point didn't amount to much. Setting 2050 as the target date also brought on much derision, and Harper quickly did a retreat, agreeing to send the bill off to committee, where it was subsequently ravaged.

Carson felt the media was largely to blame. They declared the act dead on arrival, he said, citing a CTV report. "I think the phrase was that half the people alive today will be dead when this comes to fruition." Looking back, he said the government had the right idea. "What really pisses me off is that that piece of legislation was prescient," he insisted. "Everybody now talks about 2050 as the goal to move towards." In retrospect, he felt that a different strategy should have been used. "Using the parliamentary tool was probably not the best tool to use. We ended up being captive of the minority."

Carson's efforts to manage the file was yet another demonstration of the power of the PMO. Environment was one of the departments the Conservatives held in high suspicion. They suspected that leftists were leaking information to try to paint the Tories as dinosaurs. "We had a lot of problems from Environment Canada with bureaucrats slipping stuff out to the media," recalled Keith Beardsley. That, he said, made the PMO suspicious of other departments as well. "It set a lot of the tone, at least in dealing with the bureaucrats, [that] just tainted the whole process."

In keeping with the culture of control they were bringing to the capital, the Tories sought to minimize access on the environment file. They shut down the federal website on climate change, directing people to other sites where information on the perils of global warming was scant. Opposition critics alleged that the Tories were following the advice of a well-known Republican strategist, Frank Luntz, who came to Ottawa in the spring of 2006 for strategy sessions with Harper's team. In the U.S., Luntz had advised Republicans to keep the public confused about the state of climate science.

From the outset, the government's attitude, said Mark Cameron, who did some work on the environment file, was "Let's not be boy scouts. There is a problem with many of these issues at the international level. Many of the countries will say anything, then not follow up. I don't think we wanted to make some promise and have the U.S. or China not do anything and [we] end up holding the bag. So I think our approach was pretty pragmatic."

But Cameron felt the government erred in not being more forthcoming. "I don't think the direction of the policy was a problem," he said. "But we could have laid out more of a framework on what we had in mind. I think business and the provinces would have appreciated it more [if we'd done that] rather than keeping everything in reserve."

By the start of 2007, Ambrose was out as environment minister, having been replaced in the portfolio by John Baird, who, like Flaherty, was a former Ontario cabinet minister under Mike Harris. Harper wanted one of his best communicators on the file. With his court jester's grin and blowtorch vocabulary, Baird filled the need.

HARPER HAD TOSSED Ambrose into a broad and intricate portfolio when she had no experience in the subject or in cabinet. Most newly elected prime ministers had found themselves in the same spot, having to appoint the uninitiated to important cabinet positions. Sometimes on-the-job training was required. Too much of it. But the Conservatives had even been hard-pressed to find talent for the party leadership, never mind other positions. It was symptomatic of a bigger problem: men and women with distinguished backgrounds and impressive accomplishments were not banging down the party's doors. Few showed up to run in the election, and that left Stephen Harper with a front bench of modest ability.

Though it didn't necessarily translate to better performance, pedigree used to mean more in politics. John F. Kennedy was saluted for attracting the so-called best and brightest. Many of his cabinet members had distinguished backgrounds in business, law, or letters. The Trudeau Liberals and the provincial Parti Québécois and others had attracted politicians with pedigree. But in the modern political arena, a long list of scholarly credentials was no longer considered advantageous. Ronald Reagan, who owned more horses than books, had fashioned a new model, and it wasn't a model with which intellectual elites identified. What's more, highly qualified people often avoided politics because of the indignities of the enterprise, the possibility that one's reputation would not survive the shelling. Distressingly, it had been demonstrated too many times that the low road was the surest way to victory.

The Harper cabinet featured barely a single soul of distinguished pedigree. Harper towered in talent over his executive, and it was of some comfort to him that no eminent heirs apparent were waiting in the wings. His lone figure with federal cabinet experience was Justice Minister Rob Nicholson, who often came across as hyper-partisan and closed-minded. House Leader Peter Van Loan fell into the same category, as did Treasury Board President Vic Toews. Defence

Minister Gordon O'Connor had experience in his field, but he was out of place in the Commons, poorly suited to the cut and thrust of debate. Among those who brought nuance to their performances were Stockwell Day in public safety, David Emerson in trade, and Jim Prentice, Minister of Indian Affairs and Northern Development. The Calgary MP Jason Kenney, who was not yet in a full cabinet role, was nonetheless demonstrating the power of a minister. There were no big men of Bay Street at the cabinet table, but Jim Flaherty, who had a degree from Princeton, was an articulate combatant.

Foreign affairs posed a special problem. The portfolio demanded experience in the world. Harper had only a parochial cast of characters from which to choose, and his own provincial background compounded the problem. His only trip abroad, a veteran Tory cracked, had been to Montana. His world-view was based more on ideology than experience, prompting concern among the diplomatic corps that he would fashion policy on the basis of pre-existing prejudice.

Before coming to power, however, Harper had shown some interest in foreign affairs. He and John Weissenberger would talk at length about the end of the Cold War and the state of the world. His take on foreign affairs, his close friend reasoned, was traditionally conservative, in that he saw Canada allied to the Western democracies, principally Britain and the United States, with Europe further down the list. The United Nations was no big favourite, the Harper view tilting more towards a clash-of-civilizations optic than the world as one big family. The more narrowly experienced political leaders tended to view foreign affairs through the lens of domestic politics. Harper was no exception.

It was a sad comment for a G8 country that Harper had hardly anyone with serious international experience to choose from for the foreign affairs post. He settled on his former rival Peter MacKay, the Nova Scotian who, as one wag put it, thought Mozambique was a calypso band. MacKay did have strong political assets, however—he was a clear and quick thinker, an excellent communicator, and a fast learner. Like Harper, though, he had travelled little. His strength and political experience lay primarily in the justice area.

The inexperience at the top was made worse by a foreign affairs bureaucracy and diplomatic corps that, as Harper had said—and with some accuracy—spent too much time clinking glasses on the cocktail circuit. In the view of the PMO, foreign affairs, more than any other department, was steeped in Liberal tradition, with its arrogant officials assuming that they should have the run of things, and that policy should be based on long-standing soft-power biases.

The department, in the prime minister's eyes, vied with environment for bureaucratic obstructionism. "You would want something done and you would get delay after delay," recalled Keith Beardsley, "and a thousand and one reasons why Harper shouldn't do it. And in the end, he would just get his back up and say, 'Well, we're going to do it.' And he did."

Harper gained some positive notices for acting decisively to extend the Afghan war, even though there was criticism for allowing only two days' debate on the issue. But in the summer, during the short war between Israel and Lebanon, his rawness was on display. Though Lebanese civilian casualties outnumbered those for Israel by almost ten to one, Harper announced that the Israeli response to provocations by Hezbollah was "measured." While most saw the necessity of a resolute counterattack to Islamist aggression, few saw it as measured. Harper took a beating from the commentariat, but while bending a bit on his evaluation, didn't retract it.

In the broader context, he was upbraided by many media and the diplomatic community for changing Canadian foreign policy in the Middle East from a more balanced approach to one that was determinedly one-sided. That didn't bother him. He was committed to the Israeli cause as a cornerstone of his foreign policy. Stockwell Day and

Jason Kenney had been forerunners at the Alliance Party in making this commitment, and Harper was only too pleased to further it.

As well as conforming to Harper's beliefs, the policy had other benefits. Though Muslims outnumbered Jews by two to one in Canada, the Jewish community was more politically impactful. Harper was aware, for example, that he stood to gain a major advantage in the Canadian media with his position. The country's largest media empire, Canwest, was controlled by the Aspers, who made no secret of their allegiance to Jewish causes and became enthusiastic backers of Harper on all related questions.

Harper held to a moral framing of foreign policy. In 2003, he wrote in *Report Magazine*, "The emerging debate on foreign affairs should be fought on moral grounds." Conservatives, he said, would be well served by preserving historic values and moral insights on right and wrong. "These are debates where modern Liberals (with the exception of Tony Blair) have no answers; they are trapped in their framework of moral neutrality, moral relativism and moral equivalence." The moral underpinnings, said Harper, "should not just give us the right to stand behind our allies but the duty to do so and the responsibility to put 'hard power' behind our international commitments." He was asserting the neo-conservative view, which framed issues in black-and-white as opposed to seeing them in the context of root causes, historical grievances, and the like.

His position on Israel, more uncompromising than Ottawa had ever been accustomed, became the source of a long-running dispute with traditionalists. The PMO was angered at the presumptuousness of opponents. There was this notion, recalled Mark Cameron, that the new government was supposed to follow along with the traditions that had been set. But "we were saying, 'No, we're the government and we have the right to make the policies.'"

During the Liberal Party's leadership race, which was in full throttle in the summer of 2006, Michael Ignatieff rashly alleged that

Israel had committed a war crime with its assault on Lebanon. It was a statement that almost derailed his campaign. Harper jumped on the remark. Giving free rein to his penchant for excess when on the attack, he tried to smear the other leadership candidates with the same brush. In Question Period, he declared, "This is consistent with the anti-Israel position that has been taken [by] virtually all the candidates of the Liberal leadership."

Noting that his wife was Jewish, Bob Rae demanded an apology, alleging that the PM's remarks were a divisive insult. "We cannot carry on politics in this country like this," Rae said. "It will not work. It divides Canadians. It's something for which he should be thoroughly embarrassed." Ignatieff similarly accused Harper of "playing crass politics with the issue of the Middle East. It's beneath him and his office to do so."

The so-called moral framing of foreign policy was also amply evident in the Conservatives' approach to China. For Jean Chrétien with his trade missions and Paul Martin with his abundant curiosity, China had been a focus. Although the dividends were not readily apparent in the trade numbers, both prime ministers felt they had made some inroads. Chrétien continued making long and lucrative business trips to the Middle Kingdom after leaving office. "You're looking fit," he was told one day as he passed through an Ottawa restaurant. "Gotta stay in shape," he responded. "All these China trips." Asked why he was going there, he said, "Well, that's where the action is." In the same week, Paul Martin was spotted bounding into the dining room of the Château Laurier. He had just returned from Africa and was enthusiastic about a coming trip to Beijing. "The biggest challenge we have," Martin explained, "is to ensure that we increase substantially our percentage of China's and India's growing market."

As Harper's trade minister, David Emerson was trying to sell the importance of China to his new Conservative brethren, but he was getting nowhere. He was overheard muttering that they just didn't get it. "It's like our China policy is made in Tibet," he complained. The Conservatives were alienating Beijing in a number of ways. Cabinet members had come out in full force for Taiwan Day celebrations in Ottawa. The government was singing the praises of the Dalai Lama, with MacKay lashing out against human rights abuses in Tibet. There was little follow-up on the Martin plan to create twenty new Chinese trade offices, and scheduled high-level meetings with Beijing were postponed.

Emerson was up against old-think on China, meeting principle-based resistance not just from Harper but from a calcified caucus. "Some of the characters in there were prone to make fairly extreme, if not outrageous, statements on China." They had roots, Emerson said, in organizations that dedicated themselves to rights and democracy issues, and China was a prime target. The view of the party base was clear: Why should a one-party dictatorship with a history of human rights abuses be accorded normal status, as if it were a Western democracy? Where was the moral reasoning in that?

Emerson went to work on these caucus members, as he did on the PM, but he knew it wouldn't be easy. With Harper, he noticed a considerable stubbornness. "He moves in increments," he explained. "He is not a guy who is going to do a 180 very quickly."

STEPHEN HARPER HAD TO BE cognizant of his party base because of the line he was taking on Quebec—a line that was hardly going to be greeted with cheers in the Prairies. In the spring, he'd taken a modest step, establishing a formal role for the province at UNESCO. But now, in the fall of his first year in power, he took a dramatic step, introducing a motion to grant the Québécois nation status.

The idea appeared to have been cooked up at the last moment, but in fact Harper had been thinking about it for some months. He'd seen a confrontation coming when Gilles Duceppe, the leader of the

Bloc Québécois, signalled that he would use the question of nation status as a wedge to score points against the federalists. Harper and his advisers held talks on how the matter could be handled if the Bloc moved on it. The PM hinted then—though he didn't show his hand—that he might beat them to the punch.

Harper's intergovernmental affairs minister—and the man responsible for Quebec relations—was Michael Chong, a young Conservative of Chinese heritage. The fresh-faced, Windsor-born thirty-five-year-old had worked at the Dominion Institute and as the director of information for the NHL Players' Association before entering politics and was seen as a player with potential. But he had no idea the PM was thinking of this kind of recognition for Quebec. He and Harper had had some one-on-one discussions on matters affecting the provinces, but the subject of nation status had never come up.

On the day Harper was to introduce his motion, Chong bumped into his deputy minister, Louis Lévesque, on his way into Parliament. Lévesque told him there was something afoot and described what he had heard the prime minister was about to do. Chong was taken aback. As a minister, he had got used to Harper's rules of operating. Like the others in the cabinet, he knew how top-down the operation was. He had learned not to say anything in public without first getting it approved by the PMO. But not to be informed in advance by the prime minister of a decision of this importance affecting his own portfolio was a shocker. When he finally did get the lowdown, it was not in a separate briefing, as the minister responsible, but at a party caucus meeting with two hundred other MPs, senators, and officials.

Standing before the caucus, the PM announced that the decision was final. Chong rose to vigorously challenge it, saying that it was against party tradition, and that it would give Quebec sovereigntists a pivotal card to play in any new drive for independence down the line. There was opposition from other caucus members as well. "The West wants in" had for years been a rallying cry from members bitter about the special treatment they saw Ottawa giving Quebec under Mulroney and others. And here they were "in," and the prime minister was going the appeasement route. Yet another favour for Quebec.

According to PCO officials, Harper's intention was not in fact to cater to Quebec as happened under the Liberals. "You noticed the difference right away between him and Liberals," said an official who had worked in the PCO under Martin and Chrétien. "Harper came in and one of the first things he said was that Quebec is not going to get everything it wants." He made clear, for example, his intention to cut down on federal largesse to the aerospace and defence companies in the province.

But the initiative that got all the public attention was the big pitch on nation status. Though there was opposition from segments of his caucus to the move, it wouldn't have mattered even if a clear majority had opposed it because the decision had already been made by Harper, the one-man democracy in the room. So dissenters tramped out of the caucus meeting room and, with one exception, held their tongues. When Harper announced the decision in the Commons that afternoon and it was greeted with enthusiasm in the media and in Quebec, their concerns were mollified. Their leader's crafty instincts, it seemed, had been right after all. And indeed it was a wily manoeuvre. It undercut the Bloc Québécois, removed a major grievance card from the separatists' never-depleted deck, and enhanced the reputation of Tories in Quebec, which was central to their political hopes.

With Chong the lone holdout, the PMO tried to bring him on board. Talks between the young minister and PMO officials, however, produced little progress. Chong wanted a meeting with Harper. He finally got one five days later, on the day the Commons was to vote on the motion. The meeting was tense. Harper said he had thought those from the Tory side of the party, like Chong, would favour the motion because it followed along the lines of Bob Stanfield's two-nations approach. Chong rebutted the point. He pointed out that the Stanfield policy had been defeated at the polls, and that Diefenbaker's one-Canada option had set the template for the Tories. He didn't go after Harper for not telling him in advance of the big decision, but he held his ground on the issue itself. Chong realized that as the minister on the file, he couldn't vote against the motion and stay in his post. He told Harper he was resigning from cabinet and would tell the media why. Beyond that, he said, he would not cause the prime minister any problems.

One of the few other times something like this had happened was when Jean Chrétien was finance minister to Pierre Trudeau. Returning from a summit in Bonn in 1978, Trudeau announced a major overhaul of government spending—a mini budget of sorts—without bothering to tell his finance minister. A humiliated Chrétien considered resigning but in the end stayed on. Two decades later, when a journalist raised the subject in an interview at 24 Sussex Drive, Chrétien reacted angrily. He was still irked by the memory. He said he would never do anything like that to one of his ministers.

In Chong's case, PMO officials familiar with the file said that he was at an earlier meeting where the issue of nation status was bandied about. He hadn't, they said, indicated any opposition to conjecture about a resolution recognizing Quebec. They thought he was sympathetic to Quebec nationalism because he was from the Tory side of the party and had been a Meech Lake supporter. His vehement opposition, they said, had surprised them. While they acknowledged that his not being consulted was a problem, they suspected he was also peeved because he didn't really have significant responsibilities as intergovernmental affairs minister.

In a cabinet lacking in youth, Harper had lost one of his bright lights simply because he hadn't bothered to pick up the phone or meet with him to tell him of his intentions. But the prime minister didn't sustain much criticism for the blunder. The brilliance of his gambit against the Bloc completely overshadowed the Chong resignation.

Chong and Harper talked about the issue only once after that. Chong and some others were convinced that down the line, when the sovereigntist appetite heated up again, the Harper decision would backfire on Ottawa. The sovereigntists, they felt, had been handed a beautiful question for a referendum ballot: "Do you agree that Quebec is a nation, and if so, do you authorize the government of Quebec to negotiate with the government of Canada to formalize this status?" How could the federalists mount a credible campaign, argued the Chong camp, when they had voted for nation status?

Harper, though, had been cautious enough to include the words "in a united nation" in his motion. The motion was about the Québécois as a community of people, not a separate political entity. What Harper was doing, as analyzed by the journalist Chantal Hébert, was changing the rules of engagement in the Quebec–Canada debate. He was launching a campaign to "appropriate Quebec's nationalist symbols and claim them as Canada's own." His resolution had neutralized the sovereigntist contention that the rest of Canada was determined to negate Quebec's distinct identity.

The reaction in the Prairies to the Harper move was relatively muted considering all the vitriol that had greeted Brian Mulroney when he curried favour with *la belle province*. Harper had most Conservatives so happy just to be back in power, explained Rod Love, that they were prepared to cut him some slack. He had also convinced them that the road to a majority was through Quebec. So there wasn't much bellyaching. As Love in his inimitable style put it, Harper basically told them, "Look, I've got to suck up to Quebec, so just shut up and let me get on with it."

HARPER'S QUEBEC DECISION was the second stunner of that month. It had been preceded by Jim Flaherty's announcement that the Conservatives were reversing a campaign promise to leave income trusts—tax shelters used by investors both large and small—intact because of their importance to small investors and retirees. Now, just eight months later, the finance minister announced that income trusts would be taxed. It was a bid to stop the increasing number of companies from converting to trusts, an act that Flaherty argued was costing the economy hundreds of millions in tax revenue. Only three weeks earlier, Bell Canada Enterprises had proposed the biggest trust conversion in Canadian history. Turning its Bell Canada subsidiary into a trust would cost Ottawa, according to defenders of the Flaherty move, an estimated $800 million in taxes over the next few years.

Critics wondered why a government that was in favour of trusts just a short time earlier was so opposed to them now. It had been evident during the election campaign that the trusts were a revenue-draining problem. Could it be that the Harper team had waited until after the election to announce the policy to avoid antagonizing Conservative voters, many of whom were seniors who had come to rely on income from the trusts?

In fact, the government's rationale for the flip-flop—the lost tax revenue—was not the real reason for it. When the announcement came, Tom Flanagan, still in Harper's good graces at the time, asked him the reason for the reversal. "Well, when I was in opposition," Harper replied, "no one told me that all the big corporations were about to convert to the income trust form of organization." He wasn't as worried about tax leakage, he explained to Flanagan, as he was about corporate governance. The income trust concept was fine, he believed, when used in a limited sphere. But when it was beginning to be adopted by major manufacturers and service corporations, he was persuaded that it was the wrong way to go. James Rajotte, who served as chair of the industry committee, was of the same impression. But it was not the case Harper and Flaherty put to the public because corporate governance was too complex an issue.

As in the case of the Quebec surprise, Harper's cabinet was not informed of the decision until after the fact. It was taken with only four people in the room—Harper, Kevin Lynch, Jim Flaherty, and Flaherty's deputy minister. Owing to the sensitivity of the issue, Harper opted for even tighter secrecy than usual.

Initially, the response was measured. The government was taken to task for the flip-flop, but many people agreed that something had to be done about the lost tax revenue. Before long, however, the evidence began to mount that the tax implications were significantly overstated. Revenue calculations by federal officials, it appeared, had been distorted to make the loss appear far more serious than it was. The Canadian Association of Income Trust Investors launched a ferocious campaign against Flaherty, arguing that the change in tax rules had cost Canadians $35 billion in retirement savings. William Stanbury of the University of British Columbia initiated an in-depth study of the matter for a book he was preparing. He found that faulty work by finance department officials and pressure on Harper from big-time CEOs were likely the real reasons for the new policy. The shroud of secrecy over the issue was inexcusable, he added. The government "did not hold any form of public consultation process in 2006, as the previous government did in 2005. Then, because of the controversy the policy switch engendered, the Harper team went into information-denial mode." The government, said Stanbury, interpreted the Access to Information Act in the most restrictive way possible. Many documents released under the act were completely blacked out.

There were defensible reasons in some cases for the government's furtive way of operating, but there were no good reasons in others. On the question of Quebec nation status, it had cost Harper a promising young cabinet minister. On the environment file, it had created, as Mark Cameron suggested, confusion and doubt. On income trusts, it would become more of a problem. And there were other issues, not the least of which was the Afghan detainees affair, for which the price paid for stealth would be steep.

CHAPTER NINE

Attack and Obstruct

With the Liberals having only an interim leader, the Conservatives, despite all their professed worries, operated in year one with a degree of security. But that was changing. After a ten-month campaign, the Grits finally named a new leader, selecting Stéphane Dion to head the party. Like most everyone else, Harper and the Conservative hierarchy had expected either Bob Rae or Michael Ignatieff to be crowned. They were quite pleased with the choice of Dion. Yes, he was from Quebec and could make it difficult for the Tories to make inroads there. But Ignatieff and Rae were also quite credible in the province, and they were both far better communicators than the Montreal academic, who had arrived in Ottawa by bus a decade earlier to join the Chrétien team.

Still, Harper's team wasn't about to relax. Although it was tradition for the governing party to give a new opposition leader time to breathe, Harper and his operatives were never overly concerned about playing by the established norms. Within two months of Dion's selection, they were running TV ads skewering him. As they saw it, there was little sense in waiting until an election campaign to launch a TV blitz against a chief rival. During a campaign, several parties filled the airwaves, vying for voters' attention. Why not go earlier?

The Conservatives were running a permanent campaign, and pre-writ advertising was only fitting. During Paul Martin's stewardship, they had twice used such advertising—in opposing gay marriage, and in promoting a broad range of party policies—but nothing against Martin personally. Now they decided to use it to bombard the opposition leader. With lots of cash in the treasury, they could afford to run ads in slots with a big audience, and for Dion they chose the biggest they could find—the Canadian telecast of the Super Bowl. They also wanted unique ads, not just the usual political pap, and so they dipped into footage from the Liberal leadership race. From an all-candidates debate, they found a crystallizing vignette of Michael Ignatieff zeroing in on Dion's record as environment minister. And so on Super Bowl Sunday, up popped Dion on millions of screens across the land looking entirely hapless. His arms were splayed and he had a wounded look on his blanched face—this as Ignatieff, craned like a hawk, leered at him. "Stéphane, you didn't get it done! You didn't get it done!" Then came, in pleading tones, the Dion response. "That's not fair. That's not fair." Then the voiceover, the punchline from the narrator: "Dion. Not a leader!"

Of course, no one knew yet what kind of leader Dion would be. He had shown some leadership capacity when he took on Lucien Bouchard on the unity issue in the late 1990s. He'd stood his ground then, offering trenchant retorts to every Bouchard broadside. But the Harper ad blitz was effective. He was criticized in some quarters for using personal attack ads outside an election campaign, but the pros outweighed the cons. A Nanos poll taken two months later showed Dion had an approval rating of only 17 percent, compared with 42 percent for Harper. Critically, the Liberals had no money in the bank to respond, and the Conservatives knew that. If they had been facing a well-heeled party, they would have been hesitant to run the ads, for fear of retaliation.

For Harper, the aggression felt good. The Grits had used some heavy artillery against his Reformers in the past, and these ads were payback. "The Liberal Party portrayed Preston Manning as a Klansman running around with a white sheet on his head for the better part of a decade," said Kory Teneycke, one of the PMO's sharpshooters. But the Reformers didn't exactly have clean hands either. Near the close of the 1993 election campaign, they ran an ad playing up the small deformity on the side of Jean Chrétien's mouth, the voice intoning, "Does this man look like a prime minister?" A public outcry followed, and the ad was pulled.

The strategist behind the Dion ads, an adviser of considerable importance to Harper, was Patrick Muttart, a young brainiac from Woodstock, Ontario. Muttart caught the politics bug early. As a boy, he delivered newspapers and was fascinated by the stories on page one. In his early teens, he cheered for John Turner in the 1984 Liberal leadership race, then campaigned for his local candidate, Alf Apps, who later became the president of the Liberal Party. But as he reached college age, he moved sharply to the right, becoming one of Ontario's first Reform Party members. Aware of Muttart's talent, Apps tried to persuade him to stay within the Liberal fold, but couldn't manage it.

Muttart worked for Manning before joining Harper's team. He set himself apart by studying how conservative parties had won elections in the United Kingdom, Australia, and the United States. He could always find what he called "takeaways," ideas that could be transplanted to the Canadian political arena. Although many people took it for granted that the Harper Conservatives had close political ties with the Americans, Muttart maintained this was overstated. "There was never an established working relationship between us and U.S. Republicans," he said. The big takeaways were actually from Australia. Although the voting system was entirely different there, the government of John Howard became something of a model for the

Conservatives, especially in the way it microtargeted voter blocks and designed policy to appeal to those blocks. Muttart liked that idea, and so did Harper.

After the loss in the 2004 election, Muttart concluded that the party's potential appeal was depressingly limited. Most Canadians, Tory surveys showed, viewed Harper as a right-winger who opposed same-sex marriage. That was it. So the party commissioned a major psychographics poll, psychographics being the study of market segments in terms of their values and lifestyles. This polling helped show the party potential growth areas.

Muttart studied the numbers and zeroed in on the segments most amenable to a Conservative pitch. He found, for example, that couples with more than two children were much more inclined to vote Conservative than those with small families. The party wanted to appeal to Canadians who worked hard and paid their taxes. Average working-class males, they learned, responded not to bureau-cratic-sounding Liberal promises like regional transfers but to bait like money for kids' hockey equipment and tax credits for mechan-ics. The targeting got very specific, right down to ways in which they might be able to help Quebec snowmobilers.

At PMO meetings, Muttart would decorate the wall with illus-trations of demographic groups so that whenever a policy was discussed, it could be framed in terms of its appeal to these groups. Sandra Buckler's communications shop did the reactive work, Muttart's strategic section did the proactive. Everything Muttart did was focused on what was coming next—that day, that week, that month. If Harper was giving a speech the following day, Muttart would assemble his team and map out the plan. What's the main message of the speech? Who are we trying to appeal to? How does it fit with our overall approach? He'd go around the table. He'd ask one of his assistants, Kevin Lacey, which individuals or groups he was lining up to issue statements of support for the speech. He'd go to the tech guy to discuss how the website would feature the event. Then he'd go to the tour person with questions about the podium size, the backdrop visual, and so on. The Conservatives had been enthusiastic about backdrop visuals ever since the Ronald Reagan days, when Mike Deaver set the Gipper against panoramas that made him look like he was on the silver screen.

Kevin Lacey, an East Coast political junkie and a right-wing true believer, had worked in many political offices and found that people generally got too immersed in the mess of the day. Having a PMO division focused exclusively on what was coming next and how to make it fit the overall plan, he felt, was a major advance. Like Muttart he was in his thirties, but in the Harper PMO that wasn't young. The two of them were sitting around one day, watching the passersby and remarking how they felt kind of old. Many in the PMO were a decade younger, fresh-faced ideologues who were a bit awestruck to be there—and thus ready to unflinchingly follow marching orders.

The PMO was structured on the basis of the silo system, with individual compartments and very little cross-pollination. In this way, as opposed to the more circular patterns of organization where information is more broadly shared, only the prime minister and his chief of staff knew everything. The silos reported to them, said a staffer, not to each other. That was the reason for the silos. "It was so that you could have the top controlling everything. In a certain way it was very good because no one would step on your turf."

That didn't mean there wasn't a lot of infighting, however. "A lot of staffers were still trying to step all over one another. It was petty. They were arguing over everything."

Though the prime minister often tried to appear moderate to appeal to a wider audience, Muttart and Lacey and others had no doubt he was a "movement conservative," and they loved that. They believed that no other PM had been so committed to the cause, had come from so far on the right side of the political spectrum. Below the surface Harper was doctrinaire, and they sensed that with him, sooner or later, the dial would move.

They were prepared to be aggressive on his behalf. Indeed, Lacey sometimes thought they could have gone even harder against opponents. He and Muttart both believed that the moment you showed weakness was the moment your agenda went off the rails. This tended to be Harper's view as well. James Rajotte, the astute Conservative backbencher, said the PM believed the party had been "too nice" in the past, especially during the 2000 election campaign, when Stockwell Day declined to take off the gloves, even with evidence of Liberal corruption staring him in the face.

Muttart had few qualms about using the dagger. As a student of political history, he looked at the broader perspective, at other leaders and their legacies. In the long run, he concluded, Harper would be judged on his achievements, not on how many opponents he had kneecapped to gain them.

Chief of Staff Brodie took exception to Harper's being painted as an angry man. He pointed to a time when Chrétien manhandled a protestor who got in his path, and another when he made cracks about demonstrators being pepper-sprayed. "This is the sort of thing that I always find so strange," said Brodie of the accusations. "It's not like Harper saw a bunch of people getting pepper-sprayed—and then made a bloody joke about it. It's not like he personally broke some guy's dental work—and then made a bloody joke about it."

He went on: "I'm not denying Harper is an ambitious man. Or that he is impatient. I'm not claiming he suffers fools gladly. What I'm wondering is why reporters are so fascinated by that sort of thing. Was Trudeau more patient? Didn't he give people the finger? Utter the words that were recorded as 'fuddle-duddle'? Ask out loud, 'Why should I sell your wheat?' Yes, yes, and yes. But this was all rolled into admiring profiles of his 'charm' or his 'sex appeal.'"

Harper's hard-nosed methods became a subject of controversy when, in the spring of 2007, Canwest columnist Don Martin revealed in the *National Post* that the Conservatives had prepared a secret guidebook that detailed "how to unleash chaos while chairing parliamentary committees." The manual, which ran to about two hundred pages, included instructions on how to employ dirty tricks to shut down committee hearings. It told the chairs how to set in motion debate-obstructing delays and how to select party-friendly witnesses. And if things got really tough and opposition members were on to something that could hurt the government, Conservatives were instructed to end the proceedings by storming out of the committee room.

The opposition had the proverbial field day with this one, saying this was twenty-first-century democracy, Harper-style. Embarrassingly for the prime minister, the document was revealed at a time when he was blaming the opposition parties for the dysfunctional behaviour at committee hearings. In the years previous he had taken heat for breaking his promise to allow committee members to select their own chairpersons.

Ironically, the manual had been prepared by the office of Jay Hill, then the chief whip and a politician who was respected for his fairness and low-key approach. Given the blanket vetting operation the PMO had in place, it seemed logical to assume that the manual had been approved at the highest levels. But Keith Beardsley said the news of it caught the PMO by surprise. "We were all going, 'Oh, God, why would you put that in writing?' I mean, if you want to do something like that with a committee, you call a person or go over and see them. It was just bizarre." The PMO maintained that the chief whip's office was solely responsible for the document. In an effort to find who leaked it, they had all the committee chairs return their copies.

Many Conservatives, though, couldn't understand the commotion. While Rajotte, himself a committee chairman, conceded that

Harper had gone against his word on the question of committee chairs, he thought the fuss over the manual was exaggerated. Ninety percent of what was in the book, he said, was just standard operating procedure, adding that the wise PMO strategy would have been to make the document public, thus showing there was nothing to hide. By not releasing it, Harper's operatives were as much as admitting it had damaging content.

But if there was any hand-wringing at the PMO, it was over getting caught, not over what the book revealed. Here, the team once again applied the standard yardstick: if it was something that had been done by the Liberals, then it was okay to do it again now. "I don't think anything we proposed in that manual was different than what had gone on before," argued Mark Cameron. "I remember when we were in opposition and you'd have a vote on the committee and you knew there were two or three Liberals on the committee who were sympathetic to what we wanted to do. Then all of a sudden the Liberals would yank those committee members and send in a whole bunch of parliamentary secretaries who would vote the PMO line."

Despite all the Tories' protestations, this incident played right into their critics' hands. Just as the manual appeared, they were carrying out some of its recommended tactics. At the ethics committee, Conservatives were trying to prevent an inquiry into the alleged censorship of documents on the Afghan detainees question. To put off committee appearances by hostile witnesses, Tory MPs stalled for five hours. Over at the official languages committee, the Conservative chairman called off a hearing before witnesses could appear to condemn the government's cancellation of the Court Challenges Program. When opposition MPs subsequently voted to remove the chairman, Guy Lauzon, the Tories refused to select a replacement.

The Court Challenges Program, which had been cancelled the previous year, provided funding for Canadians to defend their Charter rights before the courts. Linguistic minorities had used the program, as had ethnic and religious minorities, gays, lesbians, and the disabled. Opposition critics said terminating the program was a fitting move for a government bent on stifling dissent. John Baird bluntly defended the cancellation, saying, "I just don't think it made sense for the government to subsidize lawyers to challenge the government's own laws in courts." Later, the government would restore the part of the program that applied to linguistic minorities.

IN THIS PERIOD, having been battered with allegations of censorship, stonewalling, and the like, the government faced a controversy that would not go away: the treatment of Afghan prisoners taken by Canadian soldiers. It was a dispute that average Canadians didn't seem too concerned about, since it involved the heathen Taliban, and even those who were interested soon lost track of the narrative in the maze of details and conflicting information that sped or sometimes dribbled out. But weighty matters of international law were involved, as were, for Harper and company, serious matters of reputation.

In December 2005, General Rick Hillier had signed a detainee-transfer agreement with the government of Afghanistan. It didn't make much news; Canadians were in the midst of an election campaign. Three months later, a U.S. State Department report revealed that local Afghan authorities "continued to routinely torture and abuse detainees." The torture and abuse, the report said, "consisted of pulling out fingernails and toenails, burning with hot oil, beatings, sexual humiliation and sodomy."

Through 2006 and into 2007, Canadian troops transferred an estimated 140 prisoners to Afghan authorities. Diplomat Richard Colvin, it was later revealed, wrote memos beginning in May 2006 to Canadian officials alleging abuse of these detainees. On hearing Colvin's claims, senior military men maintained that he didn't mention any abuse to them at that time.

When the matter was first raised in the House of Commons in early 2006, Prime Minister Harper cited the agreement Ottawa had signed with the Afghan government to respect prisoners' rights under the Geneva Conventions, adding that he expected the Afghans to live up to the deal. Defence Minister Gordon O'Connor maintained that the Red Cross was responsible for supervising the treatment of the prisoners, and that if something was wrong, Ottawa would be informed and take action. But in March 2007, the Red Cross directly contradicted O'Connor, saying it had no role in monitoring the agreement between Canada and Afghanistan. A flustered O'Connor had to apologize for misleading the House.

Trying to defend the embattled minister from opposition attacks, the prime minister reached for his brass knuckles. "I can understand the passion that the leader of the opposition and members of his party feel for the Taliban prisoners," he stated. "I just wish they would show the same passion for Canadian soldiers." More than a few chins in the chamber snapped back with that one. The Conservatives had started bringing demagoguery to the table on the war issue the previous fall. Whenever opposition members criticized the war policy, assorted Tories accused them of being disloyal and of failing to support the troops. Jack Layton was disparaged by Tories in corridor talk as "Taliban Jack." Harper had painted opponents as anti-Israeli in 2006, and now he was suggesting they were anti-Canadian as well. He was gaining the reputation of a leader who couldn't see a belt without wanting to hit below it.

Stéphane Dion demanded an apology, but Harper refused. "I would like to see more support in the House of Commons from all sides for Canadian men and women in uniform," the PM said. "They have not been getting it, and they deserve it." Dion lit up. Harper, he charged, was insulting the entire Parliament, trivializing the issue of war detainees, and playing politics with the lives of soldiers.

Media critics tended to see through the PM's antics. The New Democrats wanted a negotiated settlement to the conflict and the troops brought home. It was a different way of seeing things, but it didn't mean that they weren't supporting the soldiers. Under Paul Martin, the Liberals had supported and broadened the Afghan mission and significantly bolstered military spending. It was their role now in opposition to ask questions on military policy, especially in the face of allegations such as those regarding the detainees.

A month after the O'Connor apology, Graeme Smith of *The Globe and Mail* reported that thirty detainees transferred by Canadians to Afghan troops were "beaten, whipped, frozen, choked and subjected to electric shocks during interrogations." Harper was not impressed by the new evidence, telling the opposition, "I think what's disgraceful is to simply accept the allegations of what some Taliban suspects say at face value." He continued to defend O'Connor, his beleaguered defence minister, against calls for his resignation. And he was getting increasingly frustrated with the mixed signals coming from the bureaucracy. Foreign affairs would tell him one thing, recalled Beardsley, and he would read another in the newspapers. The PMO would ask the department for quick answers and they wouldn't be forthcoming, leading to evasive responses in Question Period, where O'Connor was a confused performer. Often, House Leader Peter Van Loan stood to give answers in his place. Van Loan's modus operandi was simply to attack the questioner and the Liberal record.

At the same time, there were internal conflicts at foreign affairs. Colvin would later assert in committee testimony that he was reporting evidence of the torture of detainees, but his superiors, aware of political sensitivities, were not exactly welcoming the news. How much of his information was being passed to the political masters was unclear. If accurate information had been forwarded, it raised obvious questions about a coverup.

Harper had considerable stakes in a refurbished military and progress in the war. He wanted to see Canada flexing its muscle. Conservatives had joined with Rick Hillier in terming the 1990s "the decade of darkness" for the military because of the deep cuts to defence spending. Canada had been no different from most other nations in cutting back on military outlays. The Soviet threat, which had for decades consumed a great chunk of military spending, was gone. Ottawa was also struggling with a massive deficit in the 1990s, and all departments experienced significant reductions in their budgets. But Conservatives didn't buy those explanations.

Harper didn't want to hear any bad news about the war, and it was beginning to appear as if his government would go to considerable lengths to prevent such news from getting out. Allegations of a coverup emerged with the appearance of a *Globe and Mail* report by Paul Koring on April 25, 2007. Through an access-to-information request, Koring had received a government report on human rights abuses in Afghanistan. Prepared by Canadian diplomats in Kabul, the report, when delivered to the *Globe*, contained numerous blacked-out paragraphs. But through other sources, the newspaper was able to recover the original, unexpurgated copy. It was a reporter's dream. Koring could compare the edited report to the original to see what had been censored. Among the sentences that had been blacked out by foreign affairs was one in particular that caught his eye: "Extrajudicial executions, disappearances, torture and detention are all too common."

In the public version of the report, all references to torture and abuse in Afghan jails were blacked out. Using claims of national security, the government had edited out whatever it didn't want people to know. But now, with the revelations in Koring's story, opposition critics had enough ammunition to allege a coverup. The Harper government faced not only political fallout but also possible legal repercussions. International law prohibits nations from transferring prisoners when they know they may be tortured. Two Canadian lawyers, Michael Byers, who would later seek election for the NDP, and William Schabas, asked the International Criminal Court to investigate possible war crimes by Canadian officials.

At the start of May, a new transfer agreement allowing Canadian officials to visit Afghan prisons was signed. Meanwhile O'Connor's position was becoming untenable. Still, Harper kept fighting off demands that the defence minister step down. He liked military men, and O'Connor had established a good relationship with his family. The PM, his advisers noted, also liked him because he was prepared to speak his mind in a direct way at meetings. By the summer, however, the embarrassments were too numerous. O'Connor had lost too much public confidence to continue on. Harper moved him to the lower-profile national revenue portfolio, putting Peter MacKay in defence. He was the second major minister—after Rona Ambrose in environment—to be moved out in Harper's first eighteen months in office.

Given the evidence of stonewalling and coverup, the detainees story was attracting considerable attention, but not to the degree it might have. Many media did not choose to aggressively follow the *Globe* leads. Moreover, given all the ammunition presented to him, the new Liberal leader, Stéphane Dion, was unable to exploit the story as much as he might have. The opposition leader's demeanour was pallid and reticent, and his difficulties with the English language further diminished his impact. He was unable to get down in the trenches with Harper. "I am not a bully," Dion offered in his office one day. "I am a gentleman." But the former academic was discovering that he was not in a gentleman's game. When he was asked about the chief differences between himself and the prime minister, Dion listed off "values, orientation, behaviour." With Harper, said Dion, "it's clear that he is able to lie, as he did again and again in order to go where he wants to go." But, he added, "I am unable to do that because if I'm not sincere, I'm not me."

No one doubted Dion's sincerity. It was one quality that everyone gave him credit for. But sincerity was not enough to win in politics. Making charges stick required cutting sound bites, and Dion couldn't do anger well. "I was a very discreet person," he explained. "Now I'm in the centre of attention. I am improving myself. I understand more." He thought his language skills were improving, but they weren't. His vocabulary was sufficient, but he had a problem with elocution. He sometimes couldn't get the words out properly. In explaining, for example, the three pillars of his policy approach, he talked of "three peelers," as if he were at some strip club in Manhattan.

While Harper and his team were able to deflect some of the criticisms on the detainee file, there were still major gaps and contradictions in their story. "To be blunt, it was quite a mess," recalled Bruce Carson. "As a group I think we were caught between the department of foreign affairs and defence, and we had great difficulty trying to determine what happened over there." The controversy was sullying the government's reputation for war management and creating doubts as to its integrity. With the removal of his friend Gordon O'Connor from the defence post, Harper was able to bring round one of the detainees affair to a close. But even tougher rounds awaited him.

CHAPTER TEN

Tory Trendlines

If politics is about timing, Stephen Harper had come along at a favourable moment. Beyond the daily dramas affecting the Conservatives' hopes, it was possible to see larger forces at work, many of them advantageous to their cause. Once leafy Liberal Canada was nudging towards a new look.

When the new century began, with Jean Chrétien running the country, the Liberal consensus that had driven so much of the nation's history appeared very much intact. The party had won yet another majority government, and it far outpaced its divided conservative rivals in popular support. Canadians remained firmly ensconced in the soft centre of the political spectrum, which had always been this party's home. But the terrorist attacks of September 11, 2001, profoundly affected the dynamic, moving security issues to the top of the national agenda. In the previous decade—the first post–Cold War decade—the talk had been of peace dividends and soft power, all of which fitted comfortably into the Liberal consensus. But given the terrorist calamity and a continuing terrorist threat, no one wanted to talk soft power anymore.

John Manley, one of Chrétien's top ministers, came forward to say that Canada wasn't carrying its military weight: "You just can't sit at the G8 table and then, when the bill comes up, go to the washroom."

The attack on the United States triggered the war in Afghanistan and with it an appetite for rebuilding the Canadian Armed Forces, a long-time mainstay of the conservative agenda. The military was back in vogue, something the country had not seen for more than half a century.

There was still enough Liberal momentum to resist participation in the war in Iraq. But in Afghanistan, a modest Canadian mission escalated through the decade into a significant combat role. The tenor of the times made it easier for the Harper Conservatives to build support for the war and the military, and to take a harder line on foreign policy than might otherwise have been possible.

One indicator of how Canadian attitudes had changed was the case of Omar Khadr, the young al Qaeda supporter who was accused of killing an American in a firefight. Canadians showed a willingness to forgo their traditional judicial principles and leave the probably brainwashed teenager to the primitive prerogatives of military justice in Guantánamo Bay. Other countries had their nationals removed from the prison and brought them home to face fair trials. Harper steadfastly refused to do the same for Khadr, displaying a shameful disregard for high principles of justice. Hardened public opinion allowed him to get away with it.

At home, the heightened security fears played into the Conservatives' law-and-order proclivities. The counter-arguments of criminologists didn't matter. The public was less opposed to a lock-'em-up philosophy. Like soft power, civil liberties were out of fashion.

Another trendline of benefit to the right side of the spectrum through these times was the demographic shift. The population was aging and older voters, as pollsters testified, tended to tack Conservative. The baby boomers, drivers of a leftish ethic in decades past, turned grey, tired, and uninspired. At the same time, the youth legions, while more liberal, more green, and more multiculturally tolerant, remained politically lax. They had the look of a generation seized by a culture of entitlement, prepared to let the aging white men, stripped of their once progressive ideals, remain endlessly at the controls. The left-of-centre parties, much to the relief of the Conservatives, were unable to mobilize the younger generations.

The increasing clout of the western provinces was also playing to the Tories' advantage. With manufacturing in central Canada in decline, the West's resource riches increasingly served as the economic engine. The population was also shifting to that region of the country, the conservative heartland and the adopted home of Stephen Harper. In concert with this trend was the diminishing influence of Quebec, the province that had served the Liberal cause like no other. In simplified ideological terms, Quebec was Canada's pillar of the left, while Alberta was the pillar of the right. For thirty-three years, under three Quebec-based prime ministers—Trudeau, Mulroney, and Chrétien—the eastern pillar had predominated. Quebec dramas sucked up all the oxygen. In succession came the October Crisis, the election of the Parti Québécois, the 1980 referendum, the repatriation of the Constitution, the Meech Lake debate, the Charlottetown Accord, the referendum of 1995, the debate over the Clarity bill. Westerners were understandably exasperated as Quebec-based prime ministers continually fashioned their priorities with their home province in mind. For conservative causes, the tilt was all wrong. Quebec was in the vanguard on gay rights, freedom of choice, and opposition to capital punishment. On foreign affairs, the impact of the most European of the provinces was felt as well. Quebec's pacifist leanings were instrumental in keeping the country out of the Iraq war and Washington's missile defence program.

Had Alberta been pulling the levers of power through this period instead of Quebec, the differences can scarcely be imagined. But finally the political culture was changing, as it had in the U.S. with the decline of the influence of the northeast. By the year 2000, the sovereigntist threat had waned and Ottawa no longer had to be so solicitous. The presence of the Bloc Québécois, which could be counted on to snap up at least half the seats in the province in any federal election, made Quebec less of a prize for the federalist parties than it had once been. Stephen Harper still devoted considerable energies to luring the province, but there was no doubting where his philosophical biases were anchored.

The waning of Quebec influence in combination with demographic trends, as argued in Brian Lee Crowley's book *Fearful Symmetry,* was inclining the country to a gradual erosion of the welfare-state mentality. A shift in power, Crowley contended, was underway towards regions less disposed to tolerate the dependency system fostered by Quebec. With time Ottawa would feel less and less compelled to spend in areas of provincial responsibility.

Yet more developments enhanced the prospects for those on the right side of the spectrum. The corporate tax rate was in decline and economic nationalism was fading, a trend illustrated by the sell-off of corporate head offices. And the Canadian media, which had at one time demonstrated a detectable liberal bias, was now leaning to the right. It was a major change and, for Harper, a highly fortunate turn of events.

Whether all these trends were proof that the Canadian population itself was becoming more conservative was a matter of debate. Pollsters found mixed evidence. Canadians showed a loathing, for example, for George W. Bush's Republicanism and gave Barack Obama approval ratings that were through the roof. In the big provinces, Liberal governments predominated. But there was little doubt where the momentum lay. Canada was a different country than it had been in the heyday of Pierre Trudeau. Stephen Harper was in the right place at the right time. The country looked to be more inclined to embrace the conservative way.

COMPLICATING MATTERS, however, was the plight of conservatism under the Bush Republicans. Canadian conservatives liked to look upon the United States as something of a model, especially when the Grand Old Party was in power. But the model was in a state of deterioration. The United States had become the world's most indebted nation. It was mired in a prolonged and unpopular war in Iraq. Its reputation as a human rights leader was being ravaged by images from Guantánamo and the Abu Ghraib prison in Iraq. It was the world's largest emitter of greenhouse gases. Its reputation for fair play and collective security was being undermined by the unilateralism of the Bush–Cheney administration. As an economic power, it was rapidly losing ground to China.

Harper had arrived in power at a time when Canada could no longer rely on American economic might the way it had for so long. With the rise of the Asian powers, the neighbour was unlikely to recover the economic paramountcy it had enjoyed for so long. Canadian exports to the U.S. had continued rising throughout the twentieth century—until they accounted for roughly 85 percent of all exports—but now those numbers were declining, and the decline was forecast to continue over the long term. The era of limitless Canada–U.S. integration was drawing to a close, and public policy had to catch up to the new dynamic. The pressure to locate new markets was accumulating.

Normally, a conservative like Harper would have wanted to follow an integrationist or, to use the older term, continentalist path. As the leader of the Alliance Party, he had signalled his American allegiance, most notably with his support of the Iraq war. It was one of the differences that led Keith Martin, the British Columbia Alliance member, to move to the Liberals. Martin recalled a conversation with Harper. "He said to me, 'Keith, I can't believe that you wouldn't support our allies going to war in Iraq.'" Martin explained that inspectors had found no evidence of weapons of mass destruction, that Saddam Hussein had been neutralized for an entire decade, and that the policy of containment was working. Harper listened, Martin recalled, but maintained the view that you should still stand shoulder to shoulder with your greatest ally.

Once he became prime minister, however, Harper could see the political realities. Bush's style of conservatism was being widely rejected, and Harper could hardly build with him the type of relationship that Mulroney had with Reagan. He was friendly enough but wisely kept a distance, steering clear of any talk of partnership. What he did instead was to focus on his own flag by promoting a new patriotism, one that took inspiration from the early years of John Diefenbaker, before the Chief descended into his own hubristic inferno. This was not a defensive nationalism but a Canadianism born of a proud heritage and strong national symbols. Harper promoted the military, the monarchy, the North, family values, and traditional allies—the classic elements of conservative identity. It was the true north strong and free.

At the ninetieth anniversary of the Battle of Vimy Ridge, he ordered that the Red Ensign, used as the flag of Canada until 1965, be flown alongside the Maple Leaf. Few understood why, recalled his friend John Weissenberger, but it was because he had close relatives in both wars, and he knew what it would have meant to them to fly the older banner.

The prime minister also boasted of Canada as an "energy superpower." He highlighted classic Canadiana like hockey, the subject of a book he had been working on. He emboldened his pitch for sovereignty in the North with plans for a new deepwater port and a promise of $3 billion for patrol ships. Previous governments had tried to sell the North as the new frontier, but the timing was premature. Now, with the combination of melting ice caps and a renewed focus on natural resources (an estimated 25 percent of the world's untapped oil-and-gas reserves lay in the thawing tundra), the timing was finally right. Harper hadn't travelled through the North before becoming prime minister, but during his first big trip there he was captivated, Bruce Carson recalled, and took a deep interest thereafter. If he had a grand idea, his aides said, it was "northern development." But he was still hesitant to employ high-sounding phrases, and his communications team, Keith Beardsley said, didn't do a consistent job of getting the northern message out.

Harper in the role of great patriot had an odd ring. He hadn't come across as much of a flag-waver during his political rise, when he had the look of a regionalist and spoke negatively about the country as a socialist haven. But friends insisted that the unknown Stephen Harper was a deep believer in the greatness of the country. James Rajotte said Harper saw Canada on a grander scale than the Liberals did. The Liberals, he said, saw it as a middle country trying to exert a larger influence. "Harper would say no to that," observed Rajotte. "He would say we are a great country—period—and we should see ourselves as such."

At the "Three Amigos" summits, he didn't hesitate to take shots at the Bush administration for its approach to the Canadian border. Since 9/11, the Americans had held fast to their misguided suspicions that the terrorists had come streaming in from the great white north, that Canada's border was as porous as Mexico's, and that protective walls had to be erected. It was a far cry from the old days, when the Canada–U.S. boundary was called the world's longest undefended border. Back then, the fear was that the border would vanish, not be reinforced. Many could remember John Turner's trenchant warning in the 1988 election that the border was going to disappear with the Free Trade Agreement. A Liberal campaign ad featured a giant eraser removing the boundary line. Two decades on, the opposite was happening.

Post 9/11, there were armed guards, long inspections, and something that could scarcely have been imagined—the introduction of passports. The security measures were among the reasons exports to the United States had begun to trend downward. "You get this absolute supremacy of security trumping everything," complained Trade Minister David Emerson, annoyed at the same time that his government wasn't moving fast enough to develop alternative markets. Harper also warned Bush, in so many words, that by taking measures that limited cross-border commerce, Washington was playing into the hands of the terrorists. To his credit, the prime minister did not seek to play the terror card to his political advantage, as Bush had done. A central ingredient in the neo-conservative playbook was to inflate threats for political gain and use this as a rationale for increased defence spending. Harper was provided an opportunity to do this with the 2006 arrest of the so-called Toronto 18, terror suspects with alleged ties to a radical Islamic cell. Yet rather than dramatize the situation with Bush/Cheney fearmongering, Harper and Public Safety Minister Stockwell Day moved on.

But while not getting caught up in Bush's web, no one could accuse Stephen Harper of being a middle-of-the-road multilateralist. Soft power was not in his vocabulary, and traditionalists were hardly enthused about the approaches he was taking. They complained of his one-sided stance on the Middle East, his lack of assistance to Darfur, his silence on nuclear disarmament, his backward China policy, his support for Guantánamo, and his general disregard for the United Nations.

IN WASHINGTON, though, the PM was winning some friends with his war contribution. Having extended the Afghanistan mission for two years in the spring of 2006, he was now looking to extend it again. Canadians viewed the enterprise with ambivalence. They saw humanitarian gains but not much military progress. The war had the look of a stalemate, and critics had reason to wonder if the stalemate could be broken.

The Conservatives' management of the war had met with serious difficulties—the resignation of Defence Minister Gordon O'Connor, the ongoing detainees controversy, and the feuding between Hillier and the PMO. And Harper was not as gung-ho on the conflict as he had been in the beginning. He'd even begun to wonder whether any kind of victory was possible. But he was not about to be seen as someone who would cut and run. Through the summer of 2007, he and his team hotly debated the question of forcing an election on the issue. The Liberals were committed to ending the combat mission by 2009, and the NDP's Jack Layton wanted a complete withdrawal and a United Nations–led negotiated settlement. Though most polls indicated that Canadians wanted the troops home before long, the Conservatives were confident they could score a big win by casting the opposition as a weak-hearted lot wanting to run from the battlefield when the going gets tough.

"We were convinced," said Ian Brodie, "that we could not only win an election over extending the mission, but that an election which polarized on the mission would obliterate the Liberals." He further explained that "We had the data, and I was totally convinced of this. We spent a lot of time and money on this. [The Liberals] had put themselves in a position of extraordinary weakness." But Harper, or so Brodie contended, took the high road. He didn't take advantage of the opportunity because he didn't want a campaign that would be so divisive for the country.

Brodie's explanation runs counter to the image of Harper as someone who wouldn't hesitate to take out an opponent when given the opportunity. He favoured, said Tom Flanagan and others in the PMO, a "divide and conquer" approach. But Brodie insisted that for the good of the country, he turned his back on this approach when it came to Afghanistan. Instead of forcing an election on the issue, he chose the somewhat hawkish Liberal John Manley to head a panel to chart a future course on the war. The panel was stacked with conservatives—Derek Burney, Pamela Wallin, Paul Tellier, and Jake Epp. It soon reported back that Canada should indefinitely extend its mission, but only with additional equipment and more support from other countries. Manley was sensitive to accusations that he was being used by the Conservatives as a political tool, but he thought the assignment was too important to let partisan considerations get in the way. He met with Harper for three hours to brief him on the panel's report and was impressed by the prime minister's questions and knowledge of the file.

Dion initially rejected the report's recommendations, saying his party was holding to the 2009 withdrawal deadline. But a month later, the Liberals changed their minds and agreed to an extension to 2011. The Liberals were satisfied that they had won concessions from the Tories, and that the extended mission would put more focus on training Afghan forces and on development and reconstruction. In appointing Manley, Harper had demonstrated political savvy, winning bipartisan support for the extension after it looked like that kind of cooperation would not be possible.

THROUGH THIS PERIOD, the harmony of the Conservative Party was disrupted by the renewed outbreak of a conflict between Brian Mulroney and Karlheinz Schreiber. Schreiber was the gnomish German dealmaker who claimed in an affidavit that he made cash payments to Mulroney of $300,000 for the provision of lobbying services. The story had been around for some time, but it resurfaced in November 2007 with the filing of Schreiber's affidavit. Harper, knowing a good deal of shady Liberal history, initially responded craftily to demands from the Grits that he call an inquiry into the matter. "Do they really want to say that I, as prime minister, should have a free hand to launch inquiries against my predecessors?" he asked.

But then Schreiber, just as craftily, implicated Harper in the dealings. He alleged he was told by Mulroney that the former PM would be seeing Harper at his Harrington Lake retreat and would speak to him on behalf of Schreiber, who was fighting extradition to Germany. Harper denied this ever happened, but he was now linked, however thinly, to Schreiber and was forced to announce an independent review of the allegations. This prompted Mulroney, in an apparent fit of pique, to demand a full public inquiry to clear his name.

Mulroney gave Harper little choice but to call such a probe, and Harper obliged. But he threw poison into the mix, saying, "I think it will be incumbent on me and also on members of the government not to have dealings with Mr. Mulroney until this issue is resolved." He was declaring Brian Mulroney, his party's biggest electoral success story since John A. Macdonald, *persona non grata*. As could be expected, the quarantine was not greeted warmly by the boy from Baie Comeau. It brought on a long stage of rage.

It occasioned a rare show of some disunity in the Harper party. Mulroney had many Tory friends and maintained a large support network in Quebec. Its work on behalf of the party tailed off. But the impact did not appear to be terribly damaging until, further down the line, the PMO went for the jugular again.

When the Mulroney-Schreiber inquiry was about to begin, Harper operatives feared it may produce new evidence damaging to the reputation of the party. Any way of distancing the party even further from Mulroney would help.

Given his discontented state, Mulroney had told Senator Irving Gerstein, a party fundraiser, that he could no longer afford to be a member of what was called the Leaders' Circle, a list of top Tory donors. That word got around, and in the PMO, it got twisted around. The attack squad decided to put out the story—leak it to a few select media—that Mulroney had been asked to be removed from party lists and had let his membership lapse. They didn't bother to check with Mulroney. They had already declared him PNG. Now the bastards, as a Mulroney ally called them, wanted to excommunicate him entirely.

When he heard the reports that he was no longer a party member, Mulroney was incensed. "I've always been a Conservative, and I will die a Conservative," he declared. At a meeting of the party caucus, tempers flared when Senator Marjory LeBreton, a long-time Mulroney ally and the Conservative leader in the Senate, announced that the former PM was indeed no longer a party member. Lee Richardson, a Calgary MP and also a long-time Mulroney associate, jumped to his defence, saying this was bogus. It was a rare show under Harper of discord.

LeBreton's switch from total allegiance to Mulroney to fawning allegiance to Harper was a shocker to many. She had for years been Mulroney's eyes and ears in the Senate, calling him almost every day. But the new regime liked her and won her over. In the 2006 election, she was on the bus with the leader and proved an asset, as did Hugh Segal, who had served as Mulroney's chief of staff. LeBreton's knowledge of the party dated back to the days of Diefenbaker, whom she had worked for as well. She could put things in perspective and also helped Harper relax. When he named her Senate leader, she obeyed his every command, even when it came to the Mulroney quarantine.

After the caucus meeting, the PMO tried to put a lid on the story of Mulroney's supposedly lapsed membership, but the whole affair had a disquieting effect on the unity of the party, and it confirmed for many in Ottawa the scheming, dark-hearted nature of Harper's operation. These people would even go after their own. The only loyalties, said a veteran of three decades in the party, were to the ones who, "on a permanent basis, kissed ass." The split was such that friends of Mulroney's couldn't even get their calls to party officials returned. The wife of one of Mulroney's closest confidants was slated to be named to a position on a board. When word reached the PMO of her ties to Mulroney, her nomination was dropped.

WHEN HARPER TOOK OFFICE, the idea was that the clampdown, the censorship, the attacks on critics would last only until the team was settled in and had things under control. But it was now almost two years in, and the strategy hadn't let up. The attack squad left few targets untouched. Even academics who wrote articles critical of government policy felt the sting.

When Michael Behiels, a professor of history at the University of Ottawa, wrote a piece for the *Ottawa Citizen* opposing the government's position on Quebec nation status, Marjory LeBreton took action. She wrote a letter to the university chancellor, Huguette Labelle, asking that the school discipline Behiels and force him to issue an apology. The university resisted on the grounds of freedom of speech. "Universities have faculty members who are outspoken on a whole range of issues," said David Mitchell, the vice-president of university relations. "And they have the freedom to do so."

LeBreton also wrote a letter to the newspaper, in which she ripped into Behiels, who held the university research chair in federalism and constitutional studies. "And to think," she huffed, "he holds a position of trust in a university and teaches our young people."

Attempts to thwart or muzzle the media continued as well. At a Conservative caucus meeting in Charlottetown in August 2007, journalists assembled in the lobby of the hotel, as they usually do at such gatherings, to talk to caucus members as they passed by. The PMO communications team, however, was not prepared to allow it. Taking their cue, or so it appeared, from a police state, they had the RCMP remove the reporters from the hotel. The Mounties told *The Globe and Mail*'s Jane Taber they'd been instructed by the PMO to evict the journalists so they wouldn't bother the caucus members. When Taber re-entered the hotel to use the washroom, she found herself being trailed. "I was followed by a Delta hotel employee just to make sure that I got out," she recalled.

Earlier in the year, the PMO had also drawn criticism for trying to muzzle the judiciary. The reproach came from Antonio Lamer, the former chief justice of the Supreme Court. He was responding to a statement Harper had made saying he wanted judges who were tough on crime. Lamer agreed that in some cases judges could be too lenient, making criminals eligible for parole too early, but said the PM was still out of line. "I must say I was taken aback," said Lamer, who sat on the Supreme Court for twenty years. "The prime minister is going the wrong route as regards the independence of the judiciary. He's trying to interfere with the sentencing process."

To close 2007, the Conservatives got a little taste of their own medicine in the form of the Paillé Report. Harper had hired Daniel Paillé, a former cabinet minister in the Parti Québécois government, to conduct a probe of federal contracts for public opinion research between 1990 and 2003. Some suspected the Tories were looking for grounds to call a judicial inquiry into Liberal polling practices. The PQ was no fan of the Liberals, and Paillé's appointment gave the probe the look of a witch hunt. Auditor General Sheila Fraser had already looked into the polling practices of the Grits from 1999 to 2003 and had found nothing amiss.

But Paillé was not about to be used. To the dismay of the Conservatives, he turned the tables on them, examining not just how the Liberals awarded opinion research contracts but how the Tories did it as well. When they saw his findings, Harper staffers were hardly amused. They decided to keep the report under wraps for as long as they could. In this case it was two months before they found a day suitable to release it—a day when the news stood a good chance of being drowned out. The day was when Brian Mulroney was testifying before the Commons ethics committee on the Schreiber imbroglio.

The Mulroney story dominated the news, just as the Conservatives knew it would, but the Paillé Report did manage to find some daylight. "Probe into Liberal Polling Dings Tories Instead," read one of the headlines. In a nutshell, the report found that in 2007 the Harper government had spent almost twice as much on opinion research ($31.2 million) as the Liberals used to spend in a year ($18 million). On average, the Tories commissioned two polls per working day. That amounted to about 546 opinion polls a year. Paillé called the figure "astounding." (The Liberals actually exceeded that number on occasion, but they never spent nearly the sums on their polls that the Conservatives did.) Paillé found no reason to call a judicial inquiry into the Liberal dealings. The Conservatives' effort to impugn their rival party had cost taxpayers $610,000. Thereafter they decided to use their own party money for opinion research.

Despite these embarrassments, the Conservatives maintained a lead over their rivals as year two of their governance drew to a close. It had been a year of inertia, a year spent idling on the policy front, waiting for an election to be called. But while the Conservatives failed to put anything inspiring in the books, Stéphane Dion, beaten up by the governing side, beginning with the TV ads, had a grim first year and was in no position to challenge them. Through the autumn, Harper dangled several election possibilities at the Grits, knowing they would back away. To Dion's observation that in avoiding an election he was only doing what Harper himself had done in opposition, the prime minister said that he was pleased to be a role model for him.

CHAPTER ELEVEN

The Concentration of Power

Two years into his governance, the man who brought in the Accountability Act was already hearing complaints that he was one of the most unaccountable prime ministers ever. A couple of other words were being used more often to describe Stephen Harper: autocratic and authoritarian.

The first autocrat, or so the critics called him, to sit in the prime minister's chair was R.B. Bennett, the millionaire lawyer who had the misfortune of serving during the Great Depression. He was such a one-man show that an editorial cartoonist depicted a cabinet meeting in which every man seated at the table was R.B. Bennett.

Bennett had a quick mind, a deep storehouse of knowledge, and an ego of unyielding proportions. Upon becoming prime minister, judging his powers to be insufficient, he named himself finance minister and foreign minister as well.

The centrepiece of Bennett's 1935 election campaign—his bold shift to the left with a Canadian version of Franklin Roosevelt's New Deal—was concocted with nary a word of consultation with his cabinet. Campaigning against him was the grumpy Mackenzie King, who declared, "We have in Canada to make a choice. We must decide whether we want a dictatorship or whether we want to carry on the old system of parliamentary representation."

In his biography of Bennett, John Boyko makes clear that the claims against him were somewhat exaggerated. The bachelor Tory was an exceptional talent with a far-reaching mind, and he may well have been an outstanding prime minister had he served at any other time. Still, the *Vancouver Sun* was not alone in labelling him a cold, aloof man lacking in the sympathies and sincerities needed to be a great leader. It was the type of depiction Stephen Harper was beginning to hear with more frequency.

Bennett's reign was followed by what the academic Donald Savoie, a specialist in governance and public administration, considered Canada's golden age of cabinet government and broadly functioning democracy. This was the Keynesian era, when faith in government was at a high point, public servants had influence, and cabinet ministers had power bases that allowed them to put checks on the reach of prime ministers. In Canada this period lasted until the 1970s, when Pierre Trudeau began expanding the size and power of the PMO and the Privy Council Office. Trudeau took a dim view of the loose and unstructured operation of his predecessor, Lester Pearson—just as Stephen Harper was unimpressed with the operation of Paul Martin, whose father had served in Pearson's cabinet. Some young Liberals eventually rebelled against the power wielded by Trudeau and his inner circle. Trudeau would later acknowledge that the system became more presidentialized during his watch, explaining that "it grew out of the fact that in a modern, complex society I needed to keep myself as informed as my ministers about what they were doing, [about] what decisions the cabinet should take collectively and what the political implications were."

Brian Mulroney did not take the centralizing trend to any great new heights, but it grew again during the rule of Jean Chrétien. Jeffrey Simpson made the point with his choice of title for his book on Chrétien's exercise of power—*The Friendly Dictatorship*. The problem starts with the system itself, Simpson noted, because in

Canada it gives the prime minister more latitude than in any other advanced industrial country. "The prime minister is the Sun King around whom all revolves and to whom all must pay varying forms of tribute." With few formalized checks and balances in place, a strongman leader is capable of overwhelming this system. The key is information control. "Information is democracy's lifeblood," wrote Simpson. "Dictatorships treat information as propaganda, ensuring by every available means that people receive only information vetted by the government."

Harper and his principal officials, as Ian Brodie noted, had learned the great importance of running a tight ship from studying an earlier Simpson book on Joe Clark's government, *Discipline of Power.* But they appeared not to have paid much attention to his book on over-concentration of power under Chrétien. In following the Harper government, Simpson came to the view that Harper's excesses, which he considered deplorable, far surpassed those of Chrétien.

Chrétien had nothing like the extraordinary vetting system put in place by the Conservatives. Advisers Eddie Goldenberg and the late Jean Pelletier did wield enormous power—especially in the later years, when Chrétien faced an internal uprising from Paul Martin's supporters—but at least caucus members and civil servants felt free to talk to the media without prior approval. Nevertheless, Harper's team argued that he was no more heavy-handed than Chrétien. Harper "looked at the last bunch of prime ministers and concluded essentially that the tough guys were the most successful," said Bruce Carson. This view was shared by John Weissenberger, who was chief of staff to Immigration Minister Diane Finley. Harper, he said, could be accused of being domineering at times. "But, you know, people ask me that, and I say, 'Well, what's the alternative?' Do you want to be criticized for being too disciplined or do you want to be criticized for being scattered and chaotic?" Between the eithers and ors were happy mediums, of course. But the Conservatives—never mind all those promises of cleaning up the system—were content to explain away their abuse of power with the rationale that other PMs had done it and therefore so could Harper.

The line of reasoning hardly served to enhance the state of democracy. The system, said Savoie, had devolved into a "court government," with the leader and a few select courtiers, most of them unelected, exercising power with kingly presumption. Savoie had hoped that Harper would move away from such a model once he'd settled in to office. But in fact, he was going the other way.

ON HIS WAY TO PARLIAMENT ONE DAY, Stéphane Dion paused in front of the Château Laurier, the stately hotel where R.B. Bennett lived during his entire stewardship. Dion chatted with a journalist. "I'll tell you what I think about Harper," he said. "First, he is a man of principle. What he has said and what he has written during his adult life is what he thinks Canada needs." Canadians do not share his philosophy, however, and so to get his way Harper, Dion explained, has to resort to extraordinary means. So he is ready "to spend, for instance, more money than any Liberal prime minister before him." He is caught up in a schizophrenia, Dion added, between what his ideology requires him to do and what the philosophy of Canadians requires him to do.

"He is Straussian," Dion went on to say. "He's a Straussian who thinks people are not intelligent enough to understand what he wants do." Harper, Dion said, sees no great need to consult. Like Strauss, "he will go very far to manipulate the people."

Leo Strauss, a highly influential German-Jewish philosopher, taught political science at the University of Chicago from 1949 to 1968. His work is subject to varying interpretations, but he believed the liberal state was prone to moral relativism, and as a result, he became a favourite of neo-conservatives. Keith Martin, the former Alliance Party member turned Liberal, was convinced from his many meetings with Harper that he had Straussian leanings. This, he said, was the fundamental reason for his break with Preston Manning. "Whereas Manning was a nominal populist," Martin observed, "Stephen felt that grassroots, bottoms-up democracy was a fool's game. He felt that the best way to govern was per Leo Strauss—that a small number of people at the top determine what has to be done."

Sheila Drury, a Straussian specialist at the University of Regina, sees the philosopher as an adversary of democracy and liberalism. His disciples, she said, "love secrecy. It is fundamental to them. It has all to do with the manipulation of the democratic process." Before moving to Saskatchewan, Drury taught at the University of Calgary, where she worked, while not sharing their views, along-side Tom Flanagan and other conservative members of a right-wing group sometimes referred to as the Calgary School. She didn't know if Harper had read or followed Strauss, but she believed that he was slowly and methodically changing Canada along lines Strauss would have approved. Harper's penchant for secrecy and control and his deep animosity towards his opponents were in keeping with Strauss's thinking. What was also consistent, Drury believed, was the type of patriotism Harper promoted. She was impressed also by the Conservatives' skill at controlling the message, something that wasn't easy to do with so many new forms of instant communication. They were successful in part, she felt, because "the Liberal media was on the run." The strategy of accusing the media of having a liberal bias had worked well for Republicans south of the border, and was now being applied to Canada.

In his long conversations with Harper about political philosophy in their graduate school days, however, John Weissenberger said Leo Strauss was never mentioned. While he was at the National Citizens Coalition, according to staffer Gerry Nicholls, Harper talked a great deal about Friedrich Hayek, an Austrian economist and political philosopher, but not about Strauss. Tom Flanagan noted that while

Harper may exhibit some Straussian characteristics—his need to totally control the message was one—people could rest assured that he was not a true Straussian.

Michael Behiels saw in the prime minister an Alberta strain of influence that was authoritarian. For Harper, noted Behiels, "the executive is everything." It was an attitude common to old-style Alberta politicians like Bible Bill Aberhart. Traditionally, Behiels said, there were two schools of politics practised in Canada's most right-wing province. "There was participatory democracy practised by the old United Farmers of Alberta from 1921 to 1935. That was referendum, recall, initiative; constituency MPs with a lot of power. Voters were consulted all the time. Then, of course, Bible Bill Aberhart [gets in] in 1935 and dispenses with all that and becomes, in effect, an autocrat."

Whether Harper was a follower of Strauss or Hayek or Aberhart, or none of them, was open to debate. In his case, as with many other political leaders, it was risky to apply sweeping labels. Harper had demonstrated he could be just as pragmatic as ideological. He displayed different shades of conservatism at different times, depending on the circumstances he faced. The important consideration was where he was moored, and it could hardly be said that this place was imbued with democratic ideals, but rather with monocratic, domineering tendencies.

Some Conservatives were disappointed that Harper hadn't shown more of his right-wing colours in his first two years in office. But others, like many of the old Tories in the Senate, felt they had seen more than enough already. They didn't like what was going on but were afraid to speak out, so they swallowed hard and went quietly about their business.

One who didn't have to worry about the repercussions of speaking his mind was Senator Lowell Murray, a Maritimer who had served in the Mulroney cabinet and later as Senate leader. With the amalgamation of the two wings of the party, he chose to sit as an independent. For him, the differences in approach between Harper and Mulroney were striking. Mulroney was a *rassembleur*, a leader forever trying to widen the tent. He was enormously competitive and egotistical, but a generosity of spirit often prevailed. He could reach out to friend and foe alike. By contrast, Harper, Murray said, sought advantage by pitting one segment of society against another. His use of wedge politics was dismaying because it involved oversimplifying issues that required nuanced debate. That Harper so often resorted to it—we support the troops, you don't; we support Israel, you don't; we're in favour of law and order, you're soft on crime—reinforced Dion's view that he lacked respect for the intelligence of the masses. He felt he could get away with a debasement of the discourse.

Murray frowned upon wedge politics because of its potentially polarizing effect. You could win that way, thought Murray, but at what cost? Under Harper, he said, no one had the courage, such was the degree of intimidation, to speak out. In the old Progressive Conservative Party, he recalled, there were strong cabinet ministers like John Crosbie and Flora MacDonald and Don Mazankowski whose views had to be countenanced. But under Harper everyone was cowed, even Tory senators who were guaranteed their positions until age seventy-five. The atmosphere was so tight that they had to put up with taking orders from young ideologues in the PMO who knew next to nothing. How could they tolerate having to kowtow so much? Speaking for western Conservatives, Rod Love said, "They were just so goddamned pleased after being out of power for thirteen years to be back in that they put up with it. You got to remember that after Chrétien won another majority in 2000, some thought we'd never get back in." The atmosphere in the Harper government was "stifling," Love said. "Harper runs the tightest ship in the history of the party." But Tories realized that lack of discipline had killed their hopes in the past, so they were prepared to buckle under.

Murray also worried about what was happening to the public service. It looked to him as if the Clerks of the Privy Council were being co-opted. Clerks were supposed to act on behalf of the departments and the cabinet, not solely on behalf of the prime minister. "Someone at that level has to dare speak for cabinet prerogatives," said Murray, "even occasionally against the prime minister ... The senior civil servants expect the clerk to curb the worst instincts of the prime minister and defend the higher values, the higher standards of the public service." But to Murray, there was no sense of that happening under Harper. The clerk, he thought, had "gone native."

Murray's concerns received some validation early in 2008 when John Gomery spoke out. The judge whose inquiry into the sponsorship scandal had done so much to end the Liberal reign came forward to say the Harper government was going back on its word on accountability. Gomery had followed up his report on the sponsorship scandal with a second report that recommended changes to clean up the system. But his proposals had fallen into what he called a "black hole" of indifference. Harper had strongly supported the changes when he was in opposition. Now, said Gomery, "there's more concentration of power in the Prime Minister's Office than we've ever had before, which is quite remarkable in a minority government. But he's pulled it off."

Gomery had waited two years for evidence of change. "I am disappointed. I find it hard to swallow," he told a Commons committee. He laid the blame for the lack of progress at the feet of the PMO, saying, "It should be remembered that the political staff in the Prime Minister's Office are not elected. They are not subjected to any rules of law of which I am aware." His report had recommended curbing the PM's power to appoint senior civil servants and limiting the power of the Clerk of the Privy Council. Bureaucrats had objected to some of these changes, but Gomery said they were just protecting their own turf.

DURING THIS TIMEFRAME, several controversies—controversies having less to do with policies than methodology—saw Harper paying a price for his heavy hand.

One such storm swirled around the firing of Linda Keen, the head of the Canadian Nuclear Safety Commission. Her watchdog agency had shut down the nuclear reactor at Chalk River, Ontario, over safety concerns, involving the connection of the emergency power system to the cooling pumps. The fifty-year-old reactor generated two-thirds of the radioisotopes used in life-saving medical procedures the world over. The PMO objected to her decision and reopened the facility, with the natural resources minister, the cherubic Gary Lunn, declaring it safe to do so. A month later, in January 2008, Lunn fired Keen, saying she had lost the confidence of the government.

The Alberta-born Keen had a long-standing and good record as a public servant. She was informed of her dismissal the night before she was to appear before a Commons committee with Lunn, an event that would surely have caused commotion. The way the firing was handled prompted much derision from critics, who said this was the way things were done in banana republics. Harper argued that Keen had demonstrated "an appalling use of authority and judgment." Then the prime minister took things a step further, alleging that she had a Liberal Party bias, and that this somehow played into her decision-making. "Since when does the Liberal Party have a right, from the grave through one of its previous appointees, to block the production of necessary medical products in the country?" asked the prime minister.

Harper had reasonable grounds to believe the reactor should not have been shut down. As the Federal Court would later rule, he also had the authority to dismiss Keen from her position. Keen had a defensible position as well. Had there been an accident at Chalk River as a result of the safety breaches, she would have been pilloried until the end of time.

But the prime minister turned a legitimate difference in policy position into a partisan political war. His portrayal of Keen as a politically motivated Liberal was more fodder for those who believed he was paranoia-prone, predisposed to see enemies everywhere. Did she really want to shut down the reactor just to somehow embarrass the Conservatives?

Hundreds of civil servants, many of them without partisan political backgrounds, had been appointed by the Liberals during their thirteen years in power. It was a long leap to conclude that these appointees were secretly working to help the Liberal cause. Critics said the firing of Linda Keen would reverberate through the ranks of senior officers serving on regulatory commissions. These officers would fear that any unpopular decisions they made would result in disciplinary action.

The government's hardball tactics against all things Liberal, real or imagined, next extended to a denunciation of Ontario's business climate and its Liberal premier, Dalton McGuinty. Finance Minister Jim Flaherty, who represented the Ontario riding of Whitby–Oshawa, advised investors to stay away from the province. "Their business taxes are the highest in Canada. If Mr. McGuinty thinks that's good for the manufacturing sector in Ontario, he's wrong," said Flaherty. "If you're going to make a new business investment in Canada, and you're concerned about taxes, the last place you will go is the province of Ontario."

The comments prompted days of rancour between the two sides. Analysts were hard-pressed to find any other instance of a federal finance minister denigrating the country's largest province in such an overt way. Flaherty was reminded of the fact that he had been a member of the Harris cabinet that left the province with a $5.6-billion budget deficit.

A few months before that spasm, Flaherty had blasted municipal leaders who complained about their crumbling infrastructure and the lack of help from Ottawa. Stop whining, Flaherty told them. Ottawa is "not in the pothole business." In the same season, Peter Van Loan labelled McGuinty "the small man of Confederation" after he suggested that the number of seats in the Commons be determined by proportional representation. It wasn't just Van Loan's doing. He received permission to deliver the cheap shot from Harper.

The frequency with which the government resorted to attack politics confounded analysts, who wondered how the prime minister thought he could profit from appearing so mean-spirited. Ontario was far and away the biggest political prize for any party, and even if the criticisms had some merit, the words chosen were unwise. Polls taken after Flaherty made his comments about the province being a poor place to do business showed that almost twice as many respondents sided with McGuinty.

But the Conservative grenade hurlers couldn't help themselves. Next up to the plate was Treasury Board Secretary Vic Toews, whose target was Louise Arbour, the United Nations High Commissioner for Human Rights and a former Supreme Court justice. Arbour had a far more distinguished reputation than Toews did, but that didn't stop him from labelling her a national "disgrace" when she praised a new Arab human rights charter and chastised both sides in the conflict between Israel and Lebanon. Toews hollered "Shame on her!" when the matter was raised in the Commons.

The attack strategy was one prong in the Conservative arsenal. The other—ironclad message control—continued to be enforced with rigour. Harper appeared to be more and more cocooned. His events were screened to make certain that only supporters got in. Press conferences were limited to pre-set subjects.

The scripting extended to radio phone-in shows. Even though these shows tended to have a conservative lean anyway, the Harper operatives wanted to make sure all bases were covered. They prepared talking points for grassroots supporters on a wide range of issues. On the party website, supporters could tap in their postal codes to get a list of local talk shows to call and advice on what should be said on any given topic. On a CPAC phone-in show, the host, Dale Goldhawk, interrupted one caller to ask if he was reading from a script. Ryan Sparrow, a Conservative spokesman, defended the tactic as state-of-the-art messaging. "This is part of campaigning in the Internet age," he said. "Party activists are increasingly becoming virtual volunteers."

The Ottawa media were still trying to come to grips with the new controls. In the environment portfolio, John Baird presided over a muzzling operation of exceptional scope. Traditionally, scientists in the department were able to talk rather freely about their work at public forums or in the media. But everything now had to be reduced to "one voice," according to a PowerPoint presentation prepared by officials. Any interaction between scientists and journalists had to go through a Soviet-style monitoring maze. Reporters were asked to submit questions in writing, and answers were passed to senior managers for approval. A department official was allowed to talk to a reporter only so long as he or she stuck to the approved lines.

Climatologist Andrew Weaver, who worked with Environment Canada, had never seen anything even approaching this level of control. "They've been muzzled," he said of his colleagues. "The concept of free speech is non-existent at Environment Canada. They are manufacturing the message of science." Baird was unfazed by the criticism. He came forward on more than one occasion to proclaim with a straight face that "this is the most open and transparent government in Canadian history."

Baird was often joined in the bombast department by Jim Flaherty and Peter Van Loan, both of whom also hailed from the hardline Ontario regime of Mike Harris. Harper had given the Ontario men prominent positions in his government because of their past cabinet experience, and because he appreciated ministers who could carve their opponents to pieces. The opposition parties particularly disliked Van Loan, the former president of the Ontario PCs. On some days, he handled more questions in the House than any other minister—and did so with a flair for concealment and abusive partisan shots.

THE BROOK-NO-DISSENT ATTITUDE of the PMO was too much for some. Early in 2008, it contributed to the departure of General Rick Hillier. Though he had finished his three-year term as the Chief of Defence Staff, Hillier was still relatively young, healthy, popular with the troops, and popular with the media. Afghanistan was in large part his war. He had pressured the Martin government to move the Canadian forces to Kandahar, making the mission more combat heavy. He got his way and, if he felt wanted, there were many reasons to believe he would have liked to stay to see the mission through. He seemed such a good fit for the Conservatives. He had the American-style warrior mentality, and he had a retail politician's ability to sell the public on the war and the need for a revitalized military.

To do those things required some freedom, however, and that was too much for his political masters to bear. They wanted him out, but they wanted it done in as delicate a way as possible. When CTV's Robert Fife broke the story that Hillier wouldn't be offered a new term, there were vehement denials all around. A few months later, the report was confirmed. The prime minister wanted someone more submissive in the job. In the end, said Kory Teneycke, one of Harper's directors of communications, Hillier's ego was just too big. He was trying, he alleged, to become another General Douglas MacArthur. "I think history will be far less kind to General Hillier than the instant history of today's media," Teneycke said. "I think that's because of the blurring of the lines between that which is the job of elected officials versus the role of military commanders." Hillier was "an advocate, publicly, privately," said Teneycke, and "it was unbecoming."

Hillier's departure should have been a major controversy, a flashpoint for the opposition parties. Canada had lost its top war general, and there was little evidence to substantiate the charge that the government had another MacArthur on its hands. But the opposition was unable to put Harper on the defensive. The story never got legs. The message-control machine did its job.

The Liberals couldn't function with required resolution on this or other issues because they lacked the confidence to force an election. The atmosphere through this period, Canada's thirty-ninth Parliament, featured a level of acrimony that exceeded even normal standards. Some law and order bills were pushed through; immigration was streamlined by giving the minister fast-tracking powers; and Industry Minister Jim Prentice blocked the sale of Canada's subsidized space satellite manufacturer to U.S. interests. Yet despite all the controversies and the lack of big programs, Harper was still able to ride herd over the proceedings.

In the Commons, his team of slaggers usually got the better of opponents. Instead of asking pointed questions, Liberal MPs fell into the habit of delivering long preambles and predictable, invective-filled lectures. The lengthily worded questions were always easiest to fend off because they offered the responder a number of rebuttal angles from which to choose. Initially it appeared that the academically inclined Dion wished to bring some intellectual loftiness to the chamber. Preston Manning had made a noble effort at doing so when he took his seat as Reform leader in 1993. But the aggression coming from the other side is such that anyone trying to maintain a sense of dignity is soon beaten down by cheap and denigrating sound bites and eventually has to fight back or be labelled a weakling.

But not all of the thirty-ninth session of Parliament was given over to wrangling and bickering. In June, the Commons witnessed one of the most moving ceremonies in years when the prime minister addressed the chamber on the history of abuse suffered by Native students of residential schools.

The apology wasn't Harper's idea, but he followed up gracefully when urged to do so by Jack Layton. Earlier, the PM had issued an apology for the controversial Chinese head tax, a hated levy designed to discourage immigration from China in the late nineteenth and early twentieth century. The NDP leader told Harper what a big impact his comments had had in the Chinese community, and he suggested that an apology for the abuse that took place at the residential schools would resonate even more. When he reminded the PM that the Liberal government had never offered a full apology, it sealed the deal.

The wording of the apology, given the sensitivities, had to be just right. The Indian Affairs department and the Assembly of First Nations collaborated on a draft that the PMO found brutally long and wordy.

Harper, never known to be a wordsmith, decided to take on the task of writing it himself. According to Ian Brodie, this caused consternation in the ranks of the bureaucracy. The control freak was at it again! "Justice went ballistic and Indian Affairs was just so worried they just froze up totally. And the PCO was very, very nervous."

Some were worried about the legal risks and some feared that First Nations Chief Phil Fontaine would hate the result. "And some probably worried," said Brodie, "that the PM's inner neanderthal would emerge."

Harper took weeks to draft it, while hints began appearing in the media about a lack of consultation. The PMO sent Carson to calm temperatures, but, said Brodie, there was a lot of sweating. Harper, he said, had three priorities. The first was an apology for the injustice of taking kids from their families without cause. "Harper is a conservative, and when the state breaks up families without good cause, conservatives should be outraged." Secondly, Harper didn't want to apologize for churches or Christianity or evangelism generally. He wanted to apologize for the program and its horrible impact. Thirdly, he wanted to meet Phil Fontaine's request that the apology refer to the policy of killing the Indian in the child.

Harper was solemn as he spoke before a hushed gathering in the Commons. "Mr. Speaker, I stand before you today to offer an apology to former students of Indian residential schools ... Today we recognize that this policy of assimilation was wrong, has caused great harm, and has no place in our country." The policy, he said, had a lasting and damaging impact on Aboriginal culture, heritage, and language. He spoke of the emotional, physical, and sexual abuse and neglect of helpless children, and of their separation from their families and communities.

Hundreds of Native leaders stood quietly in the galleries and listened as the prime minister's voice wavered. The apology was met with approval from the media and the public, and most important, from the First Nations. "Now there were probably people around town who thought he was a control freak for taking over," said Brodie, "and that this was centralizing the decisions and so forth. But the result was a good one."

HARPER COULD NEVER escape the charge of manipulator-in-chief, however, and during this period he faced serious charges from a few years earlier relating to his dealings with a Conservative from British Columbia, the MP Chuck Cadman.

In 1992, Cadman, an electrical technician, lost his sixteen-year-old son, Jesse, after a stabbing attack by a group of teenagers. Cadman joined what he believed was the best party to get tough on crime—the Reform Party. Elected as an MP in 1997, he became the party's youth critic, handling the assignment with passion. He was diagnosed with a deadly skin cancer in 2003, and in the lead-up to the 2004 election, he lost the Conservative nomination. The popular Cadman, his condition worsening, ran as an independent, however, and easily won the riding, with the Conservative candidate a distant fourth. A year later, Paul Martin's minority government was facing a confidence vote on its budget, and the government's fate, incredibly, rested with Cadman, who was dying.

Cadman had to be mindful of his life insurance policy. If an election was held right away and he lost, he would no longer be a sitting MP and his family would stand to lose a lot of money on the policy when he died. In the prelude to the vote, both the Liberals and the Conservatives tried to convince him to come to their table. Two of Harper's most powerful players, Tom Flanagan and Doug Finley, went to see him—a sign of how much the Conservatives wanted his support. But half an hour before the vote, Cadman decided to throw in his lot with the Liberals, thus saving the Martin government from defeat and himself from the possibility of losing his seat.

When he was asked after the vote if he had received any overtures from the Conservatives, Cadman said the only thing they offered was a riding nomination. Less than two months later, he passed away. But in 2008, the story returned to the headlines with the publication of *Like a Rock: The Chuck Cadman Story* by Tom Zytaruk. The book alleged that the Conservatives had in fact offered Cadman several inducements, including a million-dollar life insurance policy, to vote with them. If true, such an act was illegal, tantamount to bribery. His wife, Dona Cadman, confirmed the story, saying, "If he died I'd get the million dollars. [And] there was a few other things thrown in there too."

Harper denied that such an offer had been made. But Zytaruk had a taped interview with the prime minister that complicated the situation. In it, Zytaruk talked about the insurance policy, asking Harper, "Did you know anything about that?"

"I don't know the details. I know that there were discussions," said Harper. "This is not for publication?"

"This will be for the book, not for the newspaper," Zytaruk replied.

Harper went on to say that the offer to Cadman was "only to replace financial considerations he might lose due to an election." IIis comments appeared to suggest that there was an inducement, and that Dona Cadman, who didn't have much reason to lie, was telling the truth.

The Conservatives then alleged that the Zytaruk tape might have been doctored and Harper's words distorted. In shoot-the-messenger mode, they went after Zytaruk's credibility. Harper then pressed the legal button, serving notice of a $3.5-million lawsuit against the Liberals for statements on their party website alleging that attempted bribery took place. Prime ministers normally didn't resort to such extremes. An affidavit from the highly regarded Peter Russell, a University of Toronto political science professor, said it was without precedent: "This use of legal action to silence the opposition is characteristic of authoritarian governments. It is incompatible with democratic government."

In February 2009, the Conservatives dropped the lawsuit after a court-ordered analysis of Zytaruk's tape found that the section in dispute had not been altered as the Tories had alleged. This left their case on shaky ground.

In the final analysis, it couldn't be said with any degree of certainty if Chuck Cadman was offered a bribe. But given the Conservatives' track record—their willingness to go to extremes to accomplish their political goals—it wasn't easy to accord them the benefit of the doubt.

CHAPTER TWELVE

Damage Control

Whiz kid Patrick Muttart wasn't concerned about the arrival of the liberal messiah, Barack Obama. Some thought that the liberal tides would sweep into Canada, that Obama's progressive spirit would make the Canadian leader look behind the times, that his magnetism would make Stephen Harper look even more banal. But Muttart's read on Canada–U.S. relations was different. He felt that there was little ideological or political synchronicity in the relationship. The washover effect wouldn't be significant. It wasn't something that would affect a Canadian election call.

But Harper was following the Obama surge closely. He had an abiding interest in American politics, and he knew he would likely have to deal with the next president. Though he had come to the prime minister's job with the image of having only a modest interest in external affairs, he soon changed the impression.

In the section of the Privy Council Office that dealt with foreign affairs—where about forty analysts assessed what was going on in the world—he was gaining a reputation as one of the best-informed prime ministers the senior bureaucrats had ever worked with. Harper, said Gregg Fyffe, who worked in the office for several years, took a greater interest in intelligence reports than other PMs. "He looked at the material very carefully," said Fyffe. "He was a reader and he wanted a reasonable amount of detail."

The U.S. was of particular interest to the prime minister. He wanted intelligence on a variety of issues, including, for example, the ongoing Iraq war and how it was being used by political leaders to shape their policies. Despite his ideological reputation, he didn't dispute the analyses the intelligence section sent him, noted Fyffe. "We never had any feedback that said, 'Don't say things like this or that.'" Like others, Fyffe noticed a heavy degree of centralization of the power structure under Harper. But this was part of a long-term trend and he believed there were legitimate reasons for it. In the twenty-four-hour news cycle, he noted, "just about anything can surface suddenly anywhere and upset a government's agenda." In such a different media world, the centre simply had to be more vigilant.

In the U.S. election, the Conservatives were naturally hoping that the underdog, John McCain, could pull off a surprise upset and beat Barack Obama. Harper had survived the Bush presidency nicely, maintaining a good relationship with the Republican administration without being seen to be too much in harmony with its reckless designs. "He was always very careful," noted Keith Beardsley. "He didn't want to appear like an American lackey." If McCain won, the Harper camp foresaw a much easier relationship than under Bush and some easing of bilateral stresses along the border.

Canadian issues rarely figured in American campaigns, and it was customary for Canadian governments to stay at arm's length. But occasionally, things got touchy. Prior to the 2000 campaign, Raymond Chrétien, Jean Chrétien's nephew and the Canadian ambassador in Washington, made a speech that some construed as tepidly endorsing Al Gore in his battle with George W. Bush. Since the Chrétiens were lifelong Liberals, everyone already knew this was where their sentiments lay. But the speech caused a flap, and when

Bush won the election, there was a coolness in relations that had to be overcome.

This was trivial, however, compared to what happened in the 2008 campaign. In the primaries, Obama and Hillary Clinton were campaigning hard in Ohio and taking turns trashing the North American Free Trade Agreement (NAFTA), blaming it for heavy job losses in the state. Obama went so far as to warn that NAFTA might have to be renegotiated. When two officials from the Canadian consulate in Chicago met with Austan Goolsbee, an adviser to Obama, they raised the matter. They understood from Goolsbee that Obama's words should be viewed as political posturing more than any clear statement of intent, and they passed on that interpretation in a memo to senior officials in Ottawa.

Three weeks later, Harper's chief of staff, Ian Brodie, revealed while chatting with reporters that the NAFTA-bashing should not be taken too seriously, that it was mainly rhetoric. News of this got out but didn't cause too much of a stir. Then the memo prepared by the Canadian officials was leaked to the Associated Press. The story made headlines across the U.S., embarrassing Obama, who appeared to be saying one thing publicly and another privately. Goolsbee was angry, claiming that the Canadian officials had misrepresented his words and the Canadian embassy in Washington was under the gun. Diplomatic memos were rarely leaked, especially in the middle of a presidential campaign, and since the Harper government was Conservative, many suspected that the leak was politically motivated.

Harper apologized, saying that what had happened was "blatantly unfair" and that the matter would be investigated. Clinton, meanwhile, won the Ohio primary, and her campaign manager, Mark Penn, said the dispute over Obama's alleged hypocrisy was an important factor in the outcome.

Republicans, eager to make gains, pressured their Conservative Canadian colleagues. McCain's team wanted bilateral meetings highlighting the trade issue. As trade minister, David Emerson was involved in the file. "There was a fair amount of difficulty there," he recalled. "It was awkward because we had the McCain folks open and willing to come up and engage and use the positive relationship with Canada for political gain." In the Harper ranks, he said, "there was a little less enthusiasm for the Obama crowd. It made the foreign affairs relationship a little difficult."

Meanwhile, Harper appointed Kevin Lynch, the Clerk of the Privy Council, to oversee an investigation into the leak. This led the opposition to complain that the exercise would be a sham. If the PMO was involved, they asked, would Lynch really bring in a report that embarrassed the prime minister?

As part of the investigation, Ian Brodie was questioned by a retired Mountie and a retired CSIS officer. "All I can say is that the investigative firm hired by the PCO was extremely thorough as far as I could tell," said Brodie, looking back on the controversy. He said he had shredded the memo from the diplomats after reading it. "I handled the report from the Chicago consulate as if it had been classified Secret. It didn't actually occur to me that it was unclassified, given the content," he recalled. "Once I read it, I disposed of it in a secure shred box. I certainly never released it to anyone outside the PMO. In short, I did not leak it."

In the end, Lynch's report cleared Brodie of having a hand in the leak and failed to find a culprit, saying the net was too wide. Since the investigation had been going on for little more than two months and had not yet served its purpose, critics wondered why it was already being shut down.

The Lynch report was released just before a weekend break, the time when political news attracts the least attention. But at the start of the following week, the *Toronto Star*'s Jim Travers contradicted its findings, quoting a source as saying, "This was a very deliberate piece of business for political purpose. It puts political ideology ahead of what's good for the country." Travers reported that the PMO had leaked the memo to a Republican Party contact, Frank Sensenbrenner. Sensenbrenner was the son of Congressman James Sensenbrenner and was well connected to Ottawa Tories. He even worked for a brief time at Canada's Washington embassy on congressional relations.

The *Star* reported that Sensenbrenner was introduced into Canadian diplomatic circles by Gerry Chipeur, a Calgary lawyer who had served as legal counsel to the Reform and Alliance parties and headed a group called Republicans Abroad Canada. Sensenbrenner, who got part of his early education in Toronto, attended Reform Party conventions and became acquainted with Preston Manning's inner circle. He was not trusted or welcome at the Canadian embassy, but he was backed by Harper's office, and that allowed him to remain for a time in the position. If the leak did come from the PMO, he would be a likely recipient. But Sensenbrenner denied ever seeing the memo and said he was shocked his name could even come up.

As part of the investigation, Ian Brodie was questioned in detail about both Sensenbrenners. He said he met Frank two or three times over the years at large gatherings or receptions but never actively contacted him. As for Harper, he said, "I know the father visited the PM once." As chief of staff, Brodie explained, "it was my constant and unrelenting policy always to downplay the various controversies in the Canada–U.S. relationship." His comments to reporters about the campaign chatter on NAFTA, he noted, were a perfect example of this. And while he acknowledged some personal links between Conservatives and U.S. Republicans, he added, "I think it's fair to say we were all much, much closer to the Australian Liberals."

With Sensenbrenner's denial and no one able to prove involvement of the PMO, the story tapered off. Like the Cadman affair, however, this incident left room, given the way Harper operatives worked, for plenty of suspicion. "I don't know that there was anything particularly conspiratorial about it," said David Emerson of the leak. But like most others, he couldn't be certain.

IN THE NATION'S CAPITAL, hardly a month could pass without some controversy erupting over the government's attempts to bring the system to heel. Now came another instalment, this one involving no less an authority than the auditor general. In testimony before the public accounts committee, Sheila Fraser said she had learned of a plan to effectively censor her and other agency heads by forcing them to have their public statements vetted by the PCO. "There's a draft communication policy going around," she said, "that would have all communications strategies, all communications, everything, go through Privy Council Office." Then she added: "Well, I can tell you there is no way that my press releases about my report are going to Privy Council Office or our communications strategies are going to be vetted by Privy Council Office."

If enacted, the policy would have given the PMO/PCO the power to stall, block, or alter communications that put them in a bad light. The reports of the auditors general usually revealed many examples of government ineptitude. Other agency heads who would have come under this far-reaching vetting plan included the privacy commissioner, the information commissioner, the ethics commissioner, the commissioner of official languages, and Elections Canada.

Harper and the Tories had an ongoing feud with Elections Canada over $1.2 million in alleged campaign-spending irregularities—the "in-and-out affair"—during the 2006 election campaign. In April 2008, shortly before Fraser spoke, the RCMP had raided Conservative Party headquarters at the request of Elections Canada. That raid prompted national headlines, infuriating the Tory brass. It led also to a scene they would dearly like to forget, with panicked

PMO operatives running around downtown Ottawa like the Keystone Kops, trying to elude a gaggle of reporters.

The day before the RCMP warrant for the raid was to be released to the public, PMO staffers tried to put their spin on the story, arranging for a private briefing with a few select pencil squeezers whom they felt would be more sympathetic to their cause. The briefing was supposed to take place at the Lord Elgin Hotel, but much to the plotters' irritation, the excluded reporters caught wind of it. When the Harper officials, led by Doug Finley, heard of this, they decided that rather than have these knaves present they should change hotels. And so the chosen ones were told to hightail it over to the Sheraton, a couple of blocks away.

But that ruse didn't work either. The barred reporters, including the CBC's Keith Boag, found out about the switch and promptly showed up at the Sheraton. The PMO staffers, with Ryan Sparrow in the role of bouncer, wouldn't let them in. But they were trapped, cameras awaiting them outside. Their only hope now was to find a secret way out. And so all the prime minister's men headed for the fire escape, fleeing down the hotel stairwell and charging out onto the streets to freedom.

Such was the new era of transparency.

PMO officials liked to claim that they weren't paranoid about information control, but the claim suffered a beating on that day. Harper's operatives believed that the CBC had been tipped off about the Mountie raid by the Liberals. The idea that the Liberals and Elections Canada and the CBC were working hand in hand fitted their conspiratorial imaginations like a glove. The only problem with this theory, recalled Keith Boag, was that the network's tip had come not from a Liberal source but "from one of their own, a Conservative."

Often enough, recalled Keith Beardsley, the matter of being called control freaks would be discussed at the PMO. Beardsley didn't mind the label personally. "I figured most of the dirty work was being done by others." Whenever the accusation was raised with Harper, recalled Beardsley, not much of a response was forthcoming. "He would shrug it off. It was like 'This is what I have to do. Let's get on with it.' He would just dig in his heels."

There were moments when he would show another side. When Beardsley's father died, he was driving to the funeral in Toronto when his cellphone went off. It was Harper. "Keith, you didn't tell me your dad died." Harper talked to him for forty minutes. He had lost his own father a couple of years beforehand and they shared memories of what their fathers had meant to them.

Following Sheila Fraser's revelations, the government back-pedalled on its vetting plans, saying the policy wouldn't apply to the agencies mentioned. Fraser later came forward to say that likely no ill will was intended. "I truly believe the government itself recognizes that would be inappropriate," she said. But if there had simply been some kind of misunderstanding, the PMO could have cleared it up by releasing a copy of its draft communications plan that had touched off the dispute. It declined to do so.

There were indications at this same time that the PMO also had a plan to monitor RCMP communications. On April 25, shortly after the raid on Tory headquarters, Commissioner William Elliott told the force in an internal broadcast that future communications would be under the control of a newly appointed assistant deputy commissioner. The implication was that a public servant answerable to political bosses would now be in charge.

This plan set off alarm bells. The Mounties had always handled their own communications—and with good reason. If they were investigating criminal allegations involving politicians, it would hardly be appropriate for the government to have control over what was being said. The Elliott statement stood for almost three weeks. When it appeared that news of it was about to break in the media, the commissioner made another announcement. He said a mistake had been made. A new communications position would be created. "However the position will not be an Assistant Deputy Minister's position, as had been indicated." That idea had raised questions, the commissioner said. "There is no intent for the position to be under the authority or direction of anyone other than the RCMP."

Keith Beardsley, who was preparing to leave the PMO at this time, maintained that in this instance there was nothing untoward going on. This time, it was perhaps reporters who were too conspiratorially minded.

TRY AS IT MIGHT, the PMO couldn't control everything. The starless cabinet, for one, continued to create problems. Harper had already replaced two ministers—at defence and environment—and now it was the turn of his man at foreign affairs to tumble.

Had Maxime Bernier kept his girlfriend in the background, nothing would have happened. But like some high roller at the casino tables, he paraded his prize around and the media got the clip. "The Bernier story was the triumph of the visual," recalled Kory Teneycke. "If there had not been six seconds of videotape of Julie Couillard getting out of that car with the low-cut dress, I don't think that story would have taken off. But my friends at CTV fell in love with that clip. I think they probably played it more than the Paul Henderson goal."

Bernier was touted as a minister with star potential, if only because there was so little to choose from in the Conservatives' Quebec caucus. Old-guard Tories had urged Harper to visit Quebec more often to draw support and talent to the party. He wanted to, but he didn't have the time.

Bernier, the tall, dapper MP from Beauce, made a good—if light—initial impression. He had avoided trouble in the industry portfolio, but PCO officials didn't like working with him, nor he with them. They didn't think he did his homework, and he in turn was annoyed at having to be vetted so much by the senior bureaucrats. But Bernier was a big vote-getter in Quebec, so Harper decided to promote him, moving him to foreign affairs in place of Peter MacKay. It was clear from the start, however, that foreign affairs would be a difficult assignment for him. There was too much to know, and he didn't know very much. The putdowns could be heard in the corridors. Bernier was all hat, no cattle.

In the new post Bernier made some smallish early mistakes. He called for the removal of the governor of Kandahar, in Afghanistan, when he had no business doing so. He promised to deliver aid to Myanmar on a Canadian cargo plane when no such plane was available. He got the name of the president of Haiti wrong in the House of Commons.

As for Julie Couillard, the low-cut dresses were one thing, but there was also the matter of the friends she kept. It became known that she'd had a relationship with a well-known Montreal crime figure who was gunned down in 1996 after becoming a police informant. She was later married to a top enforcer for a biker gang. The opposition charged that her liaison with the foreign minister might make her a security risk.

In defending Bernier, Harper trotted out Trudeau's old line about the state having no place in the bedrooms of the nation. He dismissed the critics as gossipy old busybodies. "I hear one of my cabinet ministers had an ex-girlfriend," he said. "It's none of my business. It's none of Mr. Duceppe's business. It's none of Mr. Dion's business."

But it became his business when it was revealed that Bernier had left state documents for a NATO summit at Couillard's home in Montreal. That same day, just hours after Peter Van Loan had backed the foreign minister, saying he was doing a terrific job, Harper accepted Bernier's resignation.

A few months later, Couillard told her story in a book, but it didn't create the sensation Conservatives feared. The most salacious parts revealed that Bernier was a vain womanizer who frequently criticized

Harper for his chubby waistline and for being a total control freak. The book may not have made much of a splash, but Bernier's doghouse likely tripled in size.

HAVING BEEN in damage-control mode through much of the spring of 2008, Harper was given an opportunity to get back on the offensive. The occasion was the introduction of Stéphane Dion's showpiece, his vaunted Green Shift, the guts of which was a carbon tax. Anything that smelled of a tax hike put the prime minister in high dudgeon.

Tax reductions were a pillar of Harper's policy making and always had been. But they were a harder sell than he'd expected. Unlike Americans, Canadians never saw tax increases as evil incarnate. Many viewed them as the price to be paid for a more civil and equitable society than the one in the United States. Harper wanted to change that perception. He pounded the tax-cut drum and kept pounding it, trying to get the country more in line with American attitudes. It was central to his drive to undermine the Liberals. He wanted to make them live in fear of raising taxes.

So even before Dion had introduced his carbon tax plan, even before Harper knew the details of it, he rolled out attack ads. They came right on the heels of his residential schools apology, thus ending any speculation about Harper becoming a softer, gentler political creature. Like the ads wherein Dion was portrayed as being a weak leader, the new carbon tax spot showed Dion again looking helpless. His arms were splayed and his face was limp. Plastered over the image in big bold letters were the words "Dion's Tax on Everything." The voiceover said that while he'd promised not to introduce a carbon tax, he was now doing just that, "so gas and everything else is going to cost you even more."

Again, the Liberals didn't have enough money in their treasury to counterattack. "The attacks are misleading and a lie," Dion said in a statement that made modest headlines for a day or so. The Tory ads, meanwhile, rolled on throughout the summer.

A week and a half after the TV spots first aired, Canadians finally got a look at what was actually in the Dion initiative. At a fancy media show, with big screens and music and green props all over the place, the Liberal leader wore a proud look as he set out his plan to the applause of his caucus. New taxes on industries that produced high carbon emissions would result in consumers paying higher prices on energy, he explained. But the government's revenues from those new taxes—an estimated $15 billion annually—would be redistributed to consumers via broad-based income tax cuts. Canadians, Dion said, would break even in the end. The bonus would be less pollution, less greenhouse gas emissions, a cleaner environment.

The biggest hurt would come with higher home-heating bills. Dion rejected the claim that the oil companies would pass their increased costs on to consumers at the pump, but his assertion was met with well-argued scepticism. He also had to defend himself for having called the carbon tax "a bad policy" when he was environment minister under Paul Martin. Explaining that an open mind is one that changes with time, he said, "My thinking evolved, and I'm showing it."

Overall, the plan got what the Liberals considered a reasonably good reception in the initial days. By taking a strong stand, Dion was countering Conservative claims that he was not a leader. His initiative was considerably bolder than anything the government was putting forward. The Liberal hope was that it would cast the party as forward-looking and progressive, while the Conservatives, with their focus on the military, law and order, and the traditional economy, would come off as a party of old-century solutions for new times. In the U.S., Obama was lighting up the campaign trail with progressive messaging.

But by putting out his big plan well before an election call, Dion gave the Conservatives ample time to discredit it. In Saskatoon, Harper raised the decibel level of his attacks, charging that the Liberal leader was out to ruin Canadians and recklessly harm the economy. "It is like the National Energy Program in the sense that the National Energy Program was designed to screw the West and really damage the energy sector—and this will do those things," said the Conservative leader. But Dion's plan, he said, "is different in that this will actually screw everybody across the country." For using language unbecoming a prime minister, Harper took some criticism. But he wasn't the type to be fazed by that—or by the charges of distortion for calling the Dion plan a tax on everything when in fact tax cuts were a centrepiece.

The Liberals had no seats in Alberta, only a sprinkling in the Prairies, and virtually no prospects of winning more. A more cynical politician than Dion would have struck hard at the oil patch—Barack Obama was bashing dirty oil as part of his campaign—pinning much of the blame for the country's environmental woes on Alberta. This would at least have ramped up Dion's support down east. It was the type of strategy his opponents used. It was wedge politics.

But as David Herle, Paul Martin's campaign director, noted, Dion didn't want to pit region against region, he wanted to lead a rational and civilized debate. And unlike his Liberal predecessors, Herle noted, he was showing courage. Previous Liberal governments had turned away from tough tax measures, fearing a backlash from industry. On Kyoto, they'd tried volunteerism, exhortation, subsidies—and got a predictably abysmal result.

Dion challenged Harper to a televised debate on climate change. If the prime minister was so incensed about the Green Shift plan, Dion said, he could meet him head on and explain exactly how it would "screw" Canadians. "And I can promise you this," added the Liberal leader, "I will be respectful." Harper, who was quick on his feet and reasonably articulate, would likely have had an advantage debating an opponent whose English was wobbly. But the PMO considered the idea only briefly before backing away. Why play on someone else's turf?

In fact, the turf actually belonged to the Green Party. The Greens were the early backers of a carbon tax, and they were gaining popularity as the global warming issue came to a head. That suited Harper just fine. Indeed, it was another good break for him because it divided the left into three parties (four, if you included the left-leaning Bloc Québécois). Led by Elizabeth May, the Greens got to 10–12 percent in the polls, but without a presence in the House of Commons, they couldn't advance much further. It frustrated May but not overly so because she had a different attitude to the political game. "What matters is that we get changes," the Green leader said. "It doesn't matter if we're the party that does them or gets the credit." She had a close working arrangement with Dion, and she was prepared to help him on his green plan. "I told him, 'If it's any use to you, I'll throw myself into the helpful mode, even though you're a different party.'" It was strange talk for a politician—and talk that was unappreciated by some in her party—but a welcome departure from traditional ego-driven politics.

Despite the promising kick-off, Dion's Green Shift started to lose momentum. Timing was a major obstacle. Gasoline and energy prices were on the rise, and recessionary winds were in the air. It was hardly the ideal moment to be proposing new levies, and summer was never an easy time to sell any initiative. To make matters worse, the Liberals lacked the funds for a big marketing campaign, and their organization on the ground was weak. As September arrived, the Conservatives' campaign against the plan, fuelled by ads that had been running in battleground areas all summer, appeared to be working. Polls began to show a majority opposing the Green Shift.

WHILE THE CARBON-TAX DEBATE HEATED UP, the prime minister made some critical changes, not to cabinet, but where they really counted—in his own office. After two and a half years at Harper's side—and a long time before that in opposition—Ian Brodie left as chief of staff. The NAFTA imbroglio was an embarrassment, but Brodie said he had long before arranged to depart on July 1.

There were rumblings as well about the future of Kevin Lynch. The Tories had relied on him a great deal in the early days because they were so inexperienced and Lynch knew the ropes. But now that the politicos had a better grasp of how things worked, they were less in need of that kind of assistance.

Under Brodie, Lynch had easy access to Harper. He just had to check with the prime minister's assistant, the highly efficient Ray Novak, and then would be ushered right in. Many believed that there needed to be a rebalancing, that Brodie was letting Lynch play too big a role. John Weissenberger recalled having "some concerns about the internal organization at PMO." It was reasonable to assume that he passed those concerns along to Harper.

Lynch was viewed as highly knowledgeable but overly territorial, and upstarts like Kory Teneycke complained that there wasn't enough attention paid to what he was up to. One of the big unwritten stories in Ottawa, Teneycke said, was the lack of accountability of the public service. "The amount of oversight by elected officials on the bureaucracy is almost non-existent ... In some cases [bureaucrats] view themselves as the government and the elected officials as an inconvenience. Their attitude," he charged, "is that we should leave government to those who know best."

As Brodie's replacement, Harper brought in Guy Giorno, a visceral hardliner and strict disciplinarian who had served as chief of staff to Mike Harris and did some work for Harper in the 2006 campaign. Teneycke had worked with Giorno at Queen's Park, as had all the Harris heavyweights in the Harper cabinet—Jim Flaherty,

John Baird, Tony Clement, Peter Van Loan. When David McGuinty, the brother of Premier Dalton McGuinty and a strong performer in the Dion caucus, heard of Giorno's appointment, he said it was clear that the Harrisites were taking over. "They're running this government," he said, "and it's the same five-man wrecking crew whose lingering effects we're still feeling in Ontario."

As recounted in John Ibbitson's book on the Harris government, *Promised Land*, Giorno considered himself a Red Tory, "until one night, in a crisis of faith, he phoned right-wing commentator Peter Worthington on a radio talk show and was converted to the radical right." Giorno rose quickly in the Harris ranks and soon found himself responsible for preparing the centrepiece of the Common Sense Revolution, the axe-wielding omnibus bill. Once the bureaucrats got hold of the file, however, it disappeared into what Ibbitson described as "a black hole of secrecy." If Giorno learned a lesson from that experience, it was not to trust the bureaucrats.

At the PMO it was now his show, and the changes were bold. He wanted tougher-minded right-wing loyalists and had to find room for them. Those leaving included two senior voices, two who hadn't been afraid to challenge the views of Harper. Beardsley was let go and Bruce Carson would soon voluntarily take his leave. They would be followed by Cameron, Muttart, and others.

Beardsley had still been briefing the prime minister for Question Period, but was no longer the issues management boss who presided at the 9 a.m. meeting. That was now done by the fiercely partisan Jenni Byrne. Beardsley noticed that at the morning meetings, in briefing Harper on the media and other developments, she wasn't giving him the full story, sometimes leaving out the bad news.

By this time Harper had also lost Tom Flanagan, whose book *Harper's Team* had been published the previous fall after the PM had tried to have Brodie intercede to block it. Even though Flanagan made many requested changes to the text and even though there were no revelations that were hurtful to Harper, its publication still embittered the prime minister to the extent that he started freezing Flanagan out. Their relationship went into decline, a descent furthered by Flanagan's frank newspaper columns in which he sometimes questioned Harper's judgment. The prime minister had deeply profited from Flanagan's management assistance and overarching wisdom through the years.

With his departure and with the loss of players like Carson and Beardsley, there were few left who could be candid with him. Power was accruing to Giorno at a rapid rate. David Angus, one of Ottawa's top lobbyists, dealt frequently with the PMO and noticed the change. "The leader has to have someone who thinks differently beside him," he said. "There has to be a ying and a yang. With Giorno, there were two birds of a feather." Giorno, Angus said, was very bright and very right—as in very right-wing. "He's someone who believes in all these wedge issues, and he surrounds himself with right-wing types."

The prime minister had been criticized for running too aggressive and too oppressive an operation. With the staff changes there was reason to believe he was about to move even further in that direction.

CHAPTER THIRTEEN

Election Turmoil

In the summer of 2008, as the party leaders criss-crossed the country stirring up apathy, political momentum was hard to find. Ever since Harper's election in January 2006, the standings of all parties had been static. The public was unenthusiastic about the leaders, the parties, politics itself. The leaders offered intelligence and erudition but were bereft of anything remotely resembling charm. With Harper and Dion, the absence of style, personality, anything to elevate them, was striking. In the past, at least one of the two major federal party leaders carried some sort of allure, whether it was the biblical rancour of Diefenbaker, the élan of Trudeau, the debonair blarney of Mulroney, or the grit of the little guy from Shawinigan. The colourlessness of Dion and Harper was that much more pronounced by comparison. It left voters even more tuned out than usual.

At the midway point of 2008, the minority Parliament had endured for two and a half years, and few expected it to function much longer. With all signs pointing to an economic downturn, pundits assumed that Prime Minister Harper would want to get to the polls before the snow fell. But the timing of a general election presented him with an unusual dilemma. In May 2007, his government had passed, with reluctant opposition support, a bill setting fixed election dates every four years. The idea was to take away the incumbent party's ability to call an election at the moment most favourable to it. Since Harper was now the incumbent, this initiative appeared selfless, like something he was doing as a favour to the other players.

Under the legislation, the date for the next election was set for October 19, 2009. As Rob Nicholson, the minister responsible, pointed out, this would be the date "if the government is able to retain the confidence of the House until then." In a minority Parliament, of course, the government could well be defeated before that date. But the legislation appeared to exclude the possibility of Harper's triggering an election of his own accord. Such a move would be in defiance of his lawmaking.

There were signs, however, that the Conservatives were in a defiant mood. In early August, the national campaign director, Doug Finley, staged a confrontation at an ethics committee hearing into his party's controversial spending in the 2006 election. Finley was scheduled to testify on the Wednesday of the week beginning August 10. But he apparently had other plans for that day and so decided to show up two days earlier. Paul Szabo, the Liberal committee chair, informed him that since other witnesses were slated to appear, he could not be accommodated. But Finley was not one to take no for an answer. "I want to appear now," he told the chair. Szabo repeatedly asked him to leave, but Finley wouldn't budge. Finally, Szabo looked over to the clerk of the committee and told him, "There's a burly security guard outside the door. Bring him in and get this guy out of the room." Two security guards came in and took Finley away.

Finley's attitude could be viewed as a reflection of Harper's lack of regard for the committees and the work they did. In his fifteen years on House committees, Szabo couldn't recall another display of arrogance like Finley's. "He doesn't get to dictate when he will be heard by this committee, just because he shows up," said NDPer Pat Martin. He and other opposition MPs enjoyed seeing Finley being frogmarched out of the room.

But Finley's audacity was nothing compared to the bullheadedness that was to come. Just a short time later, Harper decided to pull the plug on his own government and call an election in contravention of his own legislation. Reading the gloomy economic tides, the PM thought it unwise to wait until a fall session of Parliament to trigger a campaign. He also wanted to get the election out of the way before the U.S. vote at the start of November.

His camp discussed at length the potential negative fallout of bypassing the promise of fixed election dates. Bruce Carson reminded colleagues that Chrétien had called an election during the Winnipeg floods in 1997. "Half of Manitoba was under water," recalled Carson, who was working for then Conservative leader Jean Charest at the time. "But he came back and called one. It was okay for Charest to complain about it for a while, but either you're in or you're not." The timing hurt the Liberals initially, Carson reminded everyone, but Chrétien went on to win another majority. Harper and his advisers concluded that they would take the heat on the early call for a week or so, and then journalists and the opposition leaders would move on. They decided it was worth the risk.

To explain his actions, Harper charged that the opposition was unwilling to cooperate with him on his coming agenda. Parliament was dysfunctional, the prime minister declared, and the time had come to ask for a new mandate. When journalists pressed him about his legislation on election timing, he replied, "We are clear. You can only have certainty about a fixed election date in the context of a majority government." But how, Harper was asked, could he claim Parliament was dysfunctional when he had got his way all year, breezing through forty-three confidence votes? True enough, replied the prime minister, but now Stéphane Dion had introduced his Green Shift and was about to go in a different direction.

Harper scheduled meetings with the opposition leaders so it would appear that he'd tried to find a consensus. "I remember sitting down with him at 24 Sussex," said Jack Layton, recalling the encounter. "I said, 'Stephen, we supported your fixed election date. I believed you when you said the reason for this was that the government couldn't take advantage of the fact that they would know the date and others would not.'" He pointed out to Harper that Conservative MPs had already flooded the country with fliers and mailings. "You just blanketed the place and then you had all kinds of announcements all summer," he said, "then you pulled the early trigger, thinking you could take advantage of the other parties … That was precisely what you said the fixed election date was supposed to prevent."

Harper, Layton recalled, had little in the way of a response. He sat there and "just basically said that the new Parliament isn't going to work when we come back in the fall." The NDP leader remembers that day as the one when he really lost respect for the prime minister. Before leaving the residence, he told Harper, "I took you at your word, and I can't take you at your word anymore."

A heap of criticism was visited upon the PM, especially from those who knew the details of the legislation. Others, however, concluded that because his was a minority government, the fixed-election law couldn't really apply. Some constitutional experts believed the governor general could have refused to grant Harper the election call. That would have been especially true, observed Peter Russell of the University of Toronto, if the opposition parties had been prepared to offer a coalition alternative. They weren't, however, and so Michaëlle Jean acquiesced to the PM's wishes.

Harper strategists, aware that he had just enhanced his reputation for running roughshod over the system, looked for ways to counter the notion that he was a callous opportunist. They wanted to put forward a gentler, more compassionate leader. No more Mr. Ice Guy. And so on the opening day of the country's fortieth election campaign, the prime minister stood on the grounds of Rideau Hall and spoke warmly in response to the lobs thrown at him by the media. He spoke of his children and how they kept him balanced. He spoke of how he was not a man for big talk and grand slogans, just for getting the job done. He said that no matter what happened in the campaign, it had been a wonderful privilege to serve as the country's prime minister. He promised, having recently characterized Dion as being out to screw Canadians, to be nice to his opponents: "I don't see any reason to go personal and nasty against other leaders," he said as some in the fourth estate rolled their eyes.

Harper's team then released a slew of TV spots showing him as the doting dad. "I play a lot of card games with my kids," he intoned in one of them. "We go to movies." Aides had tried repeatedly to get him to indulge in this kind of hokum before but were unsuccessful. It took time with Harper. Flanagan took two years to convince him to use a teleprompter. But now they got him to do the ads, and they softened his look as well, getting him out of his staid suits and into a blue sweater. The blue sweater, Patrick Muttart's idea, became one of the most talked about props of the campaign.

The Liberal leader, meanwhile, tried to sound optimistic. Dion talked about welcoming the opportunity of this campaign. After all the calumnies he had endured from Harper and company, he believed Canadians would now have a chance to judge him fairly. "For the first time," he said, "they will see me, not the distortion that Stephen Harper tried to make of me." Harper had created "an expectation so low that I will surprise Canadians."

The Conservatives wanted the election to focus on leadership. Doug Finley was running the campaign, and the last thing he ever wanted to talk about, colleagues said, was policy. His game plan was to attack. He wanted Dion to be the ballot question.

Some in the PMO, like Mark Cameron, pushed to put more policy on the table. But Cameron wasn't surprised when he and others didn't get their way. "It was a little disappointing, but it was clear the election would be about leadership," he recalled. "The only reason

I would like to have had more policy announcements is because it would have given us more of a sense of a mandate once elected. But the feeling was that as long as the opposition was doing itself in, we really didn't want to create a target. So we created the smallest possible target we could."

While most in the PMO agreed that this was the right strategy, few were confident that Harper would win a majority government. This became evident when they did an office pool. Most predictions were for an increased minority. That's what Muttart's calculations told him, and Finley and Cameron thought the same. They would gain seats in Quebec but not many elsewhere—not even against a Liberal leader they considered so vulnerable.

In the words of columnist Greg Weston, the campaign came down to Bully Boy versus Mr. Bean, two determinedly uncharismatic leaders going head to head. It was Harper, the bland-looking authoritarian, against the sincere and feckless Dion. But the prime minister was the more experienced campaigner, he had a superior organization, and he had more money, a resource that was spent on an avalanche of publicity in the pre-writ period.

And Harper had another advantage: the left was divided to an extent rarely seen in Canada. The Greens were a bigger force in this election, the NDP had built a reliable base, and the Liberals under Dion tilted further left than usual. Harper had the centre-right and right all to himself, and he smartly played that up, comparing Dion's economic policies to Trudeau's.

Within days of the opening gun, the Tories, having apparently already forgotten Harper's words about not needing to go dirty, slammed Dion, posting an online ad that featured a bird defecating on his head. It drew a rush of criticism for its bad taste and was quickly withdrawn. The Harper team's extreme partisanship then resulted in another embarrassment. When the father of a soldier killed in Afghanistan criticized Harper for saying the mission should end in

2011, Tory spokesman Ryan Sparrow—the birds, as one wag put it, struck twice in the campaign's first week—called the man's criticism politically motivated. Sparrow was suspended for the insensitive remark.

These were small but surprising slips, especially given the discipline of the Conservatives. The control they were trying to exert was exemplified by the way they clamped down on the civil service for the duration of the campaign. It was normal for the business of government to slow down during an election, but the extent this time was extraordinary. An edict from the PCO virtually shut down Ottawa. On orders from the top, public servants withdrew from conferences and cancelled speeches even on the most harmless of subjects. The defence department was ordered to cease procurement practices. An Ottawa trade show was cancelled after speakers were ordered to pull out. Eight events at the war museum were suspended, apparently in case someone said something damaging to the Tories' election prospects.

While Harper's campaign was not off to the smoothest of starts, the Liberals looked ill-prepared. Their campaign team had demonstrated its ineptitude a year earlier in a by-election in the traditionally Liberal riding of Outremont, in Montreal, when the NDP's Thomas Mulcair scored a remarkable victory. Despite that wake-up call, the Liberals didn't appear to have made many improvements to their organization. The Dion campaign sputtered along. Turnouts at events were small, the messaging was loose, and soon there was a bigger problem. The dark turn in the world economy pushed Dion's Green Shift off centre stage. This was not the climate in which to introduce a new carbon tax.

When the polling numbers came out in the first week, they showed a surge for the Conservatives. They were up at around 40 percent—majority territory. The forecasts in the Tory office pool suddenly looked off base. The big victory appeared well within reach.

To win a majority, however, the Conservatives needed to boost their numbers in Quebec. They had made a breakthrough of sorts there in the 2006 campaign, winning ten seats from a starting point of zero. This time the province looked even more promising. Senator David Angus, who had been Brian Mulroney's chief fundraiser, felt the tide moving in the Tory direction. Angus had been contacted by Harper right after he won the Conservative Party leadership in 2004. Harper phoned and said he'd heard Angus was an important player and asked him to dinner. In short order, Angus was at Stornoway, telling the then opposition leader what he had to do to win in Quebec. Harper's granting the Québécois nation status, along with some other initiatives, had increased his standing in the province.

Angus knew that momentum could swing fast in the province. He had watched Mulroney take the Tories from two seats to fifty-seven in 1984. At the outset of that campaign, no one had predicted those kinds of numbers. Angus wasn't predicting fifty-seven seats in 2008, but he did believe major gains, enough to surpass the Bloc Québécois, were possible. He was especially enthusiastic when, in mid-September, he took an informal poll in the Quebec City area and found that Harper's numbers were taking off. When he returned to the same area a few days later, however, he was stunned. The Harper bandwagon was suddenly in reverse.

Campaigns rarely come without big surprises. Often seemingly small issues take on an importance no one would have imagined. In this campaign, the issue was Tory cuts to the arts and culture sector. When the cuts were announced in August, the temperature in Quebec's artistic community quickly began to rise. The cuts amounted to only $15 million for the province. Included in them were reductions in grants to promote Quebec culture abroad. In the Tory view, some of the culture being sponsored was of marginal taste, not promoting a good family image. This provoked a flurry of negative responses, including one from the singer Michel Rivard, who produced a video mocking anglophones in Ottawa for making decisions about a culture they knew little about.

This issue, which could well have cost the Conservatives their majority, had its roots in the sometimes difficult relationship between the PMO and the bureaucracy. At the heart of the problem, according to a Harper adviser, was the heritage department's slow response to demands to trim its budget. Long before the election campaign began, the government had initiated a program review, wherein each department was to identify the lowest-performing 5 percent of programs. Almost all other departments were quick to respond. Not heritage. There were delays and there was confusion, and ultimately, explained the adviser, "the bureaucratic process got caught in the election timing." The cuts were made without the usual degree of political oversight. "No red flag went up."

When the red flag did finally go up at the start of the campaign, the Conservatives had an opportunity to get out of the fix they were in. They could simply have announced that a mistake had been made and quickly restored the funding. It would have been a cheap price to pay, recalled one insider. "But the thinking was that heritage had operated in bad faith about the whole program-review exercise, so we didn't want to reward bad behaviour."

Staffers huddled to consider the best response to the controversy. One option was to wedge the issue—to come out on behalf of the common folk, those who don't go to wine-and-cheese parties, and pit them against artistic snobs who thrive on government handouts. But no clear decision was made. At a stopover in Saskatoon, however, this was the option Harper chose. He told reporters that ordinary Canadians couldn't relate to gala-going social climbers. "You know, I think when ordinary working people come home, turn on the TV, and see ... a bunch of people at a rich gala all subsidized by the taxpayers, claiming their subsidies aren't high enough when they know the subsidies have actually gone up, I'm not sure that is something that resonates with ordinary people."

Communications director Kory Teneycke was with the PM, but he hadn't prepped him to make such incendiary remarks. "I think it's fair to say his comment was a bit of a surprise," recalled Teneycke, adding that the mostly rural audience prompted Harper to ramp up the anti-artist talk. "My guess is that if our event that morning was in Toronto, it may not have come out as sharply."

The wedge backfired, further enraging the cultural community, so much so that the pollster Nic Nanos thought it might become the campaign's tipping point. Atom Egoyan, one of the country's most celebrated filmmakers, couldn't believe what he had heard. A great many people—ordinary people—he noted, made their living from the arts. "It's not a niche issue. It's a huge issue," he said. The NDP ran a French-language commercial referring to the PM as a culture killer: "*Conservat-tueur de la culture.*"

Charlie Angus, an Ontario New Democrat, was one of many people who couldn't understand Harper's thinking. "Why is it always that it's Harper who comes out and takes the cheap shots?" he asked. "He's got a pretty solid pack of goons who can do the spearing and the high-sticking for him." But, as Angus saw it, his instincts were too strong to hold in check. "If I was going to give him credit, I would say he's like a Thomas Hardy character. Harper's got this deep fundamental flaw, despite all his braininess, and at the end of the day, that fundamental flaw is going to do him in. It's a mean streak, a level of viciousness that comes out."

Some in Harper's inner circle agreed that he would be better off leaving the dirty work to others. If you want to float a trial balloon loaded with poison, said Keith Beardsley, you do it in such a way that you don't personally take the blame. But Harper felt so strongly sometimes that he couldn't resist the temptation.

Two-thirds of the people employed in the arts and culture sector lived in the big cities—Montreal, Toronto, and Vancouver. The Tories had no seats in those urban centres and weren't about to make a breakthrough this time, so initially there wasn't much concern about the impact. But the arts community has a greater political influence in Quebec than it does elsewhere in Canada—the sovereignty movement, for example, was accelerated by the culture sector—and the Tories weren't effective at mounting a counterattack against the negative fallout. Quebeckers were left to suspect that the cuts were part of a larger anti-culture agenda on the part of philistine neo-cons in Ottawa. The plummeting polling numbers rocked both the Tory campaign and Harper personally. All the effort he had put into creating support in the province—the key building block in his quest for a majority government—was being frittered away.

AN EMBARRASSMENT OF A MORE MODEST NATURE hit the campaign just before the televised debates. Liberals revealed that while in opposition, Harper had delivered a speech on the Iraq war that plagiarized to a healthy degree a speech by the hawkish Australian prime minister, John Howard. It was full of dire warnings about the danger of weapons of mass destruction (which of course turned out to be a figment of the White House's—and the Australian leader's—imagination). The Conservatives could have done without reminding voters that Harper had backed the Iraq invasion, but this story at least had a short shelf life. Speechwriter Owen Lippert, who was now serving as a party researcher, resigned his post and little else was heard on the matter.

The televised debates included for the first time the leader of the Green Party. Both Harper and Layton had attempted to block Elizabeth May's appearance but eventually bowed to public opinion. Harper put in a subdued performance in the French debate, while Dion scored well. In English the following evening, Harper was under bombardment throughout from the other party leaders, but he escaped without suffering much damage. It was a performance that required considerable forbearance on his part.

In the English-language debate, the economy was the focal point, and Harper defended his record with vigour. "We have not been following the same economic policies as in the United States that have led to that mess," he said. "We have not made those choices, which have been disastrous. We've made very different choices in Canada, and we have a surplus." Layton, the debate's most fiery participant, shot back: "The economy is not fine. Any Canadian will tell you that. Either you don't care or you're incompetent. Which is it?"

Elizabeth May was seated beside the prime minister for both debates, and something in Harper's possession caught her attention. "The rules for the debate," she explained, "were that you could not take in notes of any kind. But if you wanted to write down notes during the debate, there were big blank white index cards placed on the table next to each leader." Those rules were fine with her, but apparently not with the prime minister. On the first night, during the French-language debate, recalled May, "I glanced over at Harper and he had in his hands, below the level of the table, small index cards with reprinted font all over them. He was carrying notes." She saw the same printed index cards the next night, for the English debate. Harper was like a student cheating on a university exam. But, May said, "I didn't have the confidence to call him out on it because that's risky to call someone a cheater in the middle of the debates."

Had she done so, it would have caused a hellstorm that might have helped her and the other candidates. Still, the incident confirmed for her—just as the debacle over fixed election dates had for Layton—that the prime minister would "do anything. He's absolutely ruthless." She mentioned his cheating in a book she published much later, but by then it was too late and the episode received scant attention.

In an interview after he had stepped down as Harper's director of communications, Kory Teneycke was asked about the alleged cheating.

"I don't know what [May's] referring to," Teneycke said. "But who cares?" When it was pointed out that rules are rules, he replied testily: "Yeah, well, you know what? She's just lucky she was in the room. I don't think she should have been there ... The process was poorly served by her presence."

Conservative support slipped steadily from 40 percent in the first week of the campaign to the low thirties. Dion's Liberals, however, receded as well. The NDP gained ground, and the Bloc Québécois, which had looked to be in trouble when the campaign began, surged because of the opportunity handed them on the culture file.

The brief, five-week campaign had an unusual dynamic because of the news of the near-meltdown of the U.S. financial system. Harper and his strategists decided they should downplay it. "I think he was hoping that during the election we could just skate through it under pre-crisis assumptions," recalled Mark Cameron. "I don't think he really wanted to get into a really substantive debate about the economic crisis during the campaign. That probably led to some thoughts that were probably mistakes, like the comment about the stock market and things like that."

Harper tried to ease concerns, stressing that Canada was in a strong position compared to other economies. "My own belief," he said, "is if we were going to have some kind of big crash or recession, we probably would have had it by now." He vowed there would be no deficit, no big new spending programs, no increased taxes. "I think I was asked one question—whether I would run a deficit—and I said no. That's my answer."

It was an answer that was excessively optimistic. His Conservatives, reputed to be the party of economic rectitude, had already raised eyebrows all over Bay Street and elsewhere by posting a deficit in the first two months of the year. They were $500 million in hock, down from a surplus of $2.8 billion a year earlier. Starting the year in the red and then getting hit late in the year with the American economic collapse created shaky grounds for a no-deficit forecast. Scott Brison, who followed economic issues closely, said the thing that most surprised him about Harper was "how fiscally irresponsible he was." He had expected Harper, knowing that bad times were on the way, to take a cautionary approach to spending. Instead, said Brison, he shovelled the cash out the door to every political constituency he could find. "They increased spending by 20 percent in their first two years of taking office," Brison observed. "They put Canada in an economic deficit before the economic downturn."

Harper encountered criticism throughout the campaign for not having foreseen the recession coming. It was strange how he allowed himself, this being a subject of prime interest for him, to get hit with the charge. "He was preparing for that recession from the day he took over as prime minister," said Keith Beardsley. "It would be a common discussion. 'Well, we know the U.S. is going into the tank. It's all a matter of when. Let's start getting ready.'"

Politically, Harper's strategists viewed the bad economic news with concern but not despair. They knew the news was not sitting well with voters, but they also knew that Harper was seen as the best economic manager. The area where Dion outperformed him was in honesty and integrity, but even then, he failed to take advantage of the strong point. The Liberals had nothing in their platform on democratic reform, a reduction of the immense powers of the PMO, and the like.

IN A CHANGE from the 2006 election, when Harper had put forward so much policy, he didn't release a platform until the campaign's last week. His team had discussed three options. One was to staple together everything they had said in the recent past and call it a platform. The second was to flesh out more details of those measures. The third was to add new meat. They bandied about ideas and finally fell somewhere in the middle, as an adviser put it, announcing the odd new measure, like loans to the manufacturing sector, and adding these to what they already had.

Pollsters believed Harper erred, though, in not pointing the way forward. After announcing his first five priorities in 2006, he still hadn't followed up with a second five. The negativity of a campaign based mostly on trying to undermine opponents gave Canadians little to get enthusiastic about and reinforced the image of Harper as more of a schemer than a leader. The prime minister dismissed the criticism, saying his plan was to move forward in the same way he had governed. Something that is not brand new, he said, can still constitute a plan.

With the markets still tumbling, Harper stirred a ruckus late in the campaign by telling Peter Mansbridge that it was a good time to invest, and that "there are probably some great buying opportunities out there." That brought on charges that he was out of touch with reality. "Most Canadians are extremely concerned," said Jack Layton, "and yet he's trying to suggest that going out and gambling some of your money is the right strategy."

Coming into the election's final weekend, the Tories still led by a few points, but they were worried. They had made several missteps, losing the big lead they held in week one. Dion had held up slightly better than anticipated, and Harper's camp sensed that the Liberal leader had a bit of momentum. If that continued over the final few days, the result could be close. This was reflected in a flurry of activity at the Privy Council Office. "Departments prepare transition books when new governments come into play," explained a PCO official. "In the last few days, I got the sense from deputy ministers that they were thinking they might have to do material for a transition. There was a bit of movement around that."

Then, as had happened so often for Harper, the fates dealt him a great break. Going into the final weekend, Dion got caught in a mix-up with a TV interviewer in Halifax. The mishap arose when CTV's

Steve Murphy asked him, "If you were the prime minister now, what would you have done about the economy, and this crisis, that Mr. Harper has not done?" It was an awkwardly worded question, a jumbling of past and present tenses that made it difficult for someone with English as a second language to understand. Dion asked Murphy to repeat it. He asked him to repeat it repeatedly. Eventually, after three false starts in which he looked utterly confused, he gave a response. Murphy initially agreed not to air the aborted takeoff. (It sometimes happened that English-speaking leaders garbled their words at the start of French interviews, and the embarrassing outtakes were not run.) But Murphy later changed his mind. CTV Newsnet got all excited about the gaffe, decided they had a scoop, and ran the tape again and again.

Harper's plane was about to take off from Winnipeg when he got the news. He hadn't done any open media scrums his entire time on the hustings, it being a campaign in a cocoon. But now several advisers thought he should get out before the cameras and exploit Dion's misfortune. Others thought that it would look mean-spirited, and that it was better to take the high road. The news was all over the TV screens anyway.

Jack Layton's party stood to gain if the Liberals lost momentum in the final days. But he chose not to take advantage of the incident. He said he could understand what had happened. "People are tired. It's a long campaign," he said. "We've all had trouble with questions from time to time."

Harper, however, didn't see it that way. His decision was to go after Dion. "I remember pulling him back down [off the plane]," said Teneycke, "and I set something up very rapidly and had him do the scrum. That was not an easy discussion in terms of deciding whether to do that or not." Before the cameras, Harper said, "When you're running a trillion-and-a-half-dollar economy you don't get a second chance to have do-overs, over and over again. What this incident actually indicates very clearly is Mr. Dion and the Liberal Party don't really know what they would do on the economy."

The prime minister's comments made the big news shows, just as his aides had hoped. Bloc Québécois Leader Gilles Duceppe took exception, calling Harper's remarks a "low blow" that only served to illustrate the enduring "double standard" on Canada's official languages. Canadians, he said, demand that French political leaders speak English fluently, but they allow English-speaking leaders to get away with mangling French. Dion's English was arguably as good as if not better than Harper's French.

The consensus among the media was that Harper's response showed a lack of class. It said more about Harper's character, wrote Don Martin, than it did about Dion's. Teneycke had anticipated that reaction. "We didn't make any friends in the media travelling with us," he recalled. "But without the PM doing it, the story would not have got anywhere near the play."

For Dion, there was little solace in a later ruling by the Canadian Broadcast Standards Council that CTV Newsnet had violated the Broadcasters' Code of Ethics by running the restarts after the interviewer had promised not to do so.

But whatever the standards displayed in the airing and exploitation of the interview, Conservative tracking numbers showed that it did shift momentum for them. Their workers on the ground could feel it. In the riding of West Nova, where the PMO's Kevin Lacey was campaigning for Greg Kerr, door knockers reported a sudden turn. Everybody was talking about the flubbed interview, the canvassers said. Lacey had worked many campaigns, but he'd rarely seen such a quick turnaround. He had been worried that the Dion campaign was on the uptick. Now he worried no more.

Liberals reported a similar reaction. "I remember the fumbled interview," said Scott Brison. "I was door-knocking that night and things had been going quite well. And I knocked on this door and a woman said, 'Hmmm, he can't even speak English. It's terrible. What's the matter with him?' And I knocked on another door and it was like 'Holy cow, your leader, what's wrong with him?'"

In the view of Kory Teneycke, the garbled interview was a critical moment. It was "if not the most, then certainly one of the most" important moments in the campaign, he said, because it put the focus right back where the Tories wanted it. "It was the embodiment of our ballot question. This guy is not a leader. He is not worth the risk. That was our branding on the Liberals for months and months."

The election result saw the Tories increase their minority from 124 seats to 143, the Liberals fall from 103 to 77, the NDP jump from 29 seats to 37, and the Bloc end up with 48. The Conservatives were both satisfied and unsatisfied. It was a solid victory, but they knew the majority had been there for the taking. They might have won a dozen more seats in Quebec had it not been for the mistake on the culture cuts.

With the victory, Harper solidified his image as a builder of the party and a winner, but he also left more doubts about his character. He had violated his own law on fixed election dates; engaged in cheap wedge politics in demeaning gala-goers; broken the rules in the debates; and shown his ruthless streak in his handling of the Dion interview flap. His campaign, with its scant policy offerings, was a lesson in the politics of cynicism.

The Harper victory was followed by the stirring triumph of Barack Obama in the United States. With his election, momentum swung from America's rigid right to a more moderate, multilateral, and multicultural ethic. Given Obama's enormous popularity in Canada, Harper had to be cognizant of the new mood, and it appeared he was. In late November, Parliament was opened with the Speech from the Throne, in which the government called for "a spirit of solidarity [to] prevail." Harper signalled that he was prepared to embark on a less confrontational and less divisive course. He met with the premiers and found some harmony with them. He attended a Conservative conference in Winnipeg, where he warned Tories against being too ideological. He sat down with the opposition leaders to gauge their views on the course the country should chart. He appointed as House leader the much more accommodating Jay Hill, and he reached out to Barack Obama.

Given the security of an increased minority, it looked as though he was entering a comfort zone and was prepared to move ahead in a positive spirit.

CHAPTER FOURTEEN

Surviving the Coalition

Much of Stephen Harper's story involved a campaign against himself, against the opposition within. That opposition was the dark, vindictive side of his character—a side that at times he could not subdue, and that on several occasions, such as the government's budget update in November 2008, threatened to bring him down.

During meetings prior to the 2008 election campaign, Harper and his strategists debated including in their platform a measure to dramatically alter political party funding. The measure would have annulled a 2003 Liberal reform that outlawed big-money contributions from corporations and unions, replacing them with public financing to the tune of two dollars per vote for each party.

Harper's plan would have reprivatized funding and, since his party was far and away the better money collector, provided the Tories with a significant advantage. It was one more step along the road to the goal of supplanting the Liberals as the dominant party in the country. The Tory caucus and cabinet had approvingly debated the idea, and the question was whether to seek a mandate for the change by campaigning on it. In a decision they would come to regret, the Harper strategists mulled it over and said no. Leave it on the shelf for now.

After the election, the government passed up another opportunity by not including the plan in the Speech from the Throne. The next chance was the November 27 budget update, an occasion of greater interest than normal because of the cascading global economy. In the run-up to it, Harper and Finance Minister Jim Flaherty had difficulty squaring their projections over questions of a deficit and the need for fiscal stimulus for the economy. Harper was in Lima, Peru, at a summit of the Asia-Pacific Economic Cooperation group. The U.S. and Britain had already moved ahead with stimulus plans to fight the recession, and Harper was hearing from other leaders who were also embarking on such initiatives.

Relations between Harper and Flaherty were not always harmonious. Harper had an economics background, knew the files, and liked to be his own finance minister. Kevin Lynch, who knew more about the nation's finances and the global economy than Harper or Flaherty, liked to get his oar in as well.

For the budget update, it was decided that no major stimulus spending would be announced. "The fiscal update was not supposed to be a response to the economic crisis," recalled a Harper adviser. "It was supposed to be a baseline document that put out the fiscal forecast. It wasn't supposed to be a mini-budget with a lot of measures because there were still a lot of things in flux."

All seemed settled between the PMO and the finance department when, at the eleventh hour, word came from Peru that something else was to be put in the update. In the previous couple of weeks, the party financing measure had again been raised, and again it seemed it would be put off. Now a BlackBerry message came from the prime minister saying party subsidies were to be eliminated. Reaction in the PMO, as one official put it, was one of much surprise, if not consternation. Harper's advisers knew of his earlier hesitancy. While they didn't disagree with including the measure, some of them wondered why now. Politically, things were going well. They'd just won the election handily. What was the hurry?

Surprising as well was that Harper wanted it all done in one shot. When the measure had first been debated, strategists had discussed several options. Should the subsidy be phased out slowly? Should it just be reduced by half? Should there be some pre-positioning to build support for such a measure? But the PM decided to pounce. His old instincts bubbled up. He saw a chance to cripple the enemy. He couldn't resist.

"It's unusual," Tom Flanagan observed of Harper one day, "to have someone who is by nature a strategist as leader." Put him in the confines of a minority government, said Flanagan, and "everything becomes survival and tactics." This was a time when he might have been giving his full energies to the economic threat and a cooperative plan with the opposition to address it. Instead, Harper was thinking of partisan political advantage.

The Conservatives were well aware that during the election campaign, the NDP leader had raised the prospect of forming a coalition government, should another minority be returned. Stéphane Dion had categorically rejected the possibility, but that didn't stop the NDP. Feeling that the Liberal leader could change his mind, they had formed a scenarios committee, and it was quietly at work throughout the campaign, analyzing various options.

But with their increased minority, the Tories thought they had little reason to worry. The Liberals and NDP combined did not have the numbers to vote down the government. For that, they would need the Bloc Québécois. Dion had not only lost the election. He had been trounced. It wasn't the biggest defeat in Liberal history. In four previous elections, the Liberals had scored worse than Dion's seventy-seven seats, the low point being forty in 1984. But their popular vote was the lowest ever. Dion was finished, and a leadership campaign was already under way. No worries there, the Tories thought. The unsettled landscape made it a good time to go forward with the financing reform.

In delivering his fiscal update, Flaherty, an effective retail politician, lacked his customary cocky air. His body language and tone of voice gave the impression that this was a poisonous piece of work. On the opposition side, the rancour, so often fabricated, this time was genuine, and it ramped up in volume as Flaherty proceeded. The elimination of the party funding subsidy wasn't the only provocative announcement. The budget update also included measures to suspend the right of public servants to strike and to limit women's rights to appeal for pay equity. It was as if every second paragraph contained a hand grenade. As the derision from the opposition benches pelted his minister of finance, Harper glared arrogantly across the aisle, dismissively waving his arm at the critics. The physical gesture was something he rarely, if ever, made.

Within two hours, all three opposition leaders had pledged to vote against the package. The thought that they could lose a confidence vote didn't bother the Tories. They believed there was no chance the Grits wanted another election now. But then, to their astonishment, came word that the Liberals and the NDP were organizing a coalition with the Bloc. That would give the opposition side sufficient numbers to topple the government and replace it.

At first there was disbelief in Harperland. This can't be right, they thought. But it took hardly a few seconds to realize it was in fact right—that it was simple arithmetic and they had made a grave miscalculation. By overreaching, they had handed the opposition a dagger. It had the makings of a repeat of the fiasco that had claimed Joe Clark's minority in 1979. A minority government devours itself through boneheadedness. A departing Liberal leader returns to head the government.

Battered around for so long, out of power for almost three years, the Liberals were hard-pressed to contain their glee. They hadn't even begun to think of this possibility until just a couple of days before. It had been too crazy to contemplate. They'd suffered a humiliating defeat—and yet victory appeared to be just a breath away.

The New Democrats celebrated as well. They were on the verge of sitting on the governing side, holding cabinet positions, for the first time in their history. Following the 1980 election, Trudeau had offered Ed Broadbent's team cabinet spots if the NDP joined the Liberals in a semi-alliance for the sake, as Trudeau reasoned, of Canadian unity. But Broadbent turned him down, fearful that his party would lose its identity and credibility.

Brian Topp, one of Layton's chief advisers, had a Tory contact who was close to Harper. As news of the potential coalition spread, Topp emailed the contact to let him know that he was on his way to Ottawa because, as he put it, the red button was being pushed. The Conservative replied that the opposition might want to do some quick polling. The cancellation of the funding subsidy would save the treasury $26 million, he explained, and since the country was entering a recession, voters would support that kind of measure. Topp said they weren't worried about polls. Polls wouldn't be necessary—not with what was being planned.

Back came the reply: "You're gonna run the government with separatists?"

Zap! There it was. The Conservative counterattack strategy was already apparent. A coalition with separatists. But the warning didn't register loudly enough. Topp didn't sound the alarm to Jack Layton, who should already have known that the business with the Bloc would have to be handled with the utmost discretion. For one thing, Topp didn't think that Harper, who was still keen on courting Quebec and cutting into the Bloc vote, would demonize the sovereigntists. For another, he knew that Harper himself had been prepared to enter into a coalition-type arrangement with the Bloc and the NDP when the Liberals held a minority a few years earlier. He didn't think, Topp would later write, "Harper and his team were capable of bald-faced lying."

At the PMO, they'd spent half the night working on Harper's response to the insurgency. On the day after the budget update, he delivered a statement in the foyer of the House of Commons. The opposition was working on a backroom deal to overturn the results of the election, the prime minister charged, and he would do everything within his legal means to stop it. "The Liberals campaigned against a coalition with the NDP," he pointed out, "saying NDP policies were bad for the economy. And now they want to form a coalition, saying that this will strengthen the economy." He then added, "The opposition has every right to defeat the government. But Stéphane Dion does not have the right to take power without an election." This was an utterly groundless claim, one of several he would make throughout this crisis. Anyone who followed politics knew that in a minority Parliament there were several scenarios under which the leader of the opposition could take power without forcing another election.

The PM announced that the opposition would get an opportunity for a vote of confidence—a pledge he was shortly to renege on—but that it would be delayed by a week. The Liberals had what was called an Opposition Day for the start of the following week and were preparing to move the confidence motion then. But there was a loophole in the rules. The government's prerogative allowed Harper to impose the week's delay. That was absolutely critical in this instance. It gave Harper the days needed for a counter-insurgency.

On Saturday, the prime minister did an about-face and withdrew his proposal to end public subsidies for political parties. It was one of the quickest reversals on a budget statement ever seen. He then began a hell-bent-for-leather public relations blitz to undermine the credibility of the emerging coalition. A memorandum from Chief of Staff Guy Giorno urged Conservatives to "use every single tool and medium" at their disposal. It provided Tories with communications products—material for letters to the editors of newspapers, points to use on radio talk shows—to make their job easier.

But a black mood hung over the Tories and, most notably, Stephen Harper. "Everyone was depressed," recalled an adviser. "The PM was sick. I mean, he was basically ready to throw in the towel." No one had ever seen the usually domineering Harper so beaten down. He had once denounced Joe Clark for losing his 1979 minority because of a gasoline tax Clark had not campaigned on. Of that loss, Harper said, "You can be principled without being stupid." It now looked as if he was about to lose his own government because of something he had not campaigned on. He had failed to heed the Clark lesson and he had failed to exercise the discipline of power for which he was known. His highly regarded strategic capacities had let him down.

On the Monday, Harper was more despondent than the others at the PMO. Some had expected him to be geared for battle. But it was the opposite. He was resigned to defeat, prepared to give up the government. Staffers had never seen him like this, pale and shaken. He told them, in so many words, that it was over, that the government would fall.

His team tried to dissuade him from this defeatist course. They argued that they had to find a way to hang on to power. "We thought," recalled an adviser, "that once they were in office we'd lose control of events, and maybe they'd replace Dion and have a budget and win. So we felt that we had to keep control. That's what the PM eventually felt. But he was just completely gob-smacked that weekend."

The staff worked on changing his mood and convincing him to fight it out. It turned out that there was no need for that, however, because the coalition did it for him. Since 2002, when Harper came back to politics from the National Citizens Coalition, events had a uncanny habit of turning his way. And now they turned his way again, as his rivals began blowing themselves up.

The coalition leaders staged a big public signing of their agreement and decided to trot out Gilles Duceppe as if he were a full partner in the enterprise. He wasn't. The Bloc would have no cabinet seats in the proposed government. It would have no members on government committees or seats on the governing side of the chamber. The Bloc's only participation took the form of a pledge not to vote to bring down the coalition for eighteen months. But that was hardly the way it appeared. Gilles Duceppe mounted the podium with Dion and Layton and proceeded to put his signature to the document. A surreal air hung over the proceedings. The leaders of the three parties looked like a band of thieves. At the back of the room, Liberal caucus members milled around in anticipation. They answered questions from reporters about what cabinet portfolios they might get. But the sense of unease was palpable.

"That was the moment the whole thing turned on," recalled Kory Teneycke. "It was the moment we saw the three of them doing the signing of the accord. We knew then it was over for them. As we say, a picture is worth a thousand words." Recalled Jack Layton, with more than a touch of understatement, "I don't think we were sufficiently sensitive as to the impact that would have."

Mark Cameron noticed that after that press conference a total change came over the prime minister. Defeatism turned instantly into a hunger for battle. His heart was pumping and he took command. That night, the Conservatives held their annual Christmas party. The air of defeat that had threatened to engulf the government was swept away by a politician who had never been known as the life of any party. Stephen Harper gave a rousing forty-five-minute speech that left long faces gleaming. Standing ovation followed standing ovation. Never did the leader's words have such spark. Never was his look so animated. The speech attacked the coalition as an illegitimate, separatist-propelled power grab that would not be allowed to stand if he, Stephen Harper, had anything to say about it. Of the two weeks of the coalition drama, with all its vivid high-stakes tension, this was the moment that Harper's men remembered most—war cries from the leader that left everyone wired.

Harper wrote most of the lines for that speech himself, recalled Teneycke. "More than anyone else, the PM really found his voice. You talk about those things with him, but you don't have to write a speech like that. That one comes from within." It was a test run of some of the lines he planned to use in the Commons the next day.

In the chamber, when Harper was in attack mode, there was a tell-tale sign: he slouched in his chair with chin lowered. That day, he was deeply slouched. When Dion got up to ask the first question, Harper looked like he was about to strangle him.

Dion asked when the PM would meet his pledge to have a confidence vote. The Liberal leader said it would violate fundamental constitutional principles if the prime minister did not allow one. Harper fumed. "Mr. Speaker, the highest principle of Canadian democracy is that if one wants to be prime minister, one gets one's mandate from the Canadian people and not from Quebec separatists. The deal that the leader of the Liberal Party has made with the separatists is a betrayal of the voters of this country ... and we will fight it with every means that we have." His voice thundered and his backbenchers pounded their desks in fury.

Dion, his face reddened, said Harper hadn't answered the question. He hadn't. But that didn't matter. It seldom does in the House of Commons. Harper pummelled Dion again with equal rage and the Liberal leader, with his willowy academic demeanour, couldn't hold up. He was blown away like a sheet in a hurricane.

But the opposition leaders still had a big card to play. Harper's bid to discredit their dealings rested heavily on his contention that theirs was a "separatist coalition." But the opposition had in hand a letter that could be used to potentially devastating effect. Dated September 9, 2004, the letter was to Governor General Adrienne

Clarkson and had been signed by Harper, Layton, and Gilles Duceppe. It asserted that, given the minority Liberal government, Clarkson could be asked to dissolve Parliament at any time. It read in part: "We respectfully point out that the opposition parties, who together constitute a majority in the House, have been in close consultation. We believe that should a request for dissolution arise, this should give you cause, as constitutional practice has determined, to consult the opposition leaders and consider all your options before exercising your constitutional authority."

The intent of the letter was clear: should the Liberal government be defeated in the House, the governor general should bear in mind that Harper, Layton, and Duceppe might be prepared to join hands and step in.

Layton later explained that it was a shot across the bow, "a warning to Paul Martin that he better work with the opposition parties seriously." The NDP leader said he wouldn't have gone through with that coalition deal because he didn't want to make Harper prime minister. But there was no doubt in his mind, he said, that Harper, even though he had lost that election, was prepared to take over from Martin and govern a coalition. "Harper was prepared to become prime minister in some kind of relationship with the Bloc. Without question. Without question!"

The opportunity was there for the coalitionists to paint the prime minister as a hypocrite. To counter the Harper blitz, they should have taken the letter written to Clarkson, printed it up in billboard size, and brandished it everywhere. Instead, they raised it a couple of times in the House and then let it drop.

Throughout the crisis, it was a case of one side being able to sell its message, the other side not. Force of repetition can sweep the fine points of truth away. The number of distortions, half-truths, and non-truths offered by the Tories accumulated: that it was a separatist coalition, that the Liberal leader was not entitled to form a government, that the Bloc had a veto over the coalition, that the opposition would be allowed a confidence vote, that there was no Canadian flag at the coalition signing ceremony. When confronted with the latter, of photos of the Canadian flag in the chamber, the Harper men said, Oh yes, but it was off to the side. But the verities or lack thereof didn't really matter. It was the force of their campaign. It was the decibel range. It was the Harper side knowing how to stage a propaganda blitz, the other side having no idea.

The turnaround was a magnificent show of force and bluster, a credit to Harper's resilience and determination. He was often accused of retreating in gloom and despair when the going got tough. And it had looked for all intents and purposes on the Monday morning as if he would do just that again. But not this time. Within the space of only a few days, he was able to demonize the coalition to the point where public opinion moved in waves behind him. Rideau Hall was showered with thousands of anti-coalition missives. Though coalition governments had worked in Canada and Europe and elsewhere, Harper turned the very concept into villainy.

Despite the distortions he put forward, the prime minister had points in his favour. Just two months earlier, Dion had vowed there would be no coalition, just as he had once promised no carbon tax. Canadians had rejected him as their prime minister (though he was pledging to head the coalition for only a few months, until a new Liberal leader was chosen).

The coalition partners had a case as well. They had the numbers on their side. With the Green Party also supporting them, they represented 62 percent of the vote from the last election, while the Conservatives represented slightly less than 38 percent. The coalition had to drum home that point, but they didn't. They had to drum home the point that it was a two-party deal with peripheral support from a third. But they didn't. Duceppe had warned the Liberals about handling it properly. When the three leaders met in

Dion's office prior to the signing ceremony, he was heard suggesting to Liberal staff that they be careful about the staging of the press conference. English Canada, Duceppe told them, would not react favourably to his presence.

HAVING DEMONSTRATED considerable ineptitude in the crisis thus far, the Liberals now delivered Harper another prize. On the evening of December 3, the networks had agreed to broadcast statements to the nation by Harper and Dion. (The NDP wanted Layton to speak, but one network said it wasn't interested in presenting a "yard sale" of leaders.)

Harper used his time to repeat his coalition condemnations and promise recovery measures in the new budget. Then it was Dion's turn. But the Liberal leader didn't show up on time. His video arrived late. It was so late that one network didn't bother to run it all. And not only was it late, it was also the work of amateurs. The video was grainy and unfocused. Whatever Dion had to say was lost. The story was that his office was so inept that it couldn't produce a decent video.

After heckling Harper's performance, NDPers had anxiously awaited Dion's. They couldn't believe what they saw. Brian Topp's BlackBerry lit up. A message came from a supporter of Michael Ignatieff: "It's all over dude."

"How so?" Topp wrote back.

"The chief spokesman can't speak."

Scott Brison had heard a similar line about Dion at the end of the election campaign. On this night, he was alone in his Parliament Hill office. "I'm waiting for my leader to come on and I hear that 'Oops, well, we have a little delay here.' And I'm sitting there thinking, Holy shit. So then I go pour myself a Scotch, and I'm alone watching this train wreck." When Peter Mansbridge announced, "We have the tape," Brison felt better, but only for a moment. When the video came on, it was so grainy that it was "like an al Qaeda video." Two train wrecks in the space of an hour. "I finished my Scotch," said Brison, "and went and poured myself another one."

Harper's next move was to back out of his promise to give the opposition a vote of confidence and instead ask the governor general to shut down Parliament, having just re-opened it a couple of weeks earlier. Harper had turned public opinion so effectively that it was now obvious to Michaëlle Jean where Canadians stood.

While mounting their public relations blitz, the PMO had specialists looking at all conceivable options for Rideau Hall. Harper's advisers concluded that if the prime minister asked for an election, the governor general would likely turn him down. But they were quite certain that she would not turn down a request for prorogation. The PMO couldn't communicate in advance with Rideau Hall. "But we knew the GG's two constitutional advisers," recalled a Harper strategist, "and we knew from talking to others and from what they had written that they were likely to offer sound advice. And we knew there was only one sound course of action."

Most of the PM's strategists favoured the prorogation. Kory Teneycke was one who did not. He felt that if Harper lost a confidence vote in the House, the governor general would not turn power over to the coalition—not given the Bloc involvement and where public opinion stood. There would be an election, he reasoned, and Harper would score a majority. He was ready to "bet the farm" on the GG's not meeting the coalition's request. "It would be cataclysmic for the monarchy in Canada," he said, "to overturn an elected government in such a way."

Teneycke lost the argument, but he was content in the knowledge that prorogation was a good second choice. The PMO was nearly certain that the request would be granted. "The opposition had passed the Throne Speech," he noted. "All the advice we had was that constitutionally they had a very thin case." Mark Cameron felt the same, though he and his colleagues started getting nervous when Harper's meeting with Michaëlle Jean dragged on for almost two hours. When the news finally arrived that the prime minister had been granted his wish, there was a sense of relief though no great celebration. Her word, if it was no, would not necessarily have been the final word. The fight may have been far from over. The PM had warned that he intended to use every means at his disposal to stop the takeover of his government. When he got public opinion on his side, he felt there were options available. The first would have been to continue mobilizing public opinion—to stoke the outrage until thousands were marching on Parliament Hill, until the coalition was pretty much forced into calling an election to achieve legitimacy.

But there were other choices under consideration. Before Harper went to Rideau Hall, John Baird, one of his closest lieutenants, gave a remarkably candid interview to the CBC's Don Newman. The provocateur from the Mike Harris years let it be known just how little respect the Harper government had for Ottawa's institutions. The Conservatives' actions prior to this—their subordination of the civil service, the foreign service, the House committees—had made their attitude apparent. They had scant regard for the checks and balances in the system. But they had never put it in the terms Baird did with Newman. "What we want to do," he declared, "is basically take a timeout and go over the heads of Parliament, go over the head, frankly, of the governor general, go right to the Canadian people. They're speaking up loudly, right across the country, in a way I've never seen."

The way the people normally spoke was through their elected representatives in Parliament. Baird was saying this was to be circumvented—to the degree that even the governor general could be bypassed. Go over her head too!

Harper had said he would use all legal means, and what Baird suggested was an option the prime minister was considering. If the governor general had refused his request, he could have replaced her with a more compliant one, making the case to the Queen that the people of Canada were opposed in great numbers to a coalition replacing his government.

Like Baird, Kory Teneycke was also privy to Harper's thinking. In a later interview, after the dust had settled, Teneycke made the point that to turn down prorogation after a Throne Speech had been passed would have been " just unheard of." He was asked, in such an event, what other avenues the PM was prepared to explore. "Well, among them, the Queen," he said. Like Baird, Teneycke maintained that "the ultimate step in this is public opinion."

In the end, of course, any extremes to which Harper was willing to go were not tested. But his imperious attitude towards checks in the system was beginning to be noticed. What he was trying to do, wrote Lorraine Weinrib, a professor of law and political science at the University of Toronto, was to reconstruct his own constitutional framework. The current constitutional framework, she noted, is vague and informal, and rests on principles and practices inherited from the United Kingdom. It is vulnerable to a leader with an authoritarian bent. "While Harper touts the democratic principle as his ideal," she wrote, "his actions align with another principle—an all-powerful executive that makes its own rules on a play-by-play basis."

Among many examples, she cited his handling of the fixed-date election law; his attacks on the independence of certain commissions and parliamentary officers, Linda Keen being just one example; his low regard for substantive guarantees in the Charter of Rights and Freedoms, most notably on social policy; his disregard of the principle that says a government continues in office so long as it enjoys the confidence of the elected members of the House of Commons.

The prime minister's actions, Weinrib said, "reveal an understanding of democratic engagement that barely tolerates the dispersal of power, extensive public engagement and respect for equal citizenship that modern parliamentary democracies cherish." Down the road, future actions, including another closure of Parliament, would add weight to her thesis.

The governor general's decision to grant the prorogation prompted much debate. Given the way public opinion was trending, most analysts viewed it as the right call. But many constitutional experts took issue with the decision, echoing the view of a former governor general, Ed Schreyer. Schreyer came out shortly before Harper went to Rideau Hall to say that prorogation would constitute an evasion of the process of Parliament and should not be granted.

Schreyer's view was dismissed by conservatives because of his NDP background. But having served as GG, he had some familiarity with the subject. "I'll put it this way," he said, "and I will make this a plain-spoken sentence. Nothing should be done to aid and abet the evasion of submitting to the will of Parliament. It's about as basic as that." With a new parliamentary session having just begun, he said, only a genuine emergency would justify prorogation. "The only emergency seems to be a desire to avoid facing Parliament. That is not an emergency."

Though Michaëlle Jean's decision was one of dramatic, potentially government-changing significance, her reasons for it were never given. Canadians didn't find out—were not allowed to find out—because of a centuries-old convention that essentially says governors general do not have to explain their actions. In this respect, not much had changed since Upper Canada circa 1839, Lord Sydenham at the helm. Having all explanations kept secret suited this prime minister, as it would any leader. No more debate meant he could move on.

The coalition leaders moved on knowing they had fallen victim to the old cliché about loose lips sinking ships. With hindsight, they realized that if all their dealings had been kept quiet for a week, out of range of the media and the Conservatives, they could have caught the government unawares and defeated it on a confidence motion. Dion and Layton could then have made the case to the governor general that Duceppe was willing to back them for a substantial period of time.

Former NDP leader Ed Broadbent, a full participant in the coalition planning, had an experienced eye. He spent four decades in the game. To him the idea of including the Blocquistes at arm's length in the arrangement was a non-issue. He knew Harper had worked together with them from time to time. He thought their partial inclusion might even be perceived as a bonus, as in getting the enemy on side. "We totally misjudged how Harper would use that. We didn't anticipate just how devious Harper could be." In a display of non-partisanship Harper had offered Broadbent the position of ethics commissioner in 2006, but he turned it down. Despite the offer, Broadbent came to be more and more suspect of Harper's character. He penned a newspaper column after the coalition crisis in which he called Harper a liar several times and concluded by saying there's "a touch of evil" there. The last line never appeared. "The editor convinced me to take it out."

As the year came to a close, the coalition appeared moribund. Michael Ignatieff was installed as the new Liberal leader, and he was intent on winning the right to govern of his own accord. He sensed that while the Conservatives had survived the crisis and for the time being had public opinion with them, they were damaged goods.

Compared to 2007, when the economy hummed along nicely, 2008 was a harder year, a year of descent on many levels. The economy went into a plunge. The government, having spent profligately in its first two years, was running a heavy deficit and now faced the unpleasant task of having to resort to big spending. The war in Afghanistan rolled on without much progress made. Parliament had been shut down twice. From June on, it sat for less than a month.

It was the year of the gates—Cadmangate, NAFTA-gate, Bikergate, Schreibergate—and a year in which the level of sophistication in politics dipped lower. It was a year in which Harper dug himself a big hole in Quebec because of his penchant for wedge politics and a year in which the opposition leader, thankfully for the prime minister, kept hurling himself off cliffs.

Opponents of Stephen Harper had a habit of doing this. They either jumped or were pushed—by him.

CHAPTER FIFTEEN

The Keynesian Way

Having almost thrown his government overboard, Harper had sullied his reputation as a superior strategist and had disappointed many in the party. But such was his degree of dominance that there was barely a public utterance of complaint about the leader from the Conservative rank and file.

Liberals had openly challenged Jean Chrétien, even when he had a huge lead in the polls, even after winning three straight majorities. Likewise, Conservative Party members had a history of speaking their minds about leadership. Not now, however, not under the new regime. While much was being said of Harper's control fixations in the running of government, less had been made of the absolute dictatorship he exercised in the running of his party. The party was him. He had established, with Flanagan's assistance, what Flanagan called the garrison party, which was something more akin to a military machine, with everyone snapping to attention at the word of the commander-in-chief.

The mindset in the party, Flanagan said, was in some ways comparable to the garrison state of Israel. "You're constantly under threat," he said. "Politics and the military become kind of fused." The Conservatives, like Israel, had to be ready at all times "to go forth and defend their rule ... defend what you've conquered in the past." That required army discipline. With the state under siege, there could be no dissent from below. Voice a contrary opinion in the garrison party and you would be crushed by Harper's army commander, party boss Doug Finley. The last thing Harper and Finley cared about, old Tories muttered on the sidelines, was running a democratic party.

Harper's total control was manifest in many ways. Under him, no party sub-groupings were allowed. No youth wings, ethnic wings, provincial wings, regional councils. Policy conventions were now a relic of bygone years, the policy function being ceded to the leader's office. The party's national council had become a rubber stamp. Party nominations were strictly controlled by the centre, as was fundraising. In keeping with the military mindset, the party maintained a year-round campaign control centre with a war room at the ready to strike.

The garrison mentality equated with a war mentality. "It is effectively a battle on a daily basis," said Tory consultant Tim Powers, "and everything is calculated that way." The confrontational style Harper brought was even reflected, he said, at the social level. Conservatives weren't supposed to mix with Liberals. When he'd first come to Ottawa in the Mulroney years, it was much different. There was much less paranoia. The hatred for the Liberals—"I have a problem with that"—wasn't there.

Though the coalition crisis might have weakened Harper's hand, it strengthened the garrison mentality because it demonstrated the vulnerability of a minority government. Harper remained unthreatened from within. He had built up a lot of political capital in the party, having won two elections. He had also kept the Liberals at an embarrassing low.

From the party perspective it was a good record. The chances of improving upon it, however, looked dubious. Much had changed in the previous months. From his prior position of having a strong economy and a weak opposition leader, Harper now faced a recessionary economy and, so it was thought, a formidable opposition leader in Michael Ignatieff.

As a student of the economy, Harper knew well the ruin recessions could render on governments. He had only to recall the damage inflicted on the Tories through the tumult of the early 1990s. The arrival of Ignatieff concerned him. The new Liberal leader had the look of a fresh thinker, of someone a cut above normal political stock. As a relatively recent arrival to politics, he didn't carry the old Liberal baggage. His international stature gave him something of a mystique. He had the look of being a global man for the global times. And politics was becoming more global. The economic convulsions were felt worldwide, as were climate change issues. New communications technologies were tearing down every wall. The new political star, Barack Obama, was a multiethnic president of a country less dominant, more dependent on global currents.

But while the trendlines looked difficult, Harper wasn't about to take shelter from the storm. His climb began with the January 27 stimulus budget. It committed the government to $40 billion of spending over the next two years to pump up the economy, while running $60 billion in deficits. Measures included a home-renovation tax credit, an extension of employment insurance benefits by five weeks, and no less than $12 billion for infrastructure projects. Given what the prime minister and his finance minister had been saying only three months earlier, the budget was one of the more startling about-faces in the annals of Canadian finance.

With strategic pre-budget leaks, a practice Paul Martin had used to his advantage when he was finance minister, the Conservatives prepared people for the news. With countries everywhere going in the same Keynesian direction, Canadians appeared to support the plan, even if it came with the big deficit projections. Forecasts were much less dire than in the United States. Canadian unemployment was projected to rise from 6.6 percent to 7.7 percent in 2010, a good deal better than the double digits of the early 1990s. The country's economic fundamentals were superior to those of almost all other countries in the G20, and while Paul Martin could take much of the credit for that—he hadn't bought into the deregulation of financial institutions favoured by conservatives—the Harper government stood to benefit.

It was still galling, however, for conservatives to have to go the route of deep-deficit Keynesian economics, an approach Harper had repudiated in his master's thesis, during his days as a Reformer, at the National Citizens Coalition, as Alliance leader, and until this moment, as prime minister. Over the next two years, federal spending was forecast to increase by 15 percent. This was not just big government—this was giant government. The budget even contained some Trudeauvian touches, including a regional development plan, a $1 billion outlay for a Southern Ontario development agency.

But given the circumstances, Harper was seen to be taking the pragmatic course. As one Privy Council officer said of the spending splurge, "Events, dear boy, events. He had no choice." There was a choice, of course: he could have allowed the cyclical run of economic tides to heal the deficit. But the political outcry from a stay-the-course budget would have been debilitating. Besides, there were political benefits to be had from doling out the cash. Millions here, millions there was something that never hurt a party's vote-getting potential.

Of the overall budget, Jim Flaherty said: "These are not ideological things. We heard from Canadians that this is what we need to do. I'm a pragmatic person." Given the titanic folly of his economic statement, Flaherty was fortunate to still be delivering the budget. But given that he was not the driving force behind that statement, and given that finance ministers are not usually replaced during times of upheaval, he survived.

The government itself survived because Michael Ignatieff passed on an opportunity to keep the coalition intact and bring it down.

Canadians had been to the polls just a few months earlier and didn't want to go back again. The coalition idea was not popular, and the budget had gone a long way towards meeting Liberal demands. He supported it while putting the government "on probation." It was required to issue reports to Parliament on the progress of its stimulus plan—one in March, one in June, one in September. "Each of these reports will be an opportunity to withdraw our confidence should the government fail Canadians," declared Ignatieff. He thought Flaherty's document had insufficient funding for employment insurance and no credible plan for getting out of the deficit, among other flaws. Jack Layton, who was prepared to re-enter a coalition, was unenthusiastic. "When the Liberals vote for Mr. Harper with or without a fig leaf of an amendment," he opined, "they will be casting their forty-fifth straight vote to keep Stephen Harper in office. You can't do that and pretend to be the alternative to Mr. Harper."

The Liberals planned to give the Tories a lifeline until the fall. In the interim, Ignatieff would have some time to establish himself as leader and to reorganize and refinance the party. During that period, economic conditions could worsen, which would increase demands for a new government. By putting the government on probation, he was keeping the sword of Damocles at his disposal.

HARPER NOW FACED ANOTHER DIFFICULT TEST. On the heels of being sworn in as president, Barack Obama made Canada, as was tradition for new presidents, the site of his first trip outside the United States. After the Bush years, the new president appeared to be giving birth to a liberal renaissance. He had a natural affinity for a Harvard thinker and writer like Ignatieff, much more than for a conservative of Alberta culture. Harper and Obama had about as little in common as any previous presidents and prime ministers. One was a renowned communicator, the other uninspiring at the podium. One was a visionary, the other an incrementalist. One was stylish, straight off the cover of *GQ* magazine, the other a better sartorial match for the *Rotary Club Monthly*. One was a consensus builder, while the other preferred what Tom Flanagan called a divide-and-conquer strategy. As a discomfiting back story, there was also the matter of the NAFTA imbroglio, the leaked memo that had been injurious to the Obama campaign during the American primaries.

Rarely was it the case that a Conservative held office in Canada while a Democrat was president in the United States. John Diefenbaker and John Kennedy provided one earlier example, and theirs was a disastrous relationship, arguably the worst in bilateral history. R.B. Bennett fared poorly with his liberal counterpart, Franklin Roosevelt. But Harper handled Obama's visit adroitly and managed to establish a reasonably good rapport with the new president.

As soon as the two men greeted each other on the steps of Parliament's main entrance, the difference in style became apparent. A large crowd looked on, but Harper wasn't paying it much heed. On the way in, Obama stopped the prime minister to say that it might be a sensible idea to greet the throngs. They did—much to the crowd's delight.

Though he was on the defensive on the NAFTA-gate matter, Harper had the upper hand on other issues affecting the relationship. The economic wretchedness was chiefly a result of America's folly, not Canada's. The barricading of the border and the resulting slowdown in bilateral commerce was Washington's doing. In Afghanistan, it was the U.S., as Obama had already acknowledged, that took its eye off the ball by devoting too many resources to the war in Iraq.

The brief half-day visit was highlighted by a press conference where Obama was cool and compelling while Harper was well prepared to speak out on behalf of Canadian interests. With their own stimulus package, the Democrats had brought in Buy America provisions that would potentially cut into Canadian imports. Obama tried to ease Harper's concerns, but the prime minister showed resolve. Ottawa's stimulus package had actually removed duties on some imported goods, he noted. "If we pursue stimulus packages the goal of which is only to benefit ourselves at the expense of others, we will deepen the world's recession, not solve it," he asserted. Harper also let his opinion of the thickening border be known. He had opposed the Bush administration's never-ending security paranoia. Now Obama's homeland security director, Janet Napolitano, seemed to be of a Bush-like mindset, voicing at one point the wrong-headed suspicion that 9/11 terrorists had come through Canada.

The two leaders agreed to cooperate on the Afghan war, but shortly afterwards, during a trip to New York for American media exposure, the prime minister made some exceedingly candid observations. "We're not going to win this war just by staying," Harper told CNN. "Frankly, we are not going to ever defeat the insurgency." Leaders are seldom frank enough to say this kind of thing when their troops are on the battlefield. Usually they raise false hopes. But with an eye to getting out of Afghanistan before much longer, Harper was trying to lower expectations.

But neither his position on Afghanistan nor his meeting with Obama could be taken as an indication that he was softening his stance on foreign policy. Shortly after the Obama visit, the hawkish nature of the Harper world-view became apparent. His government tried to get the Cold War juices flowing again, falsely accusing Moscow of encroaching on Canadian airspace with bomber aircraft. His views on Russia remained determinedly negative, reflecting the old Reform–Alliance position. And while Obama was moving forward on disarmament, no one could remember a Canadian government as silent as Harper's on the issue. With Iran as well, Obama was initiating dialogue, while Harper was keeping it closed. In the Middle East it was the same.

Traditionally, Canadian leaders had tried to be a moderating influence on the foreign policy of American presidents. But with Harper and Obama, the roles were reversed in some areas. One was

Guantánamo. Aware that the prison's judicial standards, bordering on the medieval, were damaging the American reputation for human rights, Obama was bent on closing it down, as was the Republican candidate, John McCain. Harper differed. He had no such inclination. He gave the impression that it was fine with him.

Even to many Tories, Harper's stance on Omar Khadr was primitive. Khadr was fifteen when he killed a U.S. special forces soldier in the midst of a firefight in Afghanistan. From all appearances, the Canadian-born youth had been indoctrinated by his terrorist father and jihadists since he was nine. Accused of terrorist activities and spying, he had been incarcerated in a Guantánamo cell since 2002. He was the only citizen of a Western country to remain there; all other nations had demanded that their Gitmo detainees be returned to home soil, where they could face legitimate jurisprudence. In Ottawa's case, there was added reason to ask for Khadr's repatriation. In 2003 and 2004, when the Liberals were in power, Khadr was interrogated by Canadian foreign affairs and intelligence officials without being given access to counsel and after having been subjected to sleep deprivation. These interrogation practices, the courts ruled, offended "the most basic standards about the treatment of detained youth suspects." A U.S. marine colonel, Dwight Sullivan, who had served as the Pentagon's chief defence counsel, described the Guantánamo rules as "carefully crafted to ensure that an accused can be convicted—and possibly executed—based on nothing but a coerced confession."

In the case of Khadr, six former Canadian foreign affairs ministers, including John Manley and Joe Clark, wrote an open letter of appeal to Harper, but it was ignored. Canadian courts repeatedly ruled in favour of repatriating Khadr. Guantánamo, the courts ruled, represented a clear violation of Canada's international human rights obligations. The verdicts found that Khadr's Charter rights had been violated. Even the conservative *National Post* would headline an editorial "Bring Back Omar Khadr."

If Harper was concerned about alienating his right-wing base by bringing Khadr home, the court rulings gave him cover. He could have announced that he had no choice, that the courts had repeatedly spoken. But the prime minister decided that the word of the courts was not enough. He put forward a political argument, saying that the government, not the judiciary, should be the final arbiter of foreign policy. In this instance, the Supreme Court, while declaring that Khadr's Charter rights had indeed been violated, refused to order his repatriation. It said it would be inappropriate to dictate the diplomatic steps necessary to address the breaches of those rights. On this issue, Harper won the case. In the conduct of foreign affairs, his powers were deemed pre-eminent. But the government was still instructed by the court to fix the problem.

Throughout, the Tories refused to give their reasons for not repatriating Khadr. Wesley Wark, an Ottawa professor and the past president of the Canadian Association for Security and Intelligence Studies, was appalled at the arrogant silence. "The Harper government's view that it does not have to explain its actions," he said, "is nothing short of breathtaking." At the same time, the Harper government rebuffed requests by the Obama administration to help resettle dozens of Guantánamo detainees and close the prison. The recalcitrance was striking. It was a matter, in the case of Khadr, of supporting high standards of justice or not. Harper chose not.

Observers were beginning to note a trend in the government's attitude towards Canadian citizens abroad, especially citizens of colour. In addition to Khadr, there was the case of Abousfian Abdelrazik, who was tortured in his native Sudan and not allowed to return to Canada until he'd been holed up in Khartoum for more than a year. Abdelrazik's case contrasted sharply with the treatment of Brenda Martin, a Canadian who was convicted of money laundering by a Mexican judge but was brought home by the Conservative government to face justice here. Among those who saw a pattern of discrimination in the actions of the government was Gar Pardy, the former head of the consular services section of the foreign affairs department.

Opposition MPs were suspicious as well. Charlie Angus, an NDP MP from Northern Ontario, said he was told by an immigration official of discriminatory practices by his department. The department would periodically post photos of newcomers on advertising displays to promote immigration. "They identified who gets in these photos in terms of what ethnic groups they were interested in," said Angus. But one group, he was told, was deliberately left out of the promotion materials. "They said, 'No Muslims.' This came down from government orders."

In March 2009, the Conservatives barred entry to the British MP George Galloway, who had planned to address an anti-war group. Immigration made the case that Galloway had provided financial support to Hamas, which was designated a terrorist organization in Canada. Some found it ironic that Galloway could sit in the Parliament of the motherland but not be allowed entry to the former colony. He was accepted most everywhere else, including the United States, where he had spoken many times.

The Galloway decision followed an entry ban issued in January against William Ayers, an American who had advocated the use of violence four decades earlier and who had become an issue in Obama's campaign for the presidency. Obama had once been a friend of Ayers, who was now a respected professor of education much sought after by dissertation committees at Canadian universities. In keeping with the attitude towards the American left, Harper's government also began deporting conscientious objectors to the Iraq war, a war that Obama had opposed from the beginning.

WITH RESPECT TO THE WAR, the economy, climate change, and a range
of other issues, 2009 was the year the Conservatives had to govern
with both eyes on Washington. The bailout of Chrysler and General
Motors was a foremost example. If there wasn't enough ideological
heresy in their pumping the economy like FDR New Dealers, now
the Conservatives were coming to the rescue of major companies and
taking a stake in their ownership.

The price tag on the GM bailout was $10.5 billion, of which
$7 billion came from Ottawa and the rest from Ontario. In return,
GM agreed to keep 16 percent of its North American production in
Canada. The two governments received 11.7 percent equity in the
new company. The feds and the province had already provided a
few billion to help Chrysler as well. It was a regrettable step, Harper
explained, but the government had no choice because the country
risked losing its entire auto sector if it didn't align with Washington's
decision to use public money to restructure the industry. "The Bush
administration's decision to support the restructuring of Chrysler
and General Motors," he said, "left two options for Canada: either
participate in the restructuring of the companies or stand idly by as
they are completely restructured out of Canada."

Because the effort was bipartisan, with the Ontario Grits throwing a substantial amount of the financing into the pot, criticism was
muted. But in the western provinces, some alarm bells were sounded.
The bailout also raised questions from other companies and industries in distress, like Nortel and the British Columbia forestry sector.
If you're helping them, they wanted to know, why not us? Commentators like Andrew Coyne of *Maclean's* had a field day with the bailout. Noting that the provincial and federal governments had pledged
to sell off their stake in Chrysler and GM down the line, Coyne ran
the stock prices past his readers and concluded that if they quintu-
pled in value over the next nine years, "we could get back as much as
two cents on the dollar."

But Harper managed the bailout with effectiveness, no easy task. David Emerson, who served as chair of the finance committee as well as trade minister, had watched Harper's trajectory since he became PM and concluded that the notion he was handcuffed by right-wing economic ideology was misguided. "I wouldn't even put him in the category of a Friedman-type economist," said Emerson. "I think he is fairly mainstream about the way he thinks about the public policy issues from an economics perspective." Experience was the great teacher. He was getting a tangible sense, said the trade minister, of how things worked in the real world. "There's a pragmatism there," said Emerson, a pragmatist himself, "a realization that you have to come to the table." Harper had no choice on the auto bailout, he said. "Practical economics would lead you to hold your nose and get involved."

NOT BEING ABLE TO PROCEED for any length of time without a cabinet embarrassment, the PM then faced another one. His cabinet was notably weak on the female side. Among the many who stumbled were Rona Ambrose, Josée Verner, Bev Oda, Helena Guergis, and Lisa Raitt. One of the few who stayed out of trouble was Immigration Minister Diane Finley.

Harper had high hopes for the newly elected Lisa Raitt, who had executive experience as the president of the Toronto Port Authority. But she quickly tripped up in her handling of the crisis stemming from the shutdown of the nuclear reactor at Chalk River and the resulting global shortage of life-saving radioisotopes. Stephen Maher of the *Halifax Chronicle-Herald* produced a tape recording in which Raitt called the crisis "sexy" and talked about how Health Minister Leona Aglukkaq was having problems and seemed "terrified" of dealing with the issue. On the tape, Raitt said Aglukkaq's difficulties were good because "when we win on this, we get all the credit. I'm ready to roll the dice on this. This is an easy one. You know what solves this problem—money. And if it's just about money, we'll figure it out. It's not a moral issue." When an aide responded that it was a difficult issue because it was confusing to a lot of people, Raitt said, "But it's sexy. Radioactive leaks. Cancer."

The revelation prompted a storm of protest, with nuclear medical authorities decrying the characterization and citing countless patients who were being treated with twenty-year-old technologies because of the isotope shortage. At first Raitt showed no signs of remorse. The PM defended her, saying she was working round the clock on the issue and the opposition was playing cheap politics. Michael Ignatieff got a kick out of that. "The cheapest politics here is to call a crisis a career opportunity," he responded.

Raitt eventually got around to making a teary-eyed apology, but only after public outrage grew over her mixing of political calculus with the treatment of cancer patients. Her apology followed one by Transport Minister John Baird. In response to Toronto's complaints that it was not getting enough federal infrastructure money, Baird was overheard saying the city could "fuck off." Since Toronto had supplied the Tories with zero seats, this was probably one gaffe the PM didn't mind.

In dealing with Ignatieff, Harper had thus far resisted resorting to attack ads. Some in his office had advised him to bash the new Liberal leader right out of the gate, just as he had with Dion. But Harper had just suffered through rounds of criticism for trying to cripple the other parties with his funding gambit. Also, he had more respect for Ignatieff as a political adversary and was uncertain whether he was a suitable target for this type of attack.

But in the spring, a few months after the new Liberal leader took over, he changed his mind, unleashing commercials that targeted Ignatieff for living outside the country for a quarter century. The ads portrayed him as an arrogant elitist, as "just visiting," and as being here only for the sake of gaining power. If he didn't get it, he'd bolt back to Harvard.

Liberal fundraising efforts had shot up appreciably since the start of the year, but Ignatieff's team chose not to strike back at Harper with ads of their own. In scrums, Ignatieff suggested that seeing Canada from the outside was an advantage. "At any given time, there may be two million Canadian citizens living and working overseas," he remarked. "Is the Conservative Party saying these people are less Canadian?" It was time for "a new kind of politics ... one that relies not on spite and spin but on civility and common purpose." But his scrums could in no way compete with national TV ads. The only trouble for Harper came when Steve Murphy, the same Halifax reporter who had sent Dion into a tailspin in the last days of the election, put some tough questions to him.

Harper rarely faced challenging media queries. He was still avoiding full-fledged press conferences, and the journalists chosen for one-on-one interviews were those judged most favourable to him. Consistent, tough-minded critics of the prime minister, like Frances Russell of the *Winnipeg Free Press* or Susan Riley of the *Ottawa Citizen*, didn't have a hope of getting an interview. Those who did get them were usually cautious with their questioning, certain that if they got aggressive they would never get another.

Murphy, who had been criticized for his handling of the Dion interview, looked like he wanted to show he could be hard on the other side as well. He went at the PM on the attack ads, asking him repeatedly whether he thought Ignatieff was unqualified to lead the country because of his time away. Uncharacteristically, Harper stammered. Finally, on Murphy's fifth attempt at the question, he said, "Every, every, every, obviously every Canadian citizen is eligible to run for office."

Through most of the spring, the Liberals held a slight but precarious lead in the polls. Ignatieff was hesitant to put out new policies,

however, because he didn't want to give Harper an early chance
to pounce on them as he had done with Dion's Green Shift. He
published a book titled *True Patriot Love* as a way of suggesting that
no one should question his devotion to his country. Compared to
some of his other works, it was below standard. In it, the Liberal
leader mused about grand schemes such as a national power grid
and high-speed rail. But he never gave his visionary proposals flesh,
letting the ideas float and fall. Because he was deemed to be a thinking man's leader with innovative approaches learned from his time
abroad, his caution may have cost him. Initially there was hope that
he would capture the public imagination, but he started to look more
like a conventional politician than someone a cut above.

His caution was in evidence with regard to Barack Obama.
Despite having a good deal in common with Obama and some high-
level contacts in his administration, Ignatieff made no attempt to
cultivate the new president and link himself with the wave of liberalism south of the border. Other opposition leaders had shown
no hesitancy. Within a year of becoming leader of the Progressive
Conservative Party, Brian Mulroney was at the White House courting
President Ronald Reagan. The two men cemented their Irish bond,
and Mulroney benefited. As opposition leader, Lester Pearson built
a good rapport with President Kennedy, who then threw his weight
behind Pearson in his battles against John Diefenbaker. Ignatieff had
an issue on which he could help Obama—the president's fight for a
national health care plan. But there were sensitivities. The Liberal
leader wanted to cultivate a down-home image, having been out of
the country so long. He had got in trouble for so closely identifying
with the Americans, to the point where he used the pronoun "we"
in writing about them. Nonetheless, Obama represented a missed
opportunity for him. He couldn't leverage the president's popularity
into any advantage for his own party.

In attempting to control the agenda, the Liberal leader pushed hard on the subject of employment insurance, demanding that Harper significantly broaden the program and threatening to bring down the government if he didn't. It was an important issue, but few saw it as weighty enough to trigger an election campaign so soon after the last. Still, Ignatieff treated it with gravity. In June, he demanded that the prime minister reform the program, sounding very much as if he was going to force an election if he didn't get cooperation. Having issued the threat, he then got cold feet, particularly when Alf Apps, the Liberal party president, advised him that for many reasons, including the state of the party treasury, an election was not a good idea.

With that, Ignatieff had to pull back on his warning, and he looked timid in doing so. In trying to set himself apart from the Dion approach, in trying to convince Canadians that he had the right stuff for taking on the formidable opponent in the prime minister's chair, he had fumbled the first test.

CHAPTER SIXTEEN

Law and Order

In several cases, the learning curve took effect. The Harper players came in with long-held biases, but if enough evidence was brought forward, they could be moved to change them. The economic stimulus program and the bailouts were a prime example of their being able to set aside their ideological predispositions, as was China.

But Harperland featured many instances of ministries holding resolutely to old religion—none perhaps as glaringly as the justice department. The department, which had about two hundred researchers in its policy branch, produced sophisticated studies that, as per the normal run of things in any department, were supposed to be used to inform policy decisions. But a funny thing happened at justice. The researchers might just as well have gone on holiday.

The work they did went directly to nowhere because it either didn't conform with or directly contradicted the biases of the governing party. "We still produced a lot of stuff," said a former employee. "It just never saw the light of day." When a government starts suppressing its own research time and time again—research the public is paying for—it's serious business, he said. Some senior players in the department were bitter and frustrated, but they didn't dare raise their voices. They had their careers to look after, so they tolerated the censorship.

The Conservatives wanted to make up for many years of what they considered soft-on-crime legislation by their Liberal predecessors. New sheriffs were in town. Their crackdown measures included mandatory minimum sentences for a wide range of offences, a broadly expanded jail system, the closure of the prison farm system, the limiting of parole opportunities, and any number of other bills that set harsher punishments and sent young people to the slammer for minor offences. In its first four years, the government created or beefed up nineteen minimums.

Rob Nicholson's justice department was the most ideologically driven in memory. The Conservatives planned to expand budgets for prisons by 27 percent over three years. More space would be needed for all the incarcerations resulting from their new policies. Increased spending at justice continued even when almost all other departments were being hit with cutbacks.

Canadians could be forgiven for assuming that statistics and studies would be introduced to support the new draconian turn. But for much of this legislation, the stats and studies came primarily from outside the department and often contradicted the bills. Among the numerous studies was one by the *Criminological Digest*. Based on research covering forty years, it showed that mandatory minimum sentences do not have a deterrent effect. Many state legislatures in the U.S. were trying to unwind such sentencing, as were the parliaments in Britain and New Zealand. The American experience indicated that increased jailing was hardly the advisable approach. Incarceration rates south of the border had risen 700 percent over four decades, and there was no corresponding drop in crime. The state governments were moving away from the lock-them-up-and-leave-them strategy in a bid to reduce prison populations and soaring costs.

A 235-page analysis of Harper's corrections policy by Michael Jackson, a law professor, and Graham Stewart, the retired head of the John Howard Society, said that pandering to people's baser instincts was overtaking decades of empirical evidence. "Raw wedge politics—in place of studied evidence—is the new face of public policy for Canada," wrote the authors. The government "creates the notion that the decent treatment of prisoners is somehow putting the public at risk when in fact it's the compete reverse."

Harper appeared to have little interest in hearing what the specialists had to say. In a speech in 2008, he rejected research-based justice policies, saying those behind them were trying to "pacify Canadians with statistics ... Your personal experiences and impressions are wrong, they say; crime is really not a problem. These apologists remind me of the scene from the *Wizard of Oz* when the Wizard says, 'Pay no attention to the men behind the curtain.'"

Harper, said his friend John Weissenberger, viewed law and order as a matter of principle. "He feels that if you commit a crime the punishment should fit the crime. It's traditional conservatism in that it's the same type of idea he was raised with. It's closer to the average guy's view of law and order."

The Conservatives held to a dim view of criminologists. "In the case of crime," Ian Brodie said, trying to explain the Tory approach, "Canada had a very small community of criminologists propagating a policy perspective that didn't relate to the facts, and a bunch of people in government and the NGO community who got caught up in the thing for their own reasons." Brodie recalled a moment, shortly after their new government took over in 2006, when he, Rob Nicholson, Mark Cameron, Vic Toews, and Stockwell Day were surveying the situation and asking, "Hey, do the facts matter here?" Toews, he said, then spent years arguing with Statistics Canada that "the crime stats they collect massively understate crime in a known, systematic way." StatsCan reported on aggregate crime as reported to the police. "The problem," said Brodie, "as anyone who gives it a split second of thought realizes, is that not all crime gets reported to the police." Brodie made these remarks shortly before Harper made a highly controversial decision to scrap the mandatory long-census form, prompting the resignation of the head of Statistics Canada, Munir Sheikh.

Right-wing commentators expressed outrage over reporting on crime by media that used only modern-day StatsCan numbers. Statistics from the agency said crime went down 3 percent in 2009 compared to 2008, and 17 percent compared to a decade ago. Critics, mainly on the left, used these numbers to try to undermine the Harper argument for a new get-tough approach. The problem with the media, argued the *Toronto Sun*'s Lorrie Goldstein, is that they use the wrong base date. If they went back to 1962 they would find that the crime rate was 131 per cent higher in 2009 than that year, he said. As for violent crime, it was 321 per cent higher than in 1962. Of the more recent dip, Goldstein wrote: "The knee-jerk argument from the hug-a-thug crowd that a slightly lower crime rate automatically means we don't need as many police or prisons is akin to arguing a lower mortality rate automatically means we don't need as many doctors or hospitals."

In keeping with their preference for wedge politics, the Conservatives attempted to label opponents of their philosophy "soft on crime." It was one of Justice Minister Rob Nicholson's favourite phrases. What struck Don Davies, the NDP justice critic, was that the government was ignoring the evidence from south of the border. "If getting tough on prisons—locking people up longer and more harshly—resulted in a safer society," he pointed out, "the United States would probably be the safest country on earth."

John Geddes of *Maclean's* was among those who tried to get data from Nicholson to support the government's contention that sentencing in Canada was too light. But the department couldn't furnish such data. Nicholson, Geddes concluded, was using impressions more than facts to justify minimum sentencing. "Nicholson's office and his departmental officials," he wrote, "admit they have not compiled statistics on typical sentences in convictions for most of the crimes they have targeted."

Critics of the crackdown extended from Margaret Atwood on the left to Conrad Black on the right. In 2010, Black, who was serving a prison term in Florida, said of the government's blueprint, "A Roadmap to Strengthening Public Safety," that "it is painful for me to write that this garrotte of a blueprint from the government I generally support is flirting with moral and political catastrophe."

As if trying to paint themselves as philistines, Nicholson and Peter Van Loan took to ridiculing those who opposed their policies for being, in Van Loan's words, "university types." Those with academic credentials did not appear to be high on his list of preferred people. The Conservatives, Brodie included, were persuaded, in fact, that criticism from society's most erudite members on their tough-on-crime package was a benefit to them.

The motivation for the Tories' approach was simple enough— being tough on crime attracted votes. Post 9/11, Canadians had become more conservative on law-and-order issues, according to studies the government was prepared to believe. Because of this, the Liberals were prepared to support the Tories on many of the measures.

But Nicholson kept beating them with that hammer anyway. His constant refrain was that the opposition was trying to obstruct the Tory agenda—if not in the House, then in the Senate. Senator James Cowan produced a chapter-and-verse account of the progress of the government's legislation that hung Nicholson out to dry. "Of the twenty-one law-and-order bills introduced by this government," concluded Cowan, "eighteen died on the Order Paper because Stephen Harper decided to prorogue Parliament [in 2009]."

Nicholson appeared unfazed by criticisms that he was living in the stone age, even though he had once rejected the very approach he was now taking. As an MP in the Mulroney government in 1988, he vice-chaired a parliamentary committee that released a report opposing the use of mandatory minimum sentences except in the case of violent sexual offenders. In formulating its conclusions, the committee drew on the American experience.

The government's hard-headed approach was also seen in respect to Guantánamo and the gun registry. As for drug policy, the Tory attitude was reflected in the government's determination to shut down InSite, a safe-injection centre in Vancouver. Numerous peer-reviewed studies concluded that the supervised facility reduced drug overdoses and the spread of HIV/AIDS while increasing the number of users who sought treatment. B.C. courts ruled that the centre should remain open. But in keeping with their low regard for empirical data, the Conservatives launched legal challenges to lock its doors.

BEFORE THE CONSERVATIVES CAME TO POWER, expertise played a greater role in policy formation. More scholarship came from within the federal bureaucracy. More input, though not a great deal, came from the rank and file of the party in power.

The Conservative Party under Harper, however, saw policy-producing activities reduced almost to the point of non-existence. He occasionally sounded out the party on policy, as he did at a 2008 Winnipeg convention where some token resolutions were passed. But basically the rank-and-file members bought in to the idea that they were just there to raise money and fight.

Much had changed since 1993, when the Reform Party elected fifty-two MPs. By 2009, forty-two of those early missionaries were gone. Thus there was little pressure on Harper from the early idealists. If any of those who were still around tried to flex their muscle, they were muzzled. Lee Morrison, an original Reformer and one of Ottawa's most compelling characters, bowed out prior to the 2008 election. He saw what was happening and didn't like it. "The concepts of popular control of the party from the grassroots, open

government, MPs representing their constituents, and fiscal responsibility were replaced early on with total control from the PMO."
Stephen Harper, said Morrison, "will be remembered as an oppor-
tunistic, masterful tactician who in the course of only three years
purged the Conservative Party of its Reform ideals."

As Harper's grip tightened, any grumbling was met with the argument that extreme discipline was the only way to go, given the perils
of a minority. Grassroots democracy was a pipe dream. Many of the
newly elected Conservative MPs—the seventy-five or so who arrived
with the 2004 election—were young and easily won over by the
Harper way. His style of governance was the only one they knew, and
they were inclined to march in formation.

The old-guard Tories, many of whom resided in the Senate, had
been pleased to see the Reformers leave the party. But this new breed
of Conservative didn't appeal to them either. They were true believers with no affinity for Red Tory traditions.

When it came to the bureaucracy, the policy-making function
improved somewhat after Harper's first couple of years. Select senior
bureaucrats enjoyed some freedom and input. But these were the
exceptions. For most, it was a matter of keeping their head down
and implementing, not innovating. One who didn't do that was
Maryantonett Flumian, the head of Ottawa's Institute on Governance. She was a deputy minister when Harper came to office, but
ran afoul of the powers at the centre and didn't last long. "I grew
up in a world where deputy ministers used to go across the table at
one another's throats," she recalled. "It was a world where even the
most tightly held policy convictions were the subject of consultation,
trial balloons—all the things in a democracy that you are supposed
to avail yourself of." Harper didn't want that dynamic. "There's an
absence of checks and balances that are normally brought about by
discourse," she said. "What it amounts to is an attack on the way our
system has most successfully found accommodation. That's been a

virtue of the Canadian model: finding a way to make those accommodations through discourse. And if you remove that as a feature of the system, you wind up in some very strange places."

With the country living off the petro economy, she saw a need for broader input and broader vision. Despite Brian Mulroney's deficiencies, she said, he "was forever out there, in the country, among the public servants, having relationships and dialogue. The current leader doesn't have many of those things and probably relies on himself, or everyone who reinforces his view." The latter, she added, "tend to be the only ones left standing."

Flumian and others felt that with a change at the head of the civil service, the atmosphere might loosen up. After three years on the job, Kevin Lynch was being ushered out the door, courtesy of Chief of Staff Guy Giorno.

Lynch's power had come to be enormous—so much so that even Harper would made cracks about it. He told a story about how, before he became prime minister, he'd read the papers in the morning and get annoyed about something, and say to Laureen, "Why the hell doesn't the prime minister do something about this?" As prime minister, he said, he'd look through the papers, see something terrible happening, and say to Laureen, "Why the hell doesn't Kevin Lynch do something about this?"

Everyone around the office knew something had to give between Giorno and Lynch. The problem, recalled one PCO official who worked with Lynch, was that those in the PMO "felt they couldn't control him." Lynch hadn't wanted to leave, the official said, "Not at all. He had prepared decades for the job." Harper and Lynch— two steely-minded policy wonks—had got along very well. But when Giorno came in, he started cutting off Lynch's access to the PM. Eventually, PMO staffers recalled, "Guy just wouldn't deal with Lynch."

Giorno had his strengths, and not all the problems were his doing. But since his arrival in the middle of 2008, things hadn't exactly clicked. He'd been there for the bungling on the Quebec culture file, the mixed messaging on the global financial crisis, and the fiasco over the budget update. Around town, he was becoming known as the alienator-in-chief.

Under Giorno, everyone was put under strict watch. He wanted to see everything that went to Harper, including reports from the PCO that used to go directly to the prime minister. Harper was criticized for being a control freak with Brodie running his shop. Why he brought in a more iron-fisted replacement—someone who would be inclined to harden his image when it needed the opposite—was baffling.

Lynch was respected by his staff at the Privy Council Office. One of his few embarrassments came at the beginning of 2009, when Kevin Chan, a close deputy, resigned and went to work in the office of Michael Ignatieff, who had just taken over the Liberal leadership. Chan obviously knew a lot of the government's thinking and future plans, and people at the PMO suspected he would share them. Lynch hadn't seen the defection coming. He didn't know until the day it happened.

Word of Lynch's departure came down when Harper was out of the country, visiting the troops in Afghanistan. It was unceremonious, and it was noted too that Lynch received no award for his services, no offers of ambassadorships or the like. His replacement was a respected veteran, Wayne Wouters. The Saskatchewan native was a well-liked middle-of-the-roader, a hockey fan with an economics background. His appointment was greeted positively by the mandarinate, who saw him as less rigid and hoped he would open the communications channels. Much had been said and written over the years about the overconcentration of power in the PMO, but what the media missed, officials said, was the corresponding concentration at the PCO. Years of sloppy management under the Liberals had led to more stringent measures of control from the Clerk's office. Wouters, many hoped, would end the trend.

Kory Teneycke, no fan of bureaucracy, favoured the changeover. "I don't think I'm telling lies out of school to say that Lynch's approach was very centralized." Wouters was a more typical clerk, Teneycke thought. The government had matured and now it had to be run more traditionally, with ministers having more say.

Since taking over from Sandra Buckler as director of communications, Teneycke had established himself as a good pitchman, friendlier and more popular with the media. But it was difficult for him to get Harper to change his attitude towards journalists. That antagonism deepened with a bizarre incident that took place at the funeral of Romeo LeBlanc, a former governor general, in Memramcook, New Brunswick. News footage appeared to show Harper taking a communion wafer and putting it in his pocket, but witnesses said he ate it after he was out of the cameras' view. The Saint John *Telegraph-Journal* reported differently, with a massive headline shouting "It's a Scandal."

The story broke when the prime minister was attending a G8 summit in Italy. It embarrassed him among Catholic voters, whom the Conservatives were trying to court. "This is a low moment in journalism, whoever is responsible for this," Harper asserted. "It's just a terrible story and a ridiculous story, and not based on anything, near as I can tell."

Three weeks after the funeral, when it was clear it could not support its story, the Saint John newspaper issued an apology. Then the heads rolled. Both the editor and the publisher were dismissed. It was extraordinary retribution in which the PMO denied having a hand. It came just as representatives of the Irving company, which owned the paper, were meeting with Conservative cabinet ministers and representatives of the shipbuilding industry to negotiate a multi-billion-dollar deal in shipbuilding procurement. There were suspicions, but no one could prove it was anything more than a coincidence.

At the start of July, a short time after the communion controversy and the departure of Kevin Lynch, Kory Teneycke surprised the media world by announcing his resignation. He had been in the job for little more than a year and was leaving, he said, because of the time constraints and the needs of his young family. "I never intended to stay for a long time," he said. "I think it was the day after Canada Day. I went over to 24 [Sussex Drive] and talked to the PM about it. He understood, asked me if there was something else I wanted to do, and I indicated there wasn't." Later, in looking back on his experience, he said, "I made my share of mistakes. The government made its share of mistakes. I think it got it right more times than not." He said he wasn't disappointed overall. "I was realistic going in. People are disappointed when they believe the person they work for is somehow superhuman. They don't have a realistic conception that you are dealing with human beings."

THE PMO AND THE PCO, where all the power resides, is an enclosed world. Despite its importance, the PCO is largely unknown to the public. Its machinations are inside baseball. Reporters seldom write about it, just as they seldom write about the key players in the PMO, mainly because of lack of access to them. Instead, the media focuses on Parliament Hill and the legislative branch of government, which has seen its power erode over the decades. The real power in Ottawa, as in Washington, is in the executive branch. At the White House, there are daily briefings for reporters. In Ottawa, there is no such daily access. The media doesn't demand it, and as a result, major powerbrokers remain virtually anonymous.

An ongoing controversy at the top of the power circle centred on the alleged politicization of the Privy Council Office. The PCO employed supposedly non-partisan public servants, while the PMO employed partisan political staff. There was a fine line between political work and bureaucratic work, just as there was a fine line between using public money for political purposes rather than government functions and programs.

Sometimes, PCO officials felt pressured to carry out their jobs with an eye to helping Harper's team score political points. At one point, PCO bureaucrats were taken aback to see Jackie Bogdan, the wife of Keith Fountain, a senior official in the PMO, appointed director of communications in the PCO. "I don't want to cast aspersions," said a PCO official who has since left. "But you got the feeling that PCO communications was getting more political."

Throughout 2009, the government was promoting its stimulus funding, called the Economic Action Plan. In October, Bruce Cheadle of the Canadian Press, citing multiple sources, reported that officials at the PCO had sounded the alarm about the extent to which the PMO was pressuring them to promote the plan. The report said senior bureaucrats informed the PMO of their misgivings about having to operate the website for the plan. The complaints were pushed aside. There had always been a grey area between the PMO and the PCO, but the officials quoted in Cheadle's story said that never had the office been used for such blatant promotion. "You have a political party that is not constrained by what conventionally would be perceived as overtly partisan actions," one former insider was quoted as saying. Said another: "I can tell you every funding program across the government is being politicized. They do it for their own needs."

Cheadle's report said the PCO did not have a line-item accounting for its work on the website. The budget for it, $2 million, came from the finance department. Since the website had been developed by the PCO, with frequent input from the PMO, it was peculiar.

The PMO denied the story, saying the bureaucrats didn't raise any objections to the website because operating it was part of the PCO's role in coordinating and implementing the government's agenda. The overall cost for promoting the action plan was $34 million. It was $34 million of taxpayers' money for propaganda, the opposition alleged.

The suspicion was that Giorno was tending to his goal of having the political arm exert more command. When Kevin Lynch gave his retirement speech at a dinner that the prime minister did not attend, he notably praised Brodie. Lynch said Brodie had shown a "great understanding of the institutional roles and responsibilities of government and the public service." Observers took his comments to suggest that Brodie's replacement was not drawing similar distinctions.

In trying to discredit the Cheadle report, the Conservatives might have been more successful if not for yet another rash of developments that demonstrated how far they were prepared to go to score political points. They were soon discovered to be putting the party logo and names of MPs on infrastructure cheques distributed in ridings. This gave taxpayers the impression that the money was coming from the party and not their own pockets.

It was then revealed that they'd spent $100,000 on a town hall meeting in Cambridge, Ontario, to promote the stimulus plan. The bills included $30,000 for audio-visual equipment, $10,000 for the rights to use certain photos, $10,000 for hotels, and $50,000 in printing costs for a glossy report. Here was another example, the opposition hollered, of the Conservatives using public money for partisan gain.

Next it was disclosed that in awarding stimulus grants across the country, the Conservatives had directed more money to their own ridings than opposition ridings. Back in the days when the Chrétien government was doling out grant money, Alliance Party members raised a stink about the Grits favouring their own constituencies. Now they were caught doing the same thing.

In defending themselves, the Conservatives pointed to some opposition ridings that got big grants. But analyses by different news organizations showed a national bias in favour of Conservative ridings. Their case became all the more porous because of their reluctance to divulge details on the where and when of the grants. John Baird, the minister responsible, went into stonewalling mode. If he had nothing to hide, journalists asked, why hide it?

One Conservative candidate, Gordon Landon, made the mistake of musing publicly that the riding he was contesting wasn't getting any infrastructure funding because it was held by a Liberal. Essentially, he was telling constituents, "Elect me and the grant monies will come pouring in." His candour was too much for party central. He was dumped as the candidate for Markham-Unionville, near Toronto. He'd made his remarks on a local TV show, which was another mistake. Party rules said you had to get permission from Ottawa before doing such an interview.

ONE OF THE COMMENDABLE HARPER INITIATIVES was the creation of a Parliamentary Budget Office to monitor spending. In this case, however, the PM may have got more than he bargained for. The budget officer, Kevin Page, took his independence very seriously. He was quickly in trouble for casting doubt on the figures the Tories were putting out on the cost of the Afghan war. He also predicted greater deficits and an earlier recession than Team Harper, which was trying to keep those bad financial tidings out of view during the 2008 election campaign. Unfortunately for the Tories, his readings usually turned out to be the more accurate. Rather than giving him a measure of respect for his work, they sliced his budget in half.

Though there was bound to be some tension between Page and the PMO, if the government was putting out more accurate estimates, it wouldn't have been as pronounced. Conservatives had always knocked the Liberals for their poor record on financial forecasting—it was one of the reasons for creating the budget office in the first place.

For the $16-billion infrastructure program, Page wanted details of how the money was spent. He was initially blocked, and then, in an apparent huff, Harper's operatives sent him three boxes with 4,476 uncollated pages of documents. They knew that no one could make sense of these mountains of paperwork in any reasonable amount of time.

Obstructionism and secrecy extended, as the *Ottawa Citizen* revealed, to the government holding back data regarding the use of expensive Challenger jets by cabinet ministers. Jason Kenney had once lampooned the Grits for using these flying limousines, as he called them, saying the ministers could save taxpayers a fortune if they travelled on cheaper commercial aircraft. The defence department, which operated the jets, said it could not supply a list of passengers because it would take too long to assemble. Opposition critics wondered whatever happened to the computer age. Later the department released some information on the use of the jets but held back the data on the operating costs, citing reasons of national security.

Michel Drapeau, an access-to-information specialist who ran for the Progressive Conservatives in the 1997 federal election, was taken aback at the secrecy. "I never thought I'd say this," he remarked, "but the situation has gotten worse under the Conservatives."

THE OPPOSITION TRIED TO SCORE POINTS on the ever-increasing incidents of stonewalling, deceit, and muzzling, but they had only limited success. Conservative media tended to defend Harper with the rationale that the Liberals used to do it, so it's not so bad. The opposition parties didn't keep a running count of the abuses of power. Only by pulling together the dozens of examples and connecting the dots to show they fit a pattern would they have come up with a compelling narrative.

As the new opposition leader, Michael Ignatieff couldn't find his footing. In the summer months, despite making many public appearances, he still managed to recede from view. His office complained that the media weren't covering him. But he wasn't making pronouncements that were newsworthy. Opposition parties have the perennial problem of attracting coverage. The trick is to know what triggers a journalist's appetite. Ignatieff provided elevator music.

Liberals had a big caucus meeting scheduled in North Bay, Ontario, in early September, at which they were contemplating issuing an election ultimatum. But they had to have something to base it on and the summer saw nothing noteworthy put on the table. So when Ignatieff, against the wishes of many in his caucus, trenchantly announced, "Mr. Harper, your time is up," everyone was left to wonder, And why is that?

Iggy was pulling the plug. He was now committed to forcing an election at the first opportunity. He had a trip planned to China—upstaging the prime minister, who had passed on the Beijing Olympics and had yet to visit—but he cancelled it to keep sounding the election drums. Harper smartly responded by making the case that an election was the last thing Canadians wanted. Every poll agreed. It was barely a year since the previous campaign, and the Liberal leader had failed to make the case for a new one.

The Liberals finally released some television ads. But rather than respond to the Tories' portrayal of him as a just-visiting, power-hungry carpetbagger, Ignatieff turned the other cheek. The ads barely laid a hand on Harper. Instead, they showed the Liberal leader standing in front of a forest trotting out boy scout bromides. Frank McKenna, the former New Brunswick premier, spoke for many in the party that fall when he said the Liberals "are dealing with thugs. They've got to fight back and fight hard." But the fight, as was the case when Dion was leader, was with popguns against Harper's cruise missiles. Ignatieff versus Harper was the nobleman versus the Doberman. The PM's calumny machine was turning Iggy into a blend of Michael Dukakis and John Kerry. Harper was defining him—he wasn't defining Harper.

Ignatieff's election demand resulted in plunging Liberal polling numbers. He backed off from his brinksmanship, looking pusillanimous in doing so. "Mr. Harper, your time is up" became "Mr. Harper, you're perfectly welcome to stay." Dissension in the party reached the point where Ignatieff decided to change his senior advisory team. The well-meaning chief of staff, Ian Davey, the son of the old Liberal rainmaker Keith Davey, was dropped. He was replaced by Chrétien's old communications director, Peter Donolo. Donolo had joined Chrétien back in 1991, after Chrétien had staggered through his first year as opposition leader. That was one of the few consolations available to Ignatieff: almost all his predecessors—Pearson, Turner, Chrétien, Martin, Dion—had an equally troublesome year one as party leader. On the Conservative side, it wasn't much different. Harper had a dismal first year as Alliance leader.

While Michael Ignatieff was in full retreat, Stephen Harper was in full song. The prime minister, the same man who had dissed fancy galas a year earlier, took the stage at one of the fanciest fetes of the year, the National Arts Centre gala in the nation's capital. He astounded one and all with a worthy rendition of "With a Little Help from My Friends." His effervescent better half, Laureen, convinced him to do it in order to show those who considered him a sullen, cold-hearted man that he wasn't such a bore after all.

Looking as croonerish as possible in dark shirt and no tie, Harper walked onto the stage totally unannounced. The renowned cellist Yo Yo Ma struck up the tune and Harper sang. Though he couldn't hit the high notes, his voice carried the song well enough. His guard didn't totally come down. A reticence was apparent, the smile a bit forced. But it was a bravura showing, one that required a good deal of courage. He had never given a stage performance like that, and the possibility that it would bomb, providing a humiliating YouTube clip for the ages, must have passed through his mind a hundred times.

He needn't have worried. The audience stood and roared its approval. It was the talk of the town—of the country—for days to come. Harper's musical ability was an aspect that was hidden from view. He was so private an individual that even Tom Flanagan, who'd worked with him on and off for fifteen years, never knew he could play the piano. Around the office, it was his wry sense of humour that was occasionally in evidence. Once he had a new haircut, and someone noted it was in the style of John F. Kennedy. When this was brought to his attention by Goldy Hyder, Harper was quick to conjure up one of Kennedy's long-time maladies, joking, "Maybe that's why my back's so damn sore."

But he wasn't in this mode very often. An attitude of resolve was his more dominant trait. And so everyone realized that after the happy-pill moment at the National Arts Centre, there would be a return to the Harperland they knew so well.

CHAPTER SEVENTEEN

Padlocking Parliament

With their latest setback, the Hindenburg election threat, the Liberals were making the prime minister feel kingly again. Since the sponsorship scandal of a half-dozen years earlier, the party had yet to recover. Liberals had gone through three leaders—Martin, Dion, Ignatieff—in the space of five years. Nothing remotely like it had ever happened to them. Three leaders would normally last them four decades. Wilfrid Laurier headed the party for three decades, and Mackenzie King for almost the same amount of time. Louis St. Laurent and Lester Pearson captained the team for decade-long stretches. Pierre Trudeau and Jean Chrétien led for sixteen and thirteen years, respectively.

But now the Liberals were losing their gravitational pull, and Stephen Harper, who had made it his goal to undermine them, was making progress to that end. His politics of aggression was grinding them into the dirt. After dispensing with Paul Martin and Stéphane Dion, it looked as if he might add Ignatieff to his kill list. It was shaping up to be one of the most humiliating decades for the Grits ever. In the 1890s the old Conservatives had gone through four leaders in one decade. That stretch of ineptitude now appeared to be threatened by the Liberals.

What was frightening for the once natural governing party was that the Conservative advance was no fleeting effort that could be easily repelled. Harper was setting down stakes in Liberal turf, a prime example being the immigrant community.

Mining this field for the Tories was Jason Kenney, a forty-one-year-old, fresh-faced, amply waisted power broker from Wilcox, Saskatchewan, who was one of the party's best vote hustlers.

In 1996, the year Chrétien was putting his Shawinigan chokehold on a ratty protester, Kenney sat down with Harper, then a Reform MP, and told him that the future of Canadian conservatism lay in the immigrant communities that were changing the country. At that time, the Liberal Party owned the vote of new Canadians, but Kenney reasoned that they were a more natural fit for Conservatives. They were entrepreneurial, hard-working, wanted stability, were intolerant of crime and disorder, and had a proud devotion to family. Tory trademarks all.

When Harper became prime minister and named his first cabinet, Kenney was expected to be on the list. He didn't make it. Instead, he was given the assignment of reaching out to ethnic communities. Rather than bemoan his fate, Kenney went at his task with vigour. The first challenge was to rid the new Canadians of their impression that the Conservative Party was racist and anti-immigrant. The second was to convince them that their values in fact coincided with the Tories' entrepreneurial spirit. The third was to create policy-specific appeal. For Eastern Europeans, for example, Harper's hard line on Russia didn't hurt. For the Poles, he dropped the visa requirements to visit Canada. For the Chinese, it was the apology for the hated head tax. For the Taiwanese, it was a go-slow approach to new ties with Beijing. For Macedonians, it was a vow to never again refer to their country as the former Yugoslav Republic of Macedonia. And so on down the line.

The inexhaustible Kenney, who was eventually rewarded with the immigration portfolio, learned how to give greetings in dozens of languages. He showed up on behalf of the government at every ethnic celebration imaginable. Some groups, like the Italians and the Greeks, had historic ties to the Grits too deep to penetrate, and given the government's blanket support for Israel, there could be few inroads into the large Muslim community. But the progress made under Kenney was remarkable. In the election in the year 2000, more than two-thirds of visible minorities voted Liberal. In the 2008 election, the Conservatives did much better in ridings with large concentrations of ethnic voters, unexpectedly winning six of them. By 2010, pollsters were finding that they had virtually caught up to the Liberals in their appeal to ethnic communities. Justin Trudeau, whose father's multicultural approach had scored so heavily with new Canadians, admitted that "in the short term, yes, he has been effective at buying off certain groups."

Kenney was also the architect of a new citizenship guide that bore his party's stamp. It played more boldly to the Tory themes of the monarchy and the military and support for the rule of law, while giving scant notice to Liberal mainstays like the environment and health care. The document placed greater emphasis on the responsibilities of citizenship, advising newcomers on gender equality and issuing warnings against spousal abuse. "When you become a citizen, you're not just getting a travel document into Hotel Canada," said Kenney. "Multiculturalism doesn't just mean anything goes." He had stirred commotion in barring George Galloway's entry to Canada, taking away his right to freedom of speech—a right that virtually all other Western countries were prepared to grant him. He stirred more controversy with remarks suggesting that Ottawa should have a limited role in promoting multiculturalism. "I think it's really neat," he said, "that a fifth-generation Ukrainian can speak Ukrainian—but pay for it yourself." For him, Canada had to be a melting pot as well as a multicultural mosaic.

Given Kenney's lily-white Reform Party background and his strong social conservatism, opponents were always at the ready to throw bigotry charges at him. But they could never find a basis for it. On the Harper front bench, he was emerging as one of the top performers, playing a lead role in the attempt to reshape the political map.

ONE OF HARPER'S perennial problems in trying to expand the reach of his party was his difficulty in appearing inclusive. Coming from the broad middle of the spectrum, other Tory leaders hadn't had that problem and were thus more capable of majority victories. With his work in ethnic communities, Jason Kenney was helping enlarge the tent, but strangely, Harper was still hesitant to talk freely about having designs on a majority government. Such talk, Conservatives still believed, would scare off voters. It was remarkable. No other PM had been like this—afraid to appeal for a majority. It was as though, after four years in power, he was still an outsider. When a top adviser to Michael Ignatieff was asked where he thought Harper was vulnerable, he replied, "People think he's a dictator, a nasty bastard who is power crazy." The methods he used to win his wars—the stonewalling, the smearing of opponents, the trampling of democratic rights and principles—were cold-blooded. At times it was as though he didn't have a conscience to plague him, as though he'd spent too much time immersed in *Richard III.* "Conscience," Shakespeare wrote, "is but a word that cowards use."

The Harper methods were risky, but the government often got away with them. It was as if they'd become so commonplace that they weren't news anymore. Or news that lasted only a day and was forgotten the next. An example was duplicity with regard to the long-gun registry. A report of the Commissioner of Firearms showing that police were making very good use of the gun registry was sent to the public safety minister, Peter Van Loan. The report had to be tabled in Parliament by October 22, 2009, the statutory deadline that the deputy minister, Suzanne Hurtubise, informed Van Loan about. A vote on a private member's bill to scrap the gun registry was scheduled for two weeks later. But the report never got to the MPs in time. Van Loan's office ignored the deadline. The vote was taken and the bill was carried. Van Loan tabled the report, which might have affected the decisions of a number of members, two days after the vote. He knew the gun registry was a hit with police: the number of times they were making use of it had been rising dramatically. But it was another example of the government hiding empirical data from the people.

Stanley Tromp, a freedom of information specialist, issued a report showing that this type of abuse of power in the government was common. His report, called "Fallen Behind," catalogued no less than forty-six examples of stonewalling and the like.

To be noted among them was the stonewalling following the lethal Listeriosis outbreak. Twenty Canadians died after developing the disease, which was said to be connected to faulty food processing at a plant in Toronto. The Canadian Press made an Access to Information request to the Privy Council Office for relevant transcripts and minutes of meetings. The PCO, the office that's supposed to stay arm's length from the political activities of the government, requested a four-month delay. Then, after the four months, it wrote back to say that "the records retrieved do not fall under the scope of this request."

The reason, PCO officials explained, was that the records were handwritten notes as opposed to minutes or transcripts. CP thought this was curious because the word "transcribe" usually suggests handwriting as well. That was one thing. Another was that the Agriculture Department, responding to similar requests, had in fact released handwritten notes.

This too was a one-day story, but there were others that, much to Harper's lament, wouldn't go away. One was the Afghan detainees controversy, which reignited in the fall of 2009 with the testimony of Richard Colvin.

Colvin was the second-highest-ranked diplomat in Afghanistan in 2006 and 2007. Born in Coventry, England, he moved with his family to Hamilton at age sixteen. He graduated from McMaster and the University of Western Ontario, joined the foreign service, and rose steadily, serving in Sri Lanka, Russia, and Israel before going to Afghanistan. He was married briefly to a Russian woman. As a diplomat, he was considered conscientious, mild-mannered, and sincere. He was not a publicity seeker, not the type to step out of line.

Harper's team had done a good job of keeping the diplomatic corps in check. Observers were surprised at the amazingly small number of officials who leaked documents or spoke out of turn. During Paul Martin's tenure, leaks were common. In Harper's Ottawa, there were few to be found. Until Colvin.

On November 18, he came before a special parliamentary committee on the Afghan mission and offered testimony that captives of Canadian soldiers, many of them likely innocent, were subjected to torture. "They were picked up ... during routine military operations, and on the basis typically not of intelligence [reports] but suspicion or unproven denunciation." He added: "We detained and handed over for torture a lot of innocent people." Canada's complicity in this business, he alleged, was costly to the mission. "Instead of winning hearts and minds, we caused Kandaharis to fear the foreigners," he said. "Canada's detainee practices alienated us from the population and strengthened the insurgency."

That was damaging, but there was more to come. Colvin said that as early as May 2006, he had informed the senior military ranks of his findings, noting that they, in turn, would likely have informed General Rick Hillier. But Colvin revealed that he was then told that

Ottawa didn't want to hear his reports. Two senior officials from the Department of Foreign Affairs and International Trade warned him to stop writing memoranda.

Throughout 2006, the Harper government denied knowledge of any torture with respect to the detainees they handed over. Defence Minister Gordon O'Connor initially claimed that the Red Cross was to have informed him if there was a problem. But Colvin said the Red Cross couldn't even get their phone calls taken by the Canadian forces in Kandahar.

The day after Colvin's testimony, Defence Minister Peter MacKay rose in the House of Commons to respond. It was a tense moment. Would MacKay admit that mistakes had been made, say that Colvin's alerts should not have escaped the notice of authorities? Would he say that the government would investigate the allegations, since Colvin appeared to be making them in good faith? Or would he stick with the script the Conservatives so frequently used and attack the messenger?

The last option was a tricky one because diplomats had good public reputations, and Colvin had been on the scene in Afghanistan and appeared to have nothing to gain by coming forward. He was currently working as a senior intelligence officer at Canada's embassy in Washington, a post not given to someone who isn't trusted.

But that didn't hold the Conservatives back. They chose the attack strategy. MacKay took Colvin to the woodshed. The diplomat may have been duped, he said. There were "incredible holes" in the story he was telling. And, the defence minister added, none of the allegations of abuse involving prisoners transferred by the Canadian forces had been proven. Did Colvin have any hard evidence? he wondered. Did he actually see torture taking place? Was he an eyewitness?

After MacKay, Rick Hillier, the retired general who had led the mission, got in on the act. He couldn't recall ever coming across a report from Colvin, he declared. Then, invoking some of the colourful language for which he was noted, Hillier said it sounded as if Colvin was "howling at the moon."

The Liberals alleged a coverup. They insisted that the government call an independent inquiry into the controversy. Their demand was rebuffed. Instead of opening an inquiry, the government moved to shut one down.

Hot on the trail of the detainee file was Peter Tinsley, the head of the Military Police Complaints Commission (MPCC). Appointed in 2005, the twenty-eight-year veteran of the military had run up against a wall in his attempts to conduct public hearings on the matter. Government officials frequently withheld documents from him, and those they released were often blacked out beyond recognition. Normally when they censored documents like this, government officials said they were operating in the interests of national security. But this was a different situation. Tinsley had the security clearance to view such files. In fact, everyone who served on the MPCC had such clearance. But it did them no good. The documents they received were censored anyway.

Tinsley's term was coming up for renewal. He had been warned a couple of months earlier that he wouldn't be offered a second term, but since he was in the middle of the hearings, he thought he should or would be allowed to complete them. He had shown no political bias in his career, which included a stint as a United Nations prosecutor in Kosovo. But he was persistent in trying to get to the bottom of the detainees story. He had caused the PMO headaches even before Colvin's testimony. What might he do now?

No one would ever find out, as it happened, because he was cut loose in the middle of the storm. His departure effectively halted the public hearings. On leaving, Tinsley said that the flow of government documents to his commission had all but ended when Peter MacKay became defence minister. His departure, he said, would send a chill through the other quasi-judicial bodies whose heads were appointed by the government.

As Tinsley was exiting, the government also relieved itself of the services of Paul Kennedy, the head of the Commission for Public Complaints Against the RCMP. Kennedy had clashed with the government when he demanded more independent oversight of the Mounties. He had led an investigation into the Taser death of the Polish immigrant Robert Dziekanski at the hands of RCMP officers in Vancouver.

Tinsley cited the removal of Kennedy and Linda Keen, as well as his own dismissal, as evidence of a pattern: toe the government line or you're gone. Linda Keen had predicted that other firings would follow her own. Having watched her forecast come true, she now wondered, "Are we in an era where tribunals must be more interested in meeting the ends of the government than in doing their jobs?"

Colvin, meanwhile, saw the tides start to shift his way. The diplomatic community expressed outrage and rallied behind him. Initially, twenty-three former ambassadors signed a letter condemning the Conservatives' attempts to discredit him. Soon, that number grew to 125. Defence Minister MacKay kept repeating that there was no evidence of any prisoners being abused.

Then, in a major embarrassment for the government, General Walter Natynczyk, the successor to Rick Hillier, revealed that Canadian soldiers did in fact know the detainees they handed over could be tortured. The general read from military field notes from 2006 that said of an Afghan man, "We then photographed the individual prior to handing him over to ensure that if the Afghan national police did assault him, as had happened in the past, we would have a visual record of his condition." That one phrase, "as had happened in the past," was the giveaway.

The general was contrite, but his comments raised questions. How had he and the military brass not known this earlier? Had they known and been under pressure to keep it quiet? The *Toronto Star* reported that Sandra Buckler, under the vetting system imposed by the PMO, was behind a May 2007 statement in which Natynczyk, then vice chief of defence staff, said there had been no specific abuse complaints.

After Natynczyk made his admission, MacKay tried to hold firm, saying the government had never knowingly been complicit in torture or any violation of international law. But the Liberals' Ujjal Dosanjh hit back hard. "You stand indicted in the court of public opinion of turning a blind eye, of being wilfully blind," he charged. "Ignorance of facts is no defence."

Harper tried to reframe the debate. The opposition was disloyal, he said. It was not supporting the troops. "The opposition," he told the Commons, "is accusing our soldiers of committing war crimes." While touring the HMCS *Quebec* during a visit to Trinidad and Tobago, he elaborated: "Let me just say this: living as we do, in a time when some in the political arena do not hesitate before throwing the most serious of allegations at our men and women in uniform, based on the most flimsy of evidence, remember that Canadians from coast to coast are proud of you and stand behind you, and I am proud of you, and I stand behind you."

His government, meanwhile, continued to deny a Commons special committee the right to see unredacted documents. But on December 10, MPs took the rare step of passing a motion demanding the release of those documents, thus invoking the supremacy of Parliament. Harper was cornered. Having come under so much condemnation for running roughshod over the system, would he dare repudiate the will of the Commons?

Few should have been surprised by his decision. He said no, citing national security concerns and claiming that Parliament was impinging on the rights of the executive by demanding the documents. It was as if to say that Parliament was inferior to the executive, prompting critics to wonder, while not being entirely facetious, whether he had studied the Magna Carta in high school. He appeared once again to be constructing his own constitutional framework. In the coalition crisis, he had taken a hyper-inflated view of his own authority. Now he was doing it again.

His decision brought on an avalanche of criticism from defenders of democracy, all of whom asked how he dared place himself above the will of the people, as expressed through their elected representatives. But there was more to come. Hints from the PMO suggested that he might opt for a long adjournment of Parliament by invoking prorogation once more. That way, temperatures would be allowed to cool, there would be nothing to take attention from the Vancouver Olympics, the government would have time to prepare a new budget, and the opposition's pursuit of the government on the detainees issue would be forestalled.

Debate swirled around the prospect of prorogation for days. Conservative advisers popped up in the media to say it would be a good idea. Several pundits were of the same view, arguing that although it would be another affront to the system—dishonourable, devilish, undemocratic—it was crafty politics. Such was the extent of political contamination in Ottawa that so long as you scored political points, many observers were prepared to give you a pass. Crude politics had come to trump the integrity of the system. Often, reporters weren't holding politicians to the tough standards they used to. They had got so accustomed to leaders trampling over democratic norms that it came to be expected and accepted. It wasn't news anymore. Harper's defiance of Parliament wasn't exactly the Saturday Night Massacre of Watergate fame, but it was serious business. And yet, not many red flags went up. There were few hollering that the system couldn't be flouted this way.

Not sensing any palpable opposition, Harper went ahead and shut down Parliament again. According to PMO officials, he was reluctant to do it, but he listened to the many voices, inside his office and out, telling him he could get away with it. On the day before New Year's Eve, when few were supposed to notice, his office made the announcement. This time, Harper didn't even bother to visit the governor general to make the prorogation request. He only phoned over. And he didn't bother to announce the prorogation himself. He had his press secretary do it.

Parliament would return not in late January, as it usually did, but at the start of March. Proroguing Parliament, the PM's office maintained, would give the government time to recalibrate the agenda and prepare for a new budget. Normally the six-week Christmas break was sufficient for that kind of thing. But not this time. The government needed, or so it was claimed, a longer interval.

Harper had difficulty making the case that he needed this extra time to prepare a legislative agenda, however, because of the impact of prorogation on his existing agenda. It ravaged it, affecting thirty-six bills that were making their way through the system. Normally, the bills would have continued their journey through the legislative process when Parliament returned. But with prorogation, the government had to start over with most such bills when the new session began. Harper's proroguing set back or sent away legislation on consumer product safety, drug laws, child pornography, and a rash of law-and-order measures—legislation that, as Justice Minister Rob Nicholson endlessly complained, the opposition kept holding up.

There was a more persuasive reason for the prorogation. Harper was planning new Senate appointments that would give the Conservatives the most seats in the upper chamber. The Liberals would no longer have a majority, and so there would be less obstructionism. According to the rules, the makeup of the Senate could be changed only when Parliament was dissolved. But rather than come out and offer this rationale, the government kept pushing the less convincing recalibration line.

Because of the timing, reaction to the move was muted for a couple of days, but the storm quickly moved in. *The Globe and Mail*, which had been leading the coverage on the detainees issue, was so incensed that it went to the unusual extent of running a front-page editorial of condemnation. It hadn't run a front-page editorial in years. The *Toronto Star* headlined a column "They Used to Behead Kings for What Harper Is Doing." The prime minister, who was sensitive to what the international media said, took a pummelling abroad as well, especially from *The Economist* magazine. It came forward with an editorial accusing him of operating out of "naked self-interest."

Harper could usually look to the conservative media to defend him. But not this time. Andrew Coyne of *Maclean's* called his reasons for the shutdown "bilge." The *Ottawa Citizen*, a Canwest right-of-centre paper, ran an editorial titled "Cynical Sad Leadership." Having promised a more open and transparent government, the paper said, the Conservatives "take every opportunity to be cynical, secretive and radically partisan."

Some commentators came to the government's defence. Prorogations were common, they said, citing Jean Chrétien's repeated use of the tactic. Chrétien had prorogued Parliament, and sometimes for political advantage, but unlike Harper, he had never done it out of a desperation to keep his government alive and then followed it with another prorogation when under the gun again.

While prorogations were not uncommon, it was rare indeed, according to Queen's University's Ned Franks, to shut down Parliament so that the governing party could avoid censure, votes of confidence, investigations, and the like. Before Harper, it had happened only once, said Franks. That was in 1873, when the government of John A. Macdonald prorogued Parliament to stop a Commons investigation into the Pacific Scandal. "Stephen Harper is entering into uncharted territory, " said Franks. "Is Harper going to resort to this behaviour every time he doesn't want to face up to Parliament?"

As so many had noted, the emasculation of democracy with all power evolving to the prime minister was part of a trend that had begun decades earlier. Many had come to accept the notion that the further the country advanced in time, the more autocratic the system became. Such was the march of progress.

This was all rather stunning to a man like Jim Cross. A Westerner, Cross had worked in the office of Prime Minister Louis St. Laurent back in the 1950s. He was one of a staff of nine. "St. Laurent operated like the chairman of a board of directors," he recalled. "The cabinet ministers developed their own policies. There was no interference with cabinet by PMO staff."

In the PMO, he said, "We were taught to respect the opposition and its role in Parliament. I think back to those days. The parliamentary committees would never be interfered with. You could never send out instructions. It just wasn't done." Cross could understand to some extent how the PMO had to expand its operations with time. But what he was seeing as he looked on present-day Ottawa from his Saskatchewan home appalled him. Harper's tactics, he said, reminded him of Russian leader Vladimir Putin. "It's paranoia as far as I can see. It horrifies me. It really does. I'm afraid the democratic spirit has just evaporated."

At least some of the spirit remained. Diplomats had come together in opposition to the treatment of Colvin. Now a professors' protest against prorogation began with 175 signatures, including some of the most highly reputed legal scholars and political scientists in the country. And now the people themselves got in on the act. Harper and his advisers didn't think the public was terribly interested in the treatment, however brutal, of enemy combatants in Afghanistan. Here they were probably right. Nor, they thought, were they interested in what happened in Parliament, including its being padlocked. Here they were wrong. The prime minister had crossed the line one too many times. In the space of a month, he had got rid of the commissioner leading the charge on the Afghan detainees file; he had seen his government's denials repudiated by Canada's top general; he had defied Parliament's right to documents; and he had shut down Parliament.

The public reaction to the parliamentary suspension shocked Harper and sent him into a dark mood for an extended period. A senior adviser, coming in after the Christmas break, said he was practically climbing the walls. "I can tell you, he was one cranky guy." Harper would not lay the blame for the mess elsewhere, but, the adviser said, "I'm looking at him and I'm thinking that somebody got him into this because it wasn't him."

Although Harper had the final say on prorogation, this was a rare time when he went against his own judgment and accepted the prevailing view of those around him. PMO sources reported that Chief of Staff Guy Giorno was one of many who pushed hard for the prorogation. Opposition to Giorno was increasing. Many Conservatives wanted him replaced by someone capable of providing Harper's office with what it needed—some generosity of spirit. The *National Post* columnist John Ivison, who had a pipeline to the Conservatives, gave voice to the frustrations of many in the party with a piece that charted his record. But Harper kept his chief of staff. He liked the brutal partisans, those who were out not just to defeat opponents but to maim them. And he liked Giorno's discipline in running the PMO. He felt he had improved it.

Within a few days of his prorogation announcement, Harper went into damage-control mode. Traditionally, he did year-end interviews with the TV networks and other big media, but he had avoided most of those. He began to reach out instead to local journalists, those who didn't cover Parliament on a regular basis.

But rationalizing the shutdown was a difficult task. In the first weeks of January, the opposition capitalized on the image of a closed Parliament by going there and opening the doors themselves. The PM had given them two free months of target practice. The Liberals held a series of hearings on the major issues of the day, inviting critics such as Paul Kennedy, Linda Keen, and Peter Tinsley to air their views.

The government began to drop in the opinion polls, and ordinary citizens started to mobilize. The suspicion that Harper cared hardly a whit for democratic principles had been growing, and now it reached critical mass. Anger and outrage filled online media posts. The tools of the new social media were put to use. A Facebook protest gathered over two hundred thousand subscribers. A national day of protest was planned, belying the notion that Canadians were apathetic, that they didn't care about the functioning of their democracy.

The momentum kept building, and then in an instant it was gone. A magnitude 7.3 earthquake struck near the capital of Haiti, sending tens of thousands to their deaths. It was one of the worst natural catastrophes in a century. Images from Port-au-Prince cast a pall over everything. Suddenly, arguments over the propriety of shutting down Parliament, or any other issue of public policy, seemed trifling by comparison.

The priority became a massive aid campaign, and the prime minister set about it in a blaze of activity. No one could accuse him of sitting idle now. Among the many fortunate breaks Harper had received in his career, the timing of this tragedy ranked high. There was a month to go before the Vancouver Olympics, and until the earthquake, he was destined to be on the defensive that entire month. The opposition parties had the wind in their sails, and the national protest day was promising to be a dramatic event. But Haiti totally consumed the airwaves for two weeks running, knocking prorogation and the planned protest to the back pages.

Harper hardly had the image of a great humanitarian or friend of the United Nations. But given the opportunity to change the political channel and lead a humanitarian effort, he did so with great aplomb, winning applause from all quarters. He dispatched the military in a timely fashion; made good use of his cabinet, most notably Peter MacKay and Lawrence Cannon; was more than generous with financial aid; played host to a quickly assembled international conference on the crisis; and shared the spotlight with a shaken Michaëlle Jean, the Haitian-born governor general.

The epic catastrophe also allowed Harper to showcase the rebuilt armed forces. Canada's once sluggish and ill-equipped peacetime military was now well tuned and ready to respond to a crisis. When the 2004 tsunami struck, Canadian medics and engineers had to wait days to hitch a ride, as it was put, to get there. But this time, Canada's big new military aircraft were doing the job.

By either dexterity or good fortune or a combination of both, Stephen Harper had always shown himself capable of bouncing back from adversity. When his Alliance Party was going nowhere, events conspired to give him an opportunity to lead a drive for the unification of the right. With his budget fiasco in 2008, he looked dead and buried, but the coalition stumbled, giving him the opening to respond with dramatic force. Now, a catastrophe in a Caribbean island, of all things, provided him with an opportunity to get out of trouble once more, and again he took full advantage.

The national day of protest took place as planned, two weeks after the calamity. More than thirty-five hundred people gathered in Ottawa to demand that Parliament be immediately reconvened. Toronto had an estimated seven thousand protesters, and hundreds showed up in other cities as well. "The House of Commons is supposed to be the house of the people," shouted Jack Layton to the assembled crowd. "Mr. Harper, unlock the doors of the people's house!" Harper skirted questions about the protest, saying the government was very occupied and had a lot to do to get its agenda in place.

Harper then played host at the Vancouver Olympics. The Games got off to a dispiriting start when an athlete was killed in the luge competition, and the opening ceremonies were marred by malfunctioning stanchions, an absence of francophone content, and the tawdry sight of the torch being transported by Wayne Gretzky in the back of what looked like a pickup truck as it was chased by drunks along Vancouver streets. In the first week of the Games, the weather was bad, Canadian performances sub-par, and press reviews negative. But in the second week, the embarrassing Games turned into the spectacular Games. Canadians won record numbers of medals, the weather turned, and events ran smoothly. As any prime minister would, Harper basked in the glow, trying to get as much media attention as possible. Going into the Games, the opposition had missed an ideal opportunity to embarrass him by drawing the link between politics and sport. On the battlefield of Parliament, Harper had just run for cover when the going got tough. As an example of sportsmanship it was woebegone. If politics were an Olympic event, he would have been expelled from the Games. But the Liberals were not in the same league as the Conservatives in exploiting opportunity.

To close the Olympics, Harper the hockey fan got his wish when the Canadians beat the Americans in overtime to win the gold medal. A more ideal outcome couldn't have been imagined. It played perfectly to Harper's bid to stir a new patriotism.

His Conservatives expected to see a healthy bounce in the polls from the Olympics. They had helped fund the Own the Podium program, and the PM was everywhere in the news. But very little bounce came. Conservative numbers were down from the period before prorogation, and the prime minister's own approval ratings trailed those of his party. People hadn't forgotten what happened as the new year was about to dawn.

CHAPTER EIGHTEEN

True Colours

When Scott Brison sat down for dinner with Stephen Harper in November 2003, shortly before the merger of the conservative parties, the subject of social conservatism was on his mind. This was not long after one Alliance Party member, Larry Spenser, had made a statement in favour of criminalizing homosexuality. Brison was annoyed that Harper had allowed Spenser, an American-born former Baptist pastor, to resign voluntarily from his post as the party's family issues critic. He would have preferred to see Harper fire him.

Brison raised the gay rights issue, making reference to Elsie Wayne, a veteran Tory MP not known to have liberal views on the subject. "I've had enough troubles in the PC Party with Elsie Wayne, and I'm looking at your caucus and I see a whole bunch of Elsie Waynes." Harper responded forthrightly, Brison recalled, saying, "You've got to understand that social conservatism is an important part of our support base, and we will always have that as part of what we offer."

Though Harper clearly wanted the talented Brison to be an important player in a newly merged party, he was frank enough to make it clear that pressure from the Tories would not move him off his social conservative goals. "To Harper's credit," recalled Brison, "he didn't say I could come on board and help shape the party to be more socially progressive." Brison left the dinner saying that the party's take presented problems for him. In a short time, he crossed the floor to join the Liberals.

What was noteworthy in the years that followed, thought Brison, was that Harper remained truer to social conservative values than he did to economic conservative ones. The party had a strong social conservative cast, and the arrival of Guy Giorno as chief of staff had made the cast more influential. As well, Stephen Harper was a social conservative himself. His thinking was set forth in a 2003 article in which he reasoned that given the gains of economic conservatism, it was time to press forward on social conservatism. The success of the Reagan–Thatcher economic revolution, he noted, undermined the liberal-left consensus. "Socialists and liberals began to stand for balanced budgeting, the superiority of markets, welfare reversal, free trade and some privatization," he wrote. Now the problem was the social agenda of the modern left. "We need to rediscover Burkean or social conservatism because a growing body of evidence points to the damage the welfare state is having on our most important institutions, particularly the family." Conservatives understand, said Harper, that "politics is a moral affair."

The party's moral faction was relatively quiet over the years, as Harper was wary of political repercussions. But in 2010 the pitch changed. Harper began to show his Burkean colours. Issues previously off the table came to the fore. Abortion and gay rights and religion were in the news. The government announced a review of affirmative action programs. The justice department announced a crackdown on drugs, gambling, and illicit sex. In addition came the decision to scrap the mandatory long census form, a move motivated in part by a wish to keep the state from probing people's private lives.

Controversy began when Harper announced a new plan to make maternal health the focus of foreign assistance at the G8 and G20 summits to be held in Canada in June. That naturally raised the question of whether maternal health programs would include funding for abortions and contraceptives. Harper said no, moving the issue to the forefront of debate.

Armed with statistics estimating that 13 percent of maternal deaths worldwide were from abortions, opponents, including Secretary of State Hillary Clinton, put the prime minister on the defensive. But because of the pronounced presence of pro-lifers in his caucus, he had to walk a fine line. He had killed a private member's pro-life bill on the eve of the 2008 election, dismaying social conservatives, whose efforts in the campaign were somewhat lacklustre as a result. He couldn't issue another direct rebuff, so in defence of the summit plan he explained that he only wanted to fund maternal health projects that did not divide Canadians.

But what he had managed to do, unintentionally, was exactly what he had warned social conservatives in his party against doing—giving their beliefs a high profile. Social conservatives narrowed the party's appeal, making the tent smaller. There were some who were confident, however, that the party wouldn't suffer for it. By raising such issues, they were activating the party base, as evidenced by the thousands of anti-abortion activists who were soon demonstrating on Parliament Hill. The base was small, but the new political dynamic made winning with smaller numbers much easier. If the conservative base was 30 percent and the Liberal base on a divided left was roughly the same, the odds favoured the party with the more committed members, the better organization, the better funding.

As abortion came to the forefront, so too did other causes of the party's right side. Gay rights hit the headlines—never good news for the party—when the Harper Conservatives chose not to fund Toronto's gay pride parade. It was an issue Harper couldn't win on. In the previous year, when his government did fund the parade, it upset the theo-cons.

Then came a book from the journalist Marci Macdonald called *The Armageddon Factor: The Rise of Christian Nationalism in*

Canada. Though knocked for being overstated, it showed clearly that evangelical Christians were gaining influence in the country. Three theo-cons—Chief of Staff Guy Giorno; his deputy, Darrel Reid; and Harper's policy director, Paul Wilson—held major positions at the top of the PMO power structure. Reid was a former head of Focus on the Family Canada and Wilson was the former director of an evangelical training program in the capital. Tom Flanagan described the trio as "a social conservative echo chamber around the prime minister." Though not wishing to give them too much control, Harper, he said, had never made a secret of his wish to have the believers on board.

As part of its economic stimulus package, for instance, his government doled out funding to fourteen private Christian colleges. It wasn't something federal governments were in the habit of doing. The colleges received more than $26 million. Other funding was sprayed around to the Christian right. In Winnipeg, the Christian charity Youth for Christ secured a $3.2-million infrastructure grant for a new community centre. Manitoba NDPer Pat Martin found it strange to see stimulus money going to a group seeking converts. He sarcastically wondered if a group called Youth for Allah would be so lucky.

Some analysts, like Brian Lee Crowley of the Macdonald-Laurier Institute, saw the increased visibility of the religious right as part of a growing trend to counter the rampant secularism of the recent past. "We're entering an era in which faith, in the largest sense, is becoming a powerful political force," he observed. The people of faith who were most politically active were the evangelical Christians and the Jewish community, both very much in Harper's corner. The government was continuing with its near-unconditional support for Israel, becoming the country's foremost backer the world over now that the Bush administration was gone.

The support for Israel became a focus of furor at Rights and Democracy, the Montreal-based group funded by Ottawa. Created in the Mulroney years, it was supposed to operate at arm's length from the government in its promotion of human rights, civil society, and democratic development. The upheaval came when the Harper government stacked the board with pro-Israeli hardliners who, objecting to grants being awarded to Palestinian groups, overpowered the organization.

Complaining of psychological harassment and intimidation, staff rebelled. Board members resigned or were suspended. There was a break-in at headquarters. The president of the organization, in the midst of all the upheaval, died. Commentators portrayed it as a putsch, boardroom terror. A devastating account by Paul Wells in *Maclean's* made clear what hard-edged ideology can do to civil society.

For NGOs and the like, the term "arm's length" was taking on a new meaning in the Harper era. It meant well within reach of the brass knuckles. The intimidation tactics were too much even for some on the Conservative side. But Harper insiders like John Weissenberger and Mark Cameron maintained that the press and the public were missing something. When Canadians elect a Conservative government, they are voting in a conservative philosophy and expect to see that philosophy reflected, not just by MPs but in other areas of the government, such as boards and agencies. So, to think that Harper would just leave the organizations topped up with liberals, they said, was a bit strange.

"Yes, there is a lot of merit in having independent bodies handle certain files, but the challenge is that ultimately the government is accountable," said Weissenberger. "So if they're doing something that the minister feels is not in the interests of Canadians, then you've got to make the tough call." The board members aren't elected by the people. Not having to face the electorate, he said, they often reflect an ivory tower view that's out of touch with average Canadians. To the argument that Liberals didn't interfere with Rights and Democracy, the response was that they didn't have to; they already had the people on the board they wanted.

The ideological axe fell not only at Rights and Democracy but at several other NGOs. Kairos, the human rights arm of eleven Canadian church organizations, had its entire $7-million overseas budget chopped because, or so it certainly seemed, of its positions on the Middle East. The Canadian Council on International Co-operation, a group that coordinates public policy on foreign aid, had its budget cut by two-thirds, apparently because its director spoke out about a chill being spread through the NGO community on account of Harper's heavy hand. The group MATCH, focused exclusively on the rights of women in the developing world, was also shut down by funding cuts.

WHILE HARPER HAD TO BE SENSITIVE about pushing his ideology too hard, overall trends suggested the right was gaining more acceptance in the culture of the country. The Manning Centre for Building Democracy, a think-tank created by the founder of Reform to promote conservative values, released an opinion study by influential pollster Allan Gregg indicating that the traditional Canadian centre, the mainstream, was inclining to the right on a number of indicators. The new dynamic was being forged by a confluence of factors, the media being one of them.

In the media, conservatives had taken the balance of power and were looking to increase it. But in the spring of 2010, Harper got a major scare with the auctioning of the biggest conservative newspaper chain, Canwest. The Liberal-leaning Torstar chain was said to have the inside track on getting the conservative flagship, the *National Post*, which it likely would have buried, as well as a slew of other big-city papers. Such a sale would have had a major impact on the journalistic culture, shifting the balance from the Tories back to the Liberals. But Harper's legendary luck held. An eleventh-hour offer by a group led by the *National Post*'s chairman, Paul Godfrey, won the bidding war, keeping the papers in the conservative stable.

Quebecor Media then announced that it was time for a right-of-centre television network in Canada. The planned network was expected to be modelled after Fox News, the highly successful right-wing shout machine south of the border. Fox practised a kind of advocacy journalism that was cued on confrontation. It polarized the debate in the United States and was regarded by traditional journalists as toxic for the business. The Quebecor plan—which was spearheaded by Kory Teneycke, Harper's former director of communications—would have to pass regulatory hurdles, but the betting was that the new network would be up and running before long, giving Harper's conservatism another strong voice.

After this news broke, it was revealed that Harper had lunched in New York the previous year with Roger Ailes, the president of the Fox News Channel, and the chairman of News Corp., Rupert Murdoch. Kory Teneycke was also at the meeting. A few months later he left the PMO, and a few months after that he went to Quebecor, where he began exploring the possibility of Fox News North. "We're doing well in print," Teneycke said, analyzing conservative inroads in the media. "I think we're doing well in radio. I think we're doing all right online. But we're doing terribly on television." His view of television wasn't shared by many other analysts, but he was well on his way to doing something about it.

For a PM fixated on controlling the message, having a conservative advantage in the media was vital. In his position with Quebecor, Teneycke wasn't just working the television end—he was also overseeing the coverage of Sun Media, one of the biggest newspaper chains in the country. Although it ran egregiously counter to any pretence of objective journalism to have the former spokesman for the prime minister in such a role, there was no outcry from other media outlets. Teneycke quickly changed the reporting staff in the Ottawa bureau, dumping Greg Weston, an astute columnist who played no favourites. The chain had been getting more even-handed in its coverage before Teneycke's arrival, but it now took on the look of a product with which Teneycke's former boss could be most pleased.

In trying to make further inroads, conservatives continued their push against the CBC by accusing the network of Liberal bias. That kind of strategy—seen, for example, in the virulent campaign waged against the CBS and Dan Rather—had paid dividends for the right in the U.S. A new strike against the CBC was occasioned by a remark from the pollster Frank Graves, who did public opinion analyses for the network. With the Tories beginning to show their social conservative colours, Graves recommended that the Grits sharpen the lines of the debate between right and left by invoking what he termed "a culture war." The Liberals should, he said, pit "cosmopolitanism versus parochialism, secularism versus moralism, Obama versus Palin, tolerance versus racism and homophobia, democracy versus autocracy." Stop worrying about the West, he advised, because there was no hope for serious gains there.

Ignatieff had in fact been showing some inclination to sharpen the divide. He'd forced all his caucus members to vote against a bill to scrap the long-gun registry, had promised to kill $6 billion in corporate tax cuts, and had hit Harper hard on the question of support for abortion in developing countries. Graves said they had to go even further. The strategy of trying to be all things to all people had to be discarded. Harper had built a unified and committed party by appealing to his base. "It isn't fiscal conservatism which sustains this true-believer status," said Graves. "It's a sense of moral mission and rightness." But Liberals, he said, had no such commitment or sense of mission. They were scattered and demoralized. Hence his argument for a culture war.

That his advice touched a nerve was clear by the anger with which it was greeted in Tory circles. Led by Kory Teneycke and Doug

Finley, they launched a campaign against Graves, attempting to have the network drop him. The party officially lodged a complaint with the CBC, and Finley sent out a mass email to supporters asking them to protest and to contribute to the Tory war chest. "This episode," he wrote, "demonstrates once again that we Conservatives are up against a powerful array of vested interests. Vested interests who want us to go back to the days of Jean Chrétien and Paul Martin." The CBC didn't bend to the pressure. The network kept Graves and dismissed Finley's response as "paranoia-tinged."

A year earlier, Harper had spoken to the National Ethnic Press and Media Council of Canada. "Our government does not tell journalists what to say or attempt to intimidate those with whom it disagrees," the prime minister said with a straight face. "Instead, we believe strongly that Canadians' freedom is enhanced when journalists are free to pursue the truth, to shine light into dark corners, and to insist on the process of holding governments accountable."

In 2010, it was Michael Ignatieff's turn to address the same group. He noted that a few months after making his speech, Harper shut down Parliament and was turning the access-to-information system into denial-of-information. "He leads the most secretive government in Canadian history," he declared. In reference to its attitude on openness, Iggy pointed to an outburst made by Conservative Senator Nancy Ruth. Addressing groups that had gathered in Ottawa to oppose the government's stance on abortion in foreign aid, Ruth told them that they should just "shut the fuck up."

HARPER'S CAMPAIGN TO CONTROL THE MESSAGE and intimidate those trying to put out a different message continued with a passion into 2010. As Tom Flanagan had noted, the prime minister's suspicion of the world around him and his obsession to control it was something that was deep-seated, not to be understood and not to be changed.

Harper scored another blow against the checks and balances in the system when he issued an order stipulating that staffers and advisers in his office and other cabinet offices could not be called to testify before parliamentary committees. Harper invoked the convention of ministerial responsibility, saying that the decisions of the office were ultimately up to the ministers and they would be the only ones to testify. But critics saw it as another way of stifling democracy. Many past scandals—not the least of which was Watergate—had hinged on the testimony of advisers. In Ottawa, cabinet staffers were sometimes involved in controversial developments, and in many cases they knew more than their ministers. In some cases they could have knowledge of wrongdoing by the minister. Now they were immune from testifying.

Giving rise to the new edict was the refusal of Dmitri Soudas, Harper's new director of communications, to appear before a Commons committee on access to information. The committee was examining a controversy involving Public Works Minister Christian Paradis, whose office was suspected of interfering in the release of documents from his department. The Harper shop had long denied there was any such interference by ministers' offices. But it appeared to be caught red-handed when Sebastien Togneri, the parliamentary affairs director for Paradis, ordered the retrieval of a sensitive report that was headed to the Canadian Press. CP had asked for the report under access laws. When he heard the document was being released, Togneri shot off an email to a senior official in the information section, saying "Well, unrelease it." The document was an annual report on the real estate portfolio at public works. It was later released with 107 pages blacked out.

This was one of many such stories that made it difficult for the Harper team to sustain the line that it wasn't pressuring the public service to withhold potentially damaging documents. Its reputation took another hit with the release of a report by Suzanne Legault, the interim information commissioner, in which she graded government departments on a scale from A to F. The foreign affairs department, accused of serial obfuscation on the Afghan detainees file, may have set the all-time record for the worst grade. It didn't even merit an F. Legault said the obstructionism at foreign affairs was so blatant that she had to create a special red-alert category. Her report tended to confirm what critics had been alleging all along.

Also of major interest was the Privy Council Office, the department that was supposed to be setting the example for all others. It received a D grade. Previous governments had also fared miserably in the reports of other information commissioners. But under the Conservatives, Legault warned, the right of Canadians to obtain federal documents was running the risk of being "totally obliterated."

By coincidence, on the same day that Legault's report was released, Guy Giorno, who wielded enormous power but was rarely seen or heard from, made an appearance at a committee examining the issue. Opposition members fumbled the opportunity to hold him to account, however, consuming most of their allotted time with long soap-box preambles to their unpointed questions. Giorno coasted through the hearing, not giving an inch. The previous fall, a parliamentary committee had recommended that changes be made to the Access to Information Act to improve the system. Justice Minister Rob Nicholson nixed the recommendations, saying they were unnecessary. Giorno essentially defended that viewpoint, even with so many clear examples of abuse of the process laid out by the information commissioner and journalists.

The access-to-information system was what the Alliance Party had used with great effect to embarrass the Chrétien government on numerous controversies, including Shawinigate and the sponsorship scandal. Harper was well aware of its value. As opposition leader, he wrote in the *Montreal Gazette* in the year before he came to power: "Information is the lifeblood of a democracy. Without adequate access to key information about government policies and programs, citizens and parliamentarians cannot make informed decisions and incompetent or corrupt governance can be hidden under a cloak of secrecy."

When he became prime minister, his attitude appeared to undergo a shift of considerable proportions. It often took the Conservatives twice as long as previous governments to handle access requests. Sometimes it took six months to a year. His government started imposing prohibitive fees on requests at the foreign affairs department. Evidence that the PMO put pressure on bureaucrats to hide sensitive information accumulated. Documents were more likely to be blacked out than ever. In one case, reported by Ken Rubin, an authority on access requests, the government blocked portions of a published biography of Barack Obama that was part of a briefing for the PM. "That's how ridiculous the situation has become," said Rubin. Though other governments had resorted to similar tactics, none was in the same league as Harper's, he said.

A telling moment came at hearings of the Military Police Complaints Commission into the detainees controversy. Diplomat Richard Colvin made the point that if the pertinent documents were released by the government, they would reveal some crucial information about the whole affair. Speaking for the government, Alain Prefontaine, a justice department lawyer, announced that he had seen the uncensored documents and didn't find anything important. Glenn Stanford, the chairman of the proceedings, wondered if he was hearing Prefontaine correctly. Indeed he was, the lawyer responded. If there was nothing critical in the documents, asked Stanford, then why weren't they being released? "Because," said Prefontaine, "disclosure would be injurious to either national defence, international relations, or national security."

The embarrassments piled up. It was time for Speaker of the House Peter Milliken to issue his ruling on the power of the executive versus the power of the legislature, in response to Harper's refusal to release to Parliament the documents on the detainees affair. Milliken ruled, as most expected he would, on the side of Parliament. He said that the government had contravened the privilege of the House, a privilege that touches on the "very foundations" of the parliamentary system. "It is the view of the chair," Milliken declared, "that accepting an unconditional authority of the executive to censor the information provided to Parliament would in fact jeopardize the very separation of powers that is purported to lie at the heart of our parliamentary system and the independence of its constituent parts."

In plain English, the ruling was saying that the prime minister was acting like an autocrat and needed to learn to respect the ways of a democracy.

The defeat appeared not to bother Harper much. He still held to what he considered a good rationale for his actions—the question of national security. This provided him, or any PM who wished to use it, with a basis for operating in secret on many files.

Milliken's ruling, which was widely applauded, charged both sides to come up with a compromise on the national security question. The Conservatives were in no hurry. They wanted to delay the release of the files as long as possible, and the Liberals acquiesced to going beyond the deadline set by Milliken. Though it was not certain, reasonable observers were left to infer from the extremes to which the Tories were going to shield the documents that they had something serious to hide—it being that they had long known of the torture of the Afghan detainees and may well have been engaged in a political coverup ever since.

THE SPRING OF 2010 was yet another cynical political season when debate was dominated not so much by policy discussion, not so much by intelligent deliberation on the future course for the country, but by a series of controversies and mini-scandals, displays of extreme partisanship, and relentless government efforts at damage control.

Legislatively, the major enterprise was the budget bill. Flaherty's budget had run a smart, compromising course, maintaining enough stimulus to keep the economy moving while at the same time beginning to cut into a deficit that was estimated at more than $50 billion. But even on the budget bill, the government stood accused once again of trying to run roughshod over the system. Bill C-9 was supposed to be a budget bill, but it came with innumerable measures that had little or nothing to do with the nation's finances. It was, as critics put it, the advance of the Harper agenda by stealth, yet another abuse of the democratic process. The bill was a behemoth. It was 904 pages, with 23 separate sections and 2,208 individual clauses. It contained important measures that normally would proceed individually through the system, getting the attention they deserved. In this bill, they were hidden under a mountain.

As a Reform MP, Harper had complained of the Liberals doing this same thing. He said of one piece of legislation that "the subject matter of the bill is so diverse that a single vote on the content would put members in conflict with their own principles." The bill he referred to was 21 pages long—or 883 pages shorter than the one he was now putting before Parliament.

His omnibus bill contained measures that would facilitate the privatization of Canada Post's overseas services, make way for the sell-off of some or all of Atomic Energy Canada Ltd., and give the minister of the environment the authority to forgo environmental assessments for federally funded infrastructure projects. The Green Party's Elizabeth May accused the government of using the screen of a budget bill to gut environmental law. "This is rolling over environmental assessment in favour of development," she declared. She wondered how this could be happening against the backdrop of the ongoing oil spill in the Gulf of Mexico.

With the bill, May said, Harper was also once again spurning the Supreme Court. The Court's decision on the Red Chris mine in B.C. had the effect of saying that environmental assessments had to cover an entire proposed project, not just a component of it. With the omnibus bill, explained May, the minister of the environment could scope a project as narrowly as he wished. In the year's previous budget bill, the government had quietly gutted the Navigable Waters Protection Act, which, she noted, had been law since 1867.

Bill C-9 was seen by some observers as another example of Harper taking the lead from the U.S. system, where giant budget bills traditionally carried a great variety of measures. South of the border, however, they couldn't force through such measures by threatening to call an election. In Ottawa, Ignatieff's Liberals opposed many parts of the legislation but passed it anyway because they were afraid to go to the polls. Canadians, one wag joked, were thrown under the omnibus.

More manoeuvring that had the look of taking its inspiration from the U.S., in this case Republican America, was seen in a pitch to social conservatives with a plan to go after organized crime. The target of the new regulations were drugs, gambling, and illicit sex—a crackdown on them all.

With the plan, selling a few ounces of marijuana or keeping a common bawdy house or bookmaking could now result in several years of prison. In going after the small-time players, police and prosecutors were given new powers with respect to wiretaps, bail regimes, parole rules, and the capacity to seize proceeds from crime.

The measures were seen, particularly by the cynically minded, as helping generate enough criminals to help justify the government's new $9-billion jail-building binge. Prior to the announcement by Justice Minister Rob Nicholson, Stockwell Day, the treasury board secretary, had pointed to the increase in the number of unreported crimes as a possible justification. That prompted considerable derision, since the perpetrators of unreported crimes were unlikely to be apprehended. The jump in unreported crimes was a statistic the government liked to use in defence of its law and order campaign, but these were typically milder offences.

Sceptics also pounced on the government's use of the dire-sounding "organized crime" label when in fact the offences the Conservatives were talking about were mainly small-time stuff from prostitutes, bookies, and marijuana dealers.

The crackdown was another sign that Harper, on domestic policy, was moving rightward, that his Reform Party instincts and those of the party base were becoming more pronounced. Politically it was a difficult strategy to understand, since it was generally conceded that the Tories needed more moderate-side appeal to grow.

Noteworthy also was the way in which the prime minister leapt to the defence of dinosaurish party loyalists like Rob Anders who faced a challenge for the nomination in his Calgary riding. Anders had gained notoriety for being the only MP to vote against making Nelson Mandela an honorary citizen of Canada. He said China's hosting the 2008 Olympics was the equivalent of Hitler's Germany hosting the 1936 games. For these and other reasons, local constituents began organizing to have someone they deemed less neanderthal represent them. But Anders was a staunch long-time Harper loyalist, and the party, led by Doug Finley, crushed the democratic effort to remove him. The equivalent of a SWAT team from party headquarters seized control of the riding association, taking membership lists, funds, everything. Finley refused to explain his behaviour, but insiders said he felt the candidate who might replace Anders was too liberal.

Harper had pledged in 2006 to ensure that party nominations were conducted in a fair and democratic manner. The suppressing of the democratic initiative of the riding association was about as distant from the grassroots goals of early Reformers as could be imagined. Duff Conacher, who was charting the government's progress on

its accountability promises, cited this as yet another broken promise. According to Democracy Watch, the government had broken
approximately half of its democratic-reform pledges. Bad news for
those wanting more checks in the system came with Conacher's
announcement that he was departing the watchdog group, leaving its
future in doubt.

THE ECONOMY was starting to move briskly during this period. Job
growth was spirited, inflation was next to nil, and the banking system
was strong. In many ways, the Canadian economy was an example to
the world, and it was all splendidly timed because Canada was about
to play host to the G8 and G20 summits. Because this was a major
moment for him, the prime minister spent a great deal of time preparing for the meetings, which were being held, oddly, in two locations—
the Ontario cottage country town of Huntsville and downtown
Toronto.

The run-up to the summits was filled with embarrassing headlines. There was the matter, above all, of the billion-dollar price tag. It
included the re-creation at the international media centre of a cottage
country landscape featuring an artificial lake, fake trees, a fake dock,
and the call of a fake loon. The "fake lake" quickly became the subject
of ridicule by national and international media.

Going in, the summits were overshadowed by sideshows, and the
same happened when they began. Violent clashes between police and
protesters turned downtown Toronto into a war zone, and though
there were no serious injuries, a thousand protesters were carted off
to detention centres. As is so often the case with these confrontations,
blame was apportioned according to the ideology of those doing the
apportioning. The right said the security forces behaved commend-
ably. The left said they turned Toronto into a police state.

With all the costs and all the security nightmares, why, observers wondered, didn't they just do a video conference? One of the

arguments against the idea is that it doesn't allow for arm-twisting in the corridors. Harper benefited from that very activity in gaining an agreement at the G8 summit to increase funding for maternal and child health—without a fight over abortion spending. More significantly, at the G20 he helped steer participants to an accord that would see wealthy nations halve their deficits over the next three years to avoid debt crises that could spark another recession. The agreement was more a statement of noble intentions than anything else, since some countries had already embarked on the deficit-cutting path and one, Japan, balked at the agreement, making it a G19. Also, because the accord was non-binding, many other nations were likely to have forgotten their pledges by the time the next summit rolled around. There was also a concern, emphasized by the United States, that reducing long-term deficits sometimes comes at the expense of short-term growth. If growth started to fall off, the G20 accord would be quickly repudiated.

But it would have been a setback for the Canadian summit and for Harper personally had there been no summit accord, and if the spin doctors were to be believed, the prime minister had played a central role in achieving one. He had worked for months in advance to convince other leaders that deficit targets were necessary. Luck again was with him as an economic meltdown in Greece in advance of the summit demonstrated the dangers of not acting on debt. Initially, the chances of reaching agreement in Toronto looked grim. Brazil, Argentina, India, Japan, and others were all balking. The Canadian delegation, along with the United States and Germany, then put on a big push. Germany's Angela Merkel raised the stakes with comments to the international press about the importance of a deal. Harper convinced France's Nicolas Sarkozy to warn the summiteers of market reaction should no agreement be reached. Sarkozy also made the vital point that the targets were only voluntary, so why not sign on? With the Japanese still balking, Harper smartly decided to give them an exemption, the idea being that nineteen out of twenty isn't bad.

The summit came as further evidence that the prime minister, after years of on-the-job training, had broadened his perspective and become more of a global man. He was a far cry now from the narrow-scoped regionalist who first came to power.

Near the close of 2009 he had visited India and, at long last, China. In Beijing he suffered an extraordinary rebuke when the premier, Wen Jiabao, publicly upbraided him for staying away so long. As Harper looked on stone-faced, the premier said, "Five years is too long a time for China–Canada relations." Few could argue the point. Harper had held to ideology too determinedly and failed to see the shifting world tides. But he finally came around to accepting the word of the critics, many of them in the media, and made his way to the Middle Kingdom. He now moved quickly on the Chinese relationship and built a good rapport with the leadership.

With India he re-engaged in a way Canadian governments had not done in a long time, establishing three new trade missions, signing a civilian nuclear cooperation agreement, and making tentative steps on opening trade. With Africa, he had initially shown little interest, but changed his ways, the maternal health initiative being a case in point.

He was beginning to grasp the new reality—that the West was in relative decline and new relationships had to be fostered. "The desire to act according to certain principles has come face to face with reality," said Jennifer Welsh, a foreign policy expert at Oxford who advised the Martin government. "If that is how we define maturing, then they have matured."

With this prime minister, so much depended on the outcome of the battle within, the fight between what his ideological reflexes told him and what real-world experience taught him. In many areas the former was still winning, the issue of climate change being a foremost example, one where his government continued to doddle as emission levels intensified. His team saw the issue primarily in terms of political management, and after four and a half years they felt, in contrast to prevailing wisdom, they had done well.

A note from a former PMO insider spelled out the strategy. "Harper managed climate change closely ... Once Obama was elected, he moved Jim Prentice to the file to assure the oil and gas guys that they had someone who understood their views, and immediately declared Canada would do whatever the U.S. did; i.e. he not only borrowed Obama's credibility on the issue, he headed off the possibility of U.S. carbon tariffs on everything we sell them." Smart stuff, said the insider. "He positioned himself to say he was mimicking Obama when speaking to enviro-crazies and that he was just heading off enviro-protectionism when talking to the business community."

Though the controversies at the G20 tended to dominate media coverage, Harper emerged from the conference with his reputation enhanced. He was respected enough internationally to arbitrate accords like the one just fashioned.

These were heady times for him. To host the Olympic Games and two prestigious world summits within the space of a few months was an absolute rarity for any leader. And the high times were not yet concluded. Now came the visit of the Queen to celebrate Canada's 143rd birthday. These visits happened frequently and had taken on a more routine look, but Harper was an ardent supporter of the monarchy and wanted to show it. The royal ties played to his sense of tradition, and the monarchy remained for him a cornerstone of Canadian identity.

The timing of the Queen's visit was ideal in that she touched down when the country, despite the truncheons on Toronto streets, was in a frame of mind to celebrate. Canada had led the world with its gold medal performance at the Olympics, and the country's economy was showing the way as well. The crowds this time appeared to appreciate the Queen's presence more. She was aptly described by Ban Ki-moon, the U.N. secretary general, as the "anchor of our age," and she carried herself with warmth and dignity and a sense of history. Debates over the future of the monarchy were barely in evidence this time, and the prime minister delighted in her presence.

Four and a half years had passed since Stephen Harper came to power, and it seemed in these days that the sunless man was more comfortable in the position than ever before, that he was enjoying the power, the prestige, and the significance of high office.

It was always in the good times, however, that this prime minister tended to overreach and press forward on ideological ambitions, and this occurred again with his decision to alter the census-taking process. The backlash was unforeseen and brought with it a rash of charges that he was the all-controlling ideologue that so many imagined.

Harper's support numbers dropped. The forces arrayed against his divide-and-conquer style of governance were growing. But he had built a hardened core of conservative support, one which could sustain him, one which could continue to change Canada in fundamental ways.

CHAPTER NINETEEN

A Question of Character

It had taken only four-plus years. In that time, the liberal consensus that had dominated Canada for so long had become imperilled. It was one man's doing. Stephen Harper had come to power and implanted himself with a force that the old system could barely withstand. He undermined Liberal leaders, he undermined Liberal beliefs, he undermined Liberal support.

The old Grits cowered. The party that had brought in tax increases whenever the country was in need was now afraid to even daintily raise the prospect—even with the country in deep deficit. Such was the impact of Stephen Harper that Liberal leaders knew they would be savaged in the marketplace if they did so.

The old Grits were the party of national programs. Harper erased their national daycare program and their Kelowna Accord and their Green Shift, leaving no big thirst to bring them back.

The once progressive Liberals looked on as Harper brought forth a law-and-order regimen, a hardening of the penal system, a lower regard for civil liberties. Afraid of being labelled "soft on crime," the Liberals offered only tepid resistance.

The new Conservatism was boldly evident in the revitalized and glorified military. Though the defence build-up had begun under Paul Martin, it was the Tories who changed the mentality, moving a country that was at home with dovish soft power to one that looked upon military might with more favour.

The Harper tide meant that multiculturalism, a Trudeauvian showpiece, was less in vogue. The Conservatives introduced new limits to tolerance and gave the country a modern citizenship guide that was widely applauded. At the same time, they were cutting in to the age-old Liberal domination of immigrant communities, opening the eyes of new Canadians to a different political partner.

Politically, the Grits, as the old saying goes, didn't know what hit them. Harper was withering on the attack. He bloodied them so badly that for much of the time, they were cratering below the 30 percent mark in public support. For a party that had governed the country for two-thirds of the twentieth century, it was pure humiliation.

Harper built a better organization than the Liberals, a better campaign team, a better fundraising system. With his financial advantage, he pummelled their leaders between elections with personal attack ads. In the House of Commons, having prepared for Question Period better than any other prime minister before him, he was merciless. He repeatedly turned votes into confidence tests, knowing that the Liberals feared triggering an election. He then watched them, tails between their legs, pony up to vote for his legislation.

After taking over an Alliance Party that was bitterly divided and going nowhere in the polls in 2002, Harper fashioned a remarkable ascent. He led the drive to unify the right, he won the leadership of the new party and turned it into a contender. He led it to victory in 2006 and again in 2008. Without having another party to partner with, he led one of the longest-running minority governments the country had seen. How many other Conservative leaders had ever started from so far back and made that kind of progress?

The foremost task of any Tory leader is to advance the cause of conservatism. With his triumphs over the Liberals and his steps towards creating a new conservative order, Stephen Harper had clearly advanced the cause and could be considered a Conservative success story.

HIS SUCCESS DERIVED more from taking down opponents than from expanding his own party's support. He was better as a basher than a builder. He won with 36 percent of the vote in 2006 but by mid-2010 he was below that level. He had remained near the mid-thirties throughout all his time in office. In terms of cumulative numbers, this ranked his government among the least popular in the country's history. More political parties were in play during his tenure than at some other stages of history, and this perhaps explained some of the shortfall. But several other factors contributed to the compara-tively poor standing. Harper was unable to emotionally connect; he displayed a vindictiveness, a penchant for seizing the moral low ground, and, given his ideological proclivities, was unable to provide the big-tent appeal of the old Tory parties that had won big majorities in the past.

In terms of concrete conservative policy advances, his results were middling. Once again, his accomplishments had more to do with taking down the Liberal edifice than building one of his own. He had defined his approach as incrementalist, and he held to that design. "On policy," observed Tom Flanagan, "there just haven't been many big wins."

Economically, Harper's GST cuts were crowd-pleasers that scored politically but were hardly comforting for the long-range fiscal health of the country. His government was not to blame for the onset of the recession, nor was it to be overly credited for leading the country out of it. Global forces were the catalysts on both counts. But his govern-ment's politically motivated, pre-recession spending was not in keep-ing with conservative fiscal rectitude and was a contributing factor to the large deficit the country faced in 2010.

The upgrading of the armed forces was a Harper achievement of consequence. Progress in the war effort in Afghanistan was at best halting, however, and failed to meet the hopes of a prime minister who, with full-throated faith, pushed for two mission extensions. The support for the armed forces dovetailed with the government's drive for law and order. The Conservatives' anti-crime package and their enthusiasm for jail-building were greeted with disdain by criminologists but scored points with their ideological base.

Harper raised the profile of Canada's North while pushing the case for Arctic sovereignty. On climate change, his record was lamentable, with the government spending most of its four years in a holding pattern. Health care and education were not big priorities for the Conservatives. On immigration, efforts were made to streamline the system and the refugee backlog was being addressed.

In its achievement log the government could also include the granting of nation status to the Québécois, the apology to the Native peoples on residential schools, corporate tax reductions, the softwood lumber accord, and the Haitian earthquake rescue effort.

By mid-2010, Harper had been in office almost the same length of time as the Pearson minority, which endured from 1963 to 1968. Though hounded daily by the Tory tornado, John Diefenbaker, Pearson was able to post a record of legislative achievement of greater magnitude. It included a new Canadian flag, the unification of the armed services, the Canada Pension Plan, the Canada Assistance Plan, medicare legislation, a new immigration act, a doubling of external aid, a guaranteed minimum income plan for seniors, the foundations of a bilingual public service, the abolition of capital punishment for a trial period, the establishment of the Order of Canada, the Economic Council of Canada, the Company of Young Canadians, collective bargaining for the civil service, the liberalization of divorce laws, a new labour code, and the beginnings of constitutional reform.

But while Harper was posting no such comparable record of achievement on policy, his impact on the culture of the country was telling. His conservatism had become amply evident with the focus he brought to bear on family values, law and order, pride in the armed forces, the great north, the sport of hockey, lower taxation, the monarchy. He was often criticized for being an incrementalist, for having no vision, but it was all about the true north, strong and free.

Though he didn't put it in so many words, his idea of Canada harkened back to the era of the 1950s. With his straight-guy persona, his social conservatism, his giving free rein to the justice department to chase down the bad guys, he was trying to put in place a more puritan-styled ethic. As his associates testified, he hated what Trudeau had done with all that "hippie b.s." He believed Canada was a better place before the 1960s when Quebec, the most leftish province, took over the agenda and a series of prime ministers from that province set the country on a welfare-state course. When Harper came to power it was someone else's turn, finally, and he was determined to undo the damage.

As well as any major policy turns, a leader need be judged on his impact on the conscience of the country. In less than five years Harper's impact was being felt in ways other prime ministers hadn't registered in double that amount of time.

The ledger, with its successes and lack thereof, had to be assessed in the context of Harper's minority situation, one that often saw policy-making and long-range planning take a back seat to survival politics. It had to be assessed also in the context of the great reserves of good fortune he drew on. Playing right into his hands were the broad trendlines of the times—the post-9/11 effect, the fracturing of the left, the conservative turn of an aging population, the media trend to the right, the economic ascendancy of the western provinces, the loss of leverage of Quebec. In Canada, the times augured well for a conservative renaissance.

At the same time Harper benefited from great breaks, both in his rise to power and while in power. They included the crash of the Tory Party at their 2004 leadership convention; the dearth of competition for the Conservative leadership prize; one of the biggest scandals in Liberal Party history; the stunning RCMP intervention in the 2006 election campaign. In power, the fortune continued with Stéphane Dion's long-shot victory as Liberal leader, his interview mishap to close the 2008 campaign, his strategic blunders in the coalition crisis. Harper also benefited from an acquiescent governor general, from the early stumbles of Michael Ignatieff, from the timing of the calamity in Haiti, and from conservative media owners rising to the occasion for him.

GIVEN THE NATURE OF HIS GOVERNANCE, many would find it strange that the gods of fortune kept smiling on Stephen Harper. He amassed executive power on an unprecedented scale and often used it in a manner more befitting a despot than a democrat. "Gangster politics," someone called it. Or, peace, order, and hood government.

He had campaigned on a promise of accountability, but those who knew him realized that openness was not in his DNA. Driven by the insecurities of a minority, the constraints of a town painted Liberal for thirteen years, and his own inordinate craving for power, Harper imposed an ironclad system of control aimed at bringing the nation's capital to heel. Showing no respect for the conventions or the checks and balances of the system, he let his thirst for control get out of control.

He put in place an exhaustive vetting system that required virtually all government communications to be approved by his office or the neighbouring Privy Council Office. Nothing in the annals of Canadian governance was comparable to this degree of censorship.

He defied the will of Parliament by refusing to produce documents, asserting, in effect, that his power was sovereign. He relented only when the Speaker issued a ruling that put him in his place.

He padlocked Parliament on two occasions—out of desperate political motivation in one instance and crass political advantage in the other.

In a variety of punitive ways, he moved against NGOs, agencies, watchdog groups, and semi-independent tribunals that stood in his way. He fired their directors, stacked their boards with partisans, sued them, or closed them down entirely.

His government impeded the access-to-information system, one of the most important tools of democracy, in such a way that the information commissioner was left to wonder whether the system could even survive.

He restricted or attempted to restrict media access to a degree journalists in the nation's capital had seldom, if ever, seen.

With hostile tactics he sought to make parliamentary committees dysfunctional so that they couldn't challenge him.

The historian William Christian once observed that parliamentary democracy is what you can get away with. This prime minister clearly took that message to heart.

Having passed a law mandating fixed election dates, he found that it didn't suit his purposes and proceeded to unfix the fixed date.

To cripple opposition parties, his Conservatives came up with new attack strategies, including making a bid to strip them of public funding, using pre-writ attack ads, cheating in campaign debates, and resorting to lawsuits.

After campaigning throughout his political career against patronage and an appointed Senate, Harper made a raft of patronage appointments to give his party the most seats in the upper chamber.

He took on the military, muzzling the popular Rick Hillier. He took on the Supreme Court, spurning a ruling on Omar Khadr and issuing criticisms of soft sentences, prompting a rebuke from a former chief justice.

THE MARCH OF AUDACITIES in Harper's bid to establish control (see the Notes on pages 287 and 288 for a more complete list) never stopped. It was astonishing to behold. If the hallmark of democracy, as has been said, is the toleration of dissent, the Conservative government was a embarrassment to the word.

Harper circumvented the conventions of democracy so much that academics talked in terms of his trying to construct his own constitutional framework. Errol Mendes, one of the country's prominent constitutional scholars, went so far as to allege that Harper's "abuse of executive power is tilting towards totalitarian government and away from the foundations of democracy and the rule of law on which this country was founded." William Johnson, who had written a fair-minded biography of Harper, now concluded that the prime minister had "subverted Canadian democracy." Tom Flanagan was still supportive of Harper, but he determined that he had gone too far. "The control stuff was often too much for me when I was there," he said, "and I remain convinced that he overdoes it."

To Jack Layton, the wedge politics, which Conservatives readily admitted to employing, were what Karl Rove had used in electing George W. Bush. "It's a style designed to win by dividing," said Layton. "It's divide and conquer. It's wrong, and it's certainly not in the Canadian character. But Harper is trying to change the Canadian character, to have more people divided against one another, and I find it reprehensible."

Dictatorial control requires the stifling of dissent—the erasure or the limiting of the checks and balances in the system. Harper's success in his first years was not just in pulverizing the Liberal Party.

His more exceptional accomplishment was in the way he asserted control over the levers of power. In his drive for control, his foremost priority, as Flanagan discovered, was information control. It's why the relationship between the two men essentially ended when Flanagan wrote his book *Harper's Team*. It divulged too much information about his operation. It violated Harper's obsession with control.

Information control became the focus of a major controversy in July 2010 when Harper brought in a measure to make the mandatory census voluntary. It was a sleeper story that unexpectedly exploded on him, much like the culture cuts in Quebec in the 2008 election. Harper waited until the House adjourned for the summer to bring in his census measure, figuring he could slip it in quietly. There was no quiet. The elites recoiled. In the knowledge economy, so much was dependent on reliable census data that it was senseless, they argued, to do this. Enormous pressure was put on Harper to reverse his decision, but by the beginning of August he was holding firm.

Many were mystified as to what was behind the move. Paul Saurette, the University of Ottawa political studies professor, advanced the theory that over the decades Liberals in Ottawa had created an octopus-like configuration of bureaucracies that mined statistical data and kept piling on social programs to address society's inequalities.

Big government was the result and empirical data was a source and, therefore, for Harper-styled Conservatives, empirical data was the enemy. Sophisticated research too often got in the way of ideology. The work of Statistics Canada was not in the government's interest.

The theory would sound farfetched were it not for the many other examples of similar types of information-suppressing activity by the Harper government. These included the justice department's habitual interdiction of experts' studies; the obstructing of the access-to-information process; the approach to climate change research, one which included the shutting down of websites within and outside government; the pervasive vetting system; the concealing of a report contradicting the government's position on the long-gun registry; and a range of other information-control measures.

Former prime minister Paul Martin alleged after the move against the census that Harper was in the process of dumbing down Canada. The less the people knew, the easier it was to pull the wool over their eyes. Stéphane Dion had suggested that the prime minister was at heart a Straussian. Harper's activities were lending a modicum of credibility to the notion.

In the Saurette analysis, Harper wanted to limit not only access to information but also the credibility of information. His advisers had noted when Harper came to power that his minority status, in combination with an Ottawa infrastructure dominated by Liberal sympathizers, posed an extraordinary challenge. There was a degree of paranoia among the newcomers, a condition that can lead to excessive responses, especially when the man at the top is of a suspicious nature to begin with.

The excesses left much of the capital prostrate before him. Checks and balances? Stephen Harper weakened them all. He weakened the public service through the vetting system, his own party through the garrison structure, the media by limiting access, the NGOs and agencies by dismissals and intimidation, parliamentary committees by dysfunctional tactics, the Liberal Party through browbeating, and Parliament through extortion and prorogations.

As a strongman prime minister, he was beyond compare. He made previous alleged dictators like Jean Chrétien look like welterweights. It was no small wonder that Canadians feared what he might do with a majority government. With that kind of power he could establish a hegemony the likes of which Canadians could not imagine.

THE CENTRAL QUESTION as Harper moved towards another election campaign was whether his excesses would be his doing or his undoing. If he continued to prosper through his authoritarian methods, the frightening postulate that the way to succeed in a democracy was to suffocate democracy would find vindication.

Much of Harper's attempts at building an imperial prime ministership had proceeded without public backlash. But there were signs, with his prorogation of Christmas 2009 and with the reaction on the census, that Canadians were becoming wise to it. Polls rated his degree of secrecy and his control fixation as among the voters' deepest objections to him. But it was far from certain whether a large enough segment of the population was awakening in time.

On occasion, Harper was shrewd enough to moderate his policy stances and soften his authoritarian bent. His time in office had broadened his perspective, particularly in foreign affairs, and it seemed possible that a maturing Harper would embrace higher standards of governance. The greater likelihood, however, was that his callous instincts would prevail because they were what was bred in the bone. Over the years, several advisers had gone to him with the message that he could not continue to treat the democracy this way, that if he were to show some generosity of spirit and respect for the system, he would readily increase his standing. It didn't work. Harper could put up with being called a control freak. He didn't appear stung by the fact that while the people respected his abilities, they withheld respect for his character.

His players talked enthusiastically of divide-and-conquer strategies. As cover for abuse of power they argued that they held only a minority, that other governments engaged in similar activities, that politics was a blood sport. The rationales satisfied them. They appeared untroubled by the degree of cynicism.

So long as it was working—and in many respects it was—the downgrading of democracy would proceed.

For Stephen Harper the end justified the means, almost any means. It was what troubled so many Canadians about him. He was caught up in his own internal war. The forces of old grievances and narrow ideology pulled him in one direction. The forces of broader enlightenment pulled him in the other. The former won too many of the battles.

He was one of the more talented Canadian political leaders to come along in decades. His range of knowledge, the precision of his mind, his degree of discipline, his capacity to strategize, to work his way through whatever maze stood before him, was of an unusually high standard.

He was a leader who was capable of triumphing on the high road but who, a victim of his brooding resentments, too often surrendered himself to the low.

In his holding to such a cynical view of governance, lessons of history were to be borne in mind. Before this prime minister, many leaders paid a steep price for exceeding their bounds of authority. They would have done well to recall the adage of the philosopher Heraclitus: "Character is fate."

N O T E S

Each entry is preceded by a page number or range that indicates where text references are located. Some passages in the text were compiled with the assistance of numerous media reports, many of which are not footnoted.

Chapter One: A Different Conservative

2   Brison meeting with Harper: Author interview with Scott Brison.

3   Visceral hatred: Author interviews with David Emerson and Keith Martin.

4   PM as "sonofabitch": Email exchange with Ian Brodie. He was making a point as follows: "What's the constant theme of Harper's political career? He's tough. Can be a sonofabitch. But the constant theme is he actually is pretty good at bringing people together."

4   "This was about destruction": Author interview with Rod Love.

5   Allan MacEachen quotation: Peter C. Newman, *The Distemper of Our Times* (Toronto: McClelland & Stewart, 1968).

5   "Emotionless robot": Gerry Nicholls, *Loyal to the Core* (Freedom Press Canada Inc., 2009).

6   "He hates the Liberal Party": Author interview with Keith Beardsley.

Chapter Two: The Luck of the Draw

8   "If there was a social event": Author interview with Goldy Hyder.

9   "I found him persuasive": Tom Flanagan, *Harper's Team* (Montreal/Kingston: McGill-Queen's University Press, 2007).

9   Commitment to principle: Author interview with John Weissenberger.

9–10   The account of Harper as a silent co-author and the PMO attempt to block the Flanagan book are based on an interview with Tom Flanagan and an email exchange with Ian Brodie.

11   Fat MP's pension: Author interview with Goldy Hyder.

11   "Stephen had difficulty accepting": Preston Manning, *Think Big* (Toronto: McClelland & Stewart, 2002).

11–13   The account of Harper at the National Citizens coalition is based an interview with Gerry Nicholls as well as Nicholls's book, *Loyal to the Core*.

12   Harper on Don Newman's show: Author interview with Don Newman.

15   One day over lunch: Author interview with Rod Love.

15   "The impact of that Orchard deal": Author interview with Scott Brison.

16   "Massive leg-up to Lord": Email exchange with Ian Brodie.

Chapter Three: Enemies Everywhere

19   "You know what it was like": Author interview with Bruce Carson.

20   "I want to apologize": Author interview with Keith Beardsley, as are other Beardsley references in chapter.

21   The characterization of Harper as an outsider and introvert is from interviews with John Weissenberger and Phil Von Finckenstein, a former press aide to Preston Manning.

21   "He doesn't repose trust easily": Author interview with Tom Flanagan.

24   "They surrounded my goddamn bus": Author interview with a newspaper editor who wished that his name not be disclosed.

24   "If there was one millimetre of light": Author interview with John Weissenberger.

25   "He really was like that store owner": Author interview with Tim Powers.

26   "One is that you are older than I am": Author interview with Bruce Carson.

Chapter Four: Promises of Openness

28   "When a government starts trying to cancel dissent": The Canadian Press, April 18, 2005.

28–30   Development of accountability program from author interviews with Duff Conacher and Mark Cameron.

30–31   Zaccardelli and Shawinigate: Lawrence Martin, *Iron Man: The Defiant Reign of Jean Chrétien* (Toronto: Penguin Canada, 2003).

31–32   Election financing scheme: from interviews with Duff Conacher and Keith Beardsley and reports in *The Hill Times*.

33   "I think it's fair to say": Author interview with David Emerson.

35–37 Garth Turner saga: Garth Turner, *Sheeple: Caucus Confidential in Stephen Harper's Ottawa* (Toronto: Key Porter, 2009) and email exchange with Ian Brodie.

Chapter Five: A Day in a Life

39–46 A Day in a Life: Compiled from author interviews with Mark Cameron, Keith Beardsley, Bruce Carson, Ian Brodie, David Emerson, Paul Dewar, and other PMO and PCO officials.

Chapter Six: The Incrementalist Approach

47 "Harper and his advisers": Author interview with Bruce Carson.

47 "Small conservative reforms": Tom Flanagan, *Harper's Team.*

50 "But the problem": Author interview with David Emerson.

51 Harper family background: Michael LeBlanc, radio broadcast, CBC New Brunswick.

52 Stand Up for Canada campaign: Author interviews with PMO officials.

53 "We want to see less of you": Rick Hillier, *A Soldier First* (Toronto: Harper-Collins Publishers, 2009).

54 "The fundamental lesson": Author interview with Tim Murphy.

54–56 Comparing Harper and Martin styles: Author interview with David Emerson.

Chapter Seven: The Control Fixation

57 Tushingham episode: Compiled from media reports.

58–59 Message Event Proposal: Author interviews with Keith Beardsley and other PMO officials. Mike Blanchfield and Jim Bronskill provide a detailed account of MEPs in a Canadian Press report, June 6, 2010.

60 The vetting system: Email exchange with Ian Brodie.

61 "I think there had been under Chrétien": Author interview with Mark Cameron.

62 "If a story broke": Author interview with Keith Beardsley.

63 "He was very clear": Author interview with Don Boudria.

63–64 Finley and Byrne: Compiled from author interviews with PMO officials and Tom Flanagan.

66–67 Harper on media: Author interviews with John Weissenberger and Craig Oliver.

69   Gwyn Morgan episode: MPs reject Harper's accountability appointment, CBC News, May 16, 2006.

70–71   John Baird and Joe Fontana exchange at bar: Author at the scene.

Chapter Eight: The Green Games

74   "Mulroney called Stephen": Author interview with Tom Flanagan.

74   Layton presents Harper with book: Author interview with Jack Layton.

76   "What really pisses me off": Author interview with Bruce Carson.

77   "Let's not be boy scouts": Author interview with Mark Cameron.

79   Harper on foreign affairs: Author interview with Weissenberger.

80   "You would want something done": Author interview with Keith Beardsley.

83   "Some of the characters in there": Author interview with David Emerson.

84–87   Chong's split with Harper: Author interview with PMO and cabinet officials.

86   Chrétien and Trudeau: Lawrence Martin, *Iron Man* (Toronto: Penguin Canada, 2003).

87   "Look, I've got to suck up to Quebec": Author interview with Rod Love.

88–89   Income trust decision: Interviews with Tom Flanagan, James Rajotte, and PMO officials.

Chapter Nine: Attack and Obstruct

91–93   Reasoning behind Conservative attack ads compiled from interviews with PCO officials.

93   "The Liberal Party portrayed Preston Manning": Author interview with Kory Teneycke.

96   "It's not like Harper": Email exchange with Ian Brodie.

97–98   Secret manual on parliamentary committees: Don Martin's scoop, "Tories have book on political wrangling," appeared in the *National Post*, May 7, 2007. Account compiled also from interviews with James Rajotte, Keith Beardsley, and Mark Cameron.

99–104 Afghan detainees chronology compiled from daily media reports.

103   "I am not a bully": Author interview with Stéphane Dion not expressly for this book but for a column in *The Globe and Mail*.

Chapter Ten: Tory Trendlines

109   "Keith, I can't believe that you …": Author interview with Keith Martin.

110–111 Harper's patriotism, compiled from interviews with John Weissenberger, James Rajotte, and Keith Beardsley.

113 "We were convinced": Author email exchange with Ian Brodie. The chief of staff's certainty on the point about Harper being able to trounce the opposition on a war election was not consistent with polls at the time showing the population evenly divided or somewhat against the war.

114–117 Account of Mulroney–Schreiber affair is from author interviews with PMO officials and Mulroney associates as well as media reports.

117 Description of attempted disciplining of Michael Behiels is taken from interviews with Behiels and LeBreton for a column that I wrote for *The Globe and Mail.*

118 "I must say I was taken aback": "Former chief justice of Canada accuses PM of trying to 'muzzle' the judiciary," Janice Tibbetts, Canwest News Service, February 19, 2007.

118–119 Account of Paillé Report is from media reporting on the issue and author interviews with pollsters.

Chapter Eleven: The Concentration of Power

120–121 Description of R.B. Bennett: John Boyko, *Bennett: The Rebel Who Challenged and Changed a Nation* (Toronto: Key Porter Books, 2010).

121 For an account of the evolution of the overconcentration of power in Canada, read Donald Savoie's *Court Government and the Collapse of Accountability* (Toronto: University of Toronto Press, 2008).

122 "The tough guys were the most successful": Author interview with Bruce Carson.

122 "Well, what's the alternative?": Author interview with John Weissenberger.

123 "I'll tell you what I think about Harper": Author interview with Stéphane Dion.

123–125 Account of Harper's philosophical tendencies is taken from interviews with Keith Martin, Sheila Drury, Gerry Nicholls, Michael Behiels, John Weissenberger, Tom Flanagan, and Stéphane Dion.

125–126 Harper's style compared to Mulroney's: Author interview with Lowell Murray.

126 "Harper runs the tightest ship in the history of the party": Author interview with Rod Love.

128–129 Linda Keen controversy compiled from media accounts and interviews with PMO officials.

131   John Baird presided over a muzzling operation of exceptional scope: "Muzzle Placed on Federal Scientists," *The Vancouver Sun,* February 1, 2008. Related reference to environment department's media operation— "putting journalists through a Soviet-styled monitoring maze"—is not entirely facetious. Having been a Moscow correspondent before the fall of Communism, I can report that the vetting system under the Harper government does have similarities.

133   "I think history will be far less kind": Author interview with Kory Teneycke.

134   "Justice went ballistic and Indian Affairs …": Email exchange with Ian Brodie.

135–137 Cadman affair account is taken from interviews with PMO officials, Tom Flanagan, and media accounts.

Chapter Twelve: Damage Control

138–139 Harper and the PCO: Author interview with Gregg Fyffe.

141   "There was a fair amount of difficulty there": Author interview with David Emerson.

141   "In short, I did not leak it": Email exchange with Ian Brodie. Travers's column, "Signs point to PMO in NAFTA leak," appeared in the *Toronto Star* on May 27, 2008.

142   "Anything particularly conspiratorial": Author interview with David Emerson.

143   "Well, I can tell you there is no way": "Auditor balks at vetting by PMO," Bruce Campion-Smith, *Toronto Star,* May 1, 2008.

143–144 Keystone Kops saga compiled from media reports and author interview with Keith Boag.

144   "I figured most of the dirty work": Author interview with Keith Beardsley.

146   "If there had not been six seconds of videotape": Author interview with Kory Teneycke.

148   "The attacks are misleading and a lie": Conservatives' use of pre-writ advertising is analyzed in Tom Flanagan's paper, "Political Communication and the Permanent Campaign."

151   "What matters is that we get changes": Author interview with Elizabeth May.

152–154 Account of changes at PMO is compiled from author interviews with Kory Teneycke, Keith Beardsley, Mark Cameron, other PMO officials, and lobbyist David Angus.

Chapter Thirteen: Election Turmoil

156   "There's a burly security guard": Interview with Paul Szabo. Also "Security escorts Tory official from Commons hearing," Glen McGregor, Canwest News Service, August 11, 2008.

157   "But he came back and called one": Author interview with Bruce Carson.

157   "I remember sitting down with him …": Author interview with Jack Layton.

161   An edict from the PCO virtually shut down Ottawa: See "Tories tighten muzzle on campaign," *Ottawa Citizen*, September 20, 2008.

162–165 Quebec culture drama is compiled from author interviews with Tory caucus members, PMO officials, and media accounts.

164   "I think it's fair to say": Author interview with Kory Teneycke.

164   "He's got a pretty solid pack of goons": Author interview with New Democrat Charlie Angus.

165   The arts community has a greater political influence in Quebec: "Tories' arts cuts spark ire in Quebec," Chantal Hébert, *Toronto Star*, August 29, 2008.

165–167 Allegations of Harper cheating in debates: Author interviews with Elizabeth May and Kory Teneycke.

168   "They increased spending by 20 percent": Author interview with Scott Brison.

168   "He was preparing for that recession from the day he took over": Author interview with Keith Beardsley. For the roller-coaster ride of quotations on the question of the recession and deficits, see "Quotes then and now: Harper, Flaherty," Canwest News Service, November 28, 2008.

169–170 Mishap with Dion interview: Author interviews with Scott Brison, Kory Teneycke, and other PMO officials. Also: "A Dion gaffe that shows Harper's mean streak," Don Martin, *National Post*, October 9, 2008.

Chapter Fourteen: Surviving the Coalition

175–176 Harper's message from Peru: Interview with a PMO official.

176   "Everything becomes survival and tactics": Author interview with Tom Flanagan for a *Globe and Mail* column.

178–179 Brian Topp's contacts with Tories: Brian Topp, *How We Almost Gave the Tories the Boot* (Toronto: James Lorimer and Company, 2010).

181   "That was the moment the whole thing turned on": Author interview with Teneycke.

183   "Harper was prepared": Interview with Jack Layton.

185   "I'm waiting for my leader": Author interview with Scott Brison.

188   "Well, among them, the Queen": Author interview with Kory Teneycke.

188–189 Lorraine Weinrib's analysis saying that Harper was trying to create his own constitutional framework is from her essay, "Prime Minister Harper's Parliamentary Time-out," which appears in *Parliamentary Democracy in Crisis* (Toronto: University of Toronto Press, 2009, edited by Peter H. Russell and Lorne Sossin).

189   "I'll put it this way": Author interview with Ed Schreyer for a column that appeared in *The Globe and Mail.*

190   "We totally misjudged how Harper ...": Author interview with Ed Broadbent.

Chapter Fifteen: The Keynesian Way

192   "Politics and the military become kind of fused": Description of the garrison party is primarily from an interview with Tom Flanagan. Flanagan came up with the phrase, one that is so apt in capturing the Conservative Party under Stephen Harper.

193   "It is effectively a battle on a daily basis": Author interview with Tim Powers.

197   Background on relations between Canadian and American leaders: Lawrence Martin, *The Presidents and the Prime Ministers* (Toronto: Doubleday, 1982).

200   "Nothing short of breathtaking": See "Repatriation Games—Canada's government doesn't compare well to Britain in dealing with Guantanamo Bay detainees," Wesley Wark, *Ottawa Citizen,* February 22, 2010. See also "What the think-thinkers don't get," Dan Gardner, *Ottawa Citizen,* February 24, 2010.

201   "They identified who gets in these photos": Author interview with NDP caucus member Charlie Angus.

203   "I think he is fairly mainstream": Author interview with David Emerson.

Chapter Sixteen: Law and Order

210   "Raw wedge politics": "Tories ignore taxpayer-funded crime research," Bruce Cheadle, The Canadian Press, March 14, 2010.

210   "Hey, do the facts matter here?" Email exchange with Ian Brodie.

211   The problem with the media: Lorrie Goldstein, *Toronto Sun,* June 20, 2010.

211   But the department couldn't furnish such data: John Geddes's report, "Are We Really Soft on Crime," appeared in *Maclean's*, November 16, 2009.

212   "It is painful for me to write …": Conrad Black's analysis, which appeared in the *National Post*, was particularly unwelcome for the Harperites. Black, the founder of the *Post*, had served more than two years in prison and wrote on the subject with conviction.

212   Canadians had become more conservative on law-and-order issues: Pollsters couldn't agree on whether Canadians were becoming more conservative in the broad sense, but one effect of 9/11 they certainly agreed on was that on crime they had indeed moved to the right.

212   "Of the twenty-one law-and-order bills": Senator James Cowan's analysis appeared in the *National Post* on March 3, 2010.

212   "Eighteen died on the Order Paper": For Senator Cowan's demolition of Rob Nicholson, see "Soft on truth, not tough on crime," James Cowan, March 3, 2010.

213   Much had changed since 1993: See "Manning's Reformers Fade Away," John Ivison, *National Post*, February 23, 2010.

214   "I grew up in a world": Author interview with Maryantonett Flumian.

215   "Why the hell doesn't the prime minister do something about this?" Anecdote told to author by Kory Teneycke.

216   Lynch was respected by his staff at the Privy Council Office: "Top bureaucrat Lynch bids adieu," L. Ian Macdonald, *The Montreal Gazette*, May 9, 2009.

218   "I never intended to stay for a long time": Author interview with Kory Teneycke.

219   "I can tell you every funding program across the government is being politicized": See "Bureaucrats objected to government ad campaign," Bruce Cheadle, The Canadian Press, October 8, 2009.

220   Conservatives had directed more money to their own ridings: For anyone witnessing the anger of Conservatives in lashing out at the Chrétien Liberals for steering grant monies to their own ridings a decade earlier, this was a particularly ironic development.

221   Landon episode: "Tory candidate dumped for frank TV comments," *Toronto Star*, September 29, 2009.

Chapter Seventeen: Padlocking Parliament

227–229 The account of Kenney and new Canadians is based on interviews with PMO officials and Liberal Herb Dhaliwal. See also Kevin Libin's profile of Kenney in the *National Post* on March 27, 2009, and Joe Friesen's report in *The Globe and Mail,* January 29, 2010.

229 Firearms report: For detailed account, see "Key gun-registry report was withheld: documents," Dean Beeby, The Canadian Press, May 30, 2010. See also "Tories sniped at firearm data," February 22, 2010.

231 As a diplomat, he was considered conscientious, well-mannered: See "Richard Colvin: Portrait of a whistleblower," Thonda MacCharles, *Toronto Star,* November 21, 2009.

237 Harper's proroguing set back or sent away legislation: For a detailed account see "Kill Bill," Andrew Mayeda, *Ottawa Citizen,* January 9, 2010.

238 Before Harper, it had happened only once: Harper's prorogation is put in historical perspective in "In a (parliamentary) league of our own," Richard Foot, *Ottawa Citizen,* January 17, 2010.

239 "The cabinet ministers developed their own policies": Author interview and correspondence with Jim Cross.

241 The Liberals held a series of hearings on the major issues: "Watchdogs describe coming under attack by Conservative government," Colin Freeze, *The Globe and Mail,* March 8, 2010.

231–241 The Colvin saga and related developments are compiled from media reports and author interviews with PMO officials.

Chapter Eighteen: True Colours

244 "I see a whole bunch of Elsie Waynes": Author interview with Scott Brison.

246 *The Armageddon Factor:* For analysis, see "Religious right is back in the spotlight," Frances Russell, *Winnipeg Free Press,* May 19, 2010. As an example of the way in which the right was flexing its muscle in Canadian journalism, Russell, a trenchant critic of Harper's authoritarian ways, was being pressured by her editors to ease off.

247 "A social conservative echo chamber": Author interview with Tom Flanagan. Darrel Reid left the PMO in 2010. See also "A Risky Right Turn," Michael Den Tandt, QMI Agency, May 21, 2010.

248 The press and the public were missing something: Author interviews with John Weissenberger and Mark Cameron.

251   Uproar over culture war: The controversy was triggered by an interview
        Graves gave the author for a *Globe and Mail* column. See "The Pollster,
        the senator and the forces of darkness," Dan Leger, *The Halifax Chron-
        icle-Herald,* May 3, 2010, and "Cranking up the culture war," Susan
        Riley, *Ottawa Citizen,* April 30, 2010.

257   "This is rolling over environmental assessment": Author interview with
        Elizabeth May. Also "Budget bill dare goes step too far, 'This turns legis-
        lative process into a farce,'" John Ivison, *National Post,* May 26, 2010.

260   Fake lake: The story, which caused the government many headaches, was
        first revealed by *Sun* columnist Greg Weston. When Kory Teneycke, the
        former Harper spokesman, took over running the Sun chain, Weston was
        out of his job as columnist.

Chapter Nineteen: A Question of Character

267   "On policy, there just haven't been many big wins": Author interview
        with Tom Flanagan.

268   Accomplishments in Lester Pearson's minority: A more complete list can
        be found in Peter C. Newman's *The Distemper of Our Times* (Toronto:
        McClelland & Stewart, 1968).

272   The march of audacities: It included the following: The in-and-out
        money shuffle. The David Emerson appointment. The unprecedented
        vetting system. Naming an unelected senator to cabinet. The Tushing-
        ham censorship. The elimination of the Access to Information database.
        The scrapping of the appointments commission. The Cadman affair. The
        nixing of the Court Challenges Program. NAFTA-gate. The misinfor-
        mation campaign on Afghan detainees. Reversals on half of the prom-
        ised accountability measures. The secret handbook on how to obstruct
        committees. The launching of personal attack ads between elections.
        The smearing of opponents for being anti-Israeli and not supporting the
        troops. The attempt to censor publication of a book by Tom Flanagan.
            In addition: Attacking Elections Canada. Attacking Dalton McGuinty
        as the small man of Confederation. Declaring Ontario the last place to
        invest. Ordering police to remove journalists from a hotel lobby to
        prevent coverage of a Tory caucus meeting. Labelling Louise Arbour
        a national disgrace. Attempting to discipline an academic for criticiz-
        ing the government. Making a bid to vet even the press releases of the
        auditor general. Scripting supporters' calls to radio talk jocks. Blocking

information on cabinet ministers' use of government jets. Hiding justice department studies on crime.

In addition: Belittling gala-goers. Releasing an online attack ad featuring a bird defecating on the opposition leader's head. Plagiarizing the Australian prime minister's speech. Hiding a firearms report to prevent embarrassment on the gun registry. Downgrading Diane Ablonczy for her support of gay pride week. Smearing the bank executive Ed Clark as a Liberal hack for his statement on the deficit. The Rights and Democracy fiasco. Attempting to strip political parties of public funding. Alleging that the opposition leader has no right to form a government. Declaring Brian Mulroney *persona non grata*. Slashing the budget of the Parliamentary Budget Officer.

In addition: Putting Tory logos on government cheques for stimulus funding. Withholding details of stimulus funding. Granting stimulus funding disproportionately to Tory ridings. Firing the nuclear agency head Linda Keen. Halting Peter Tinsley's probe on Afghan detainees. Ousting Paul Kennedy from the Commission for Public Complaints Against the RCMP. Smearing Richard Colvin. Defying Parliament's right to documents. Padlocking Parliament. Snuffing out democratic challenge to MP Rob Anders. Barring cabinet staffers from testifying before committees. The record-breaking omnibus budget bill. The move on Statistics Canada.

272   "It's a style designed to win by dividing": Author interview with Jack Layton.

273   An octopus-like configuration: Paul Saurette's analysis appeared in *The Mark*, July 23, 2010.

INDEX

North American Free Trade
    Agreement (NAFTA), 140–42,
    197
Novak, Ray, 152

O

Obama, Barack, 108, 138–41,
    149, 150, 172, 194, 201, 206,
    263
    visit to Canada, 196–99
O'Connor, Gordon, 53, 79,
    100–4, 113, 232
Oda, Bev, 203
oil spill (Gulf of Mexico), 257
Oliver, Craig, 66–67
Ontario, 129–30
Orchard, David, 15
Osbaldeston, Gordon, 23
Ottawa Citizen, 238
Owen, Stephen, 69

P

Pacific Scandal, 238
Page, Kevin, 221–22
Paillé, Daniel, 118
Paillé Report, 118–19
Paradis, Christian, 253
Pardy, Gar, 201
Parks Canada, 58
Parliamentary Budget Office,
    221–22
party financing reform, 174–79
patriotism, 52, 110–11, 269

Pearson, Lester, 25, 46, 51, 67,
    121, 206
    achievements of, 268
Pelletier, Jean, 60, 122
Powers, Tim, 25, 193
Prefontaine, Alain, 255
Prentice, Jim, 79, 133, 263
Priorities and Planning
    Committee, 41
Privy Council Office, 42, 143,
    218–21, 230, 254. *See also*
    bureaucracy
Progressive Conservative Party, 2,
    13, 14
    merger with Alliance Party,
        15–17, 73
    and new breed of
        Conservative, 214
prorogation of Parliament,
    186–89, 236–43, 271
psychographics, 94
Public Appointments
    Commission, 68–69
Putin, Vladimir, 42, 239

Q

Quebec
    and arts and culture cuts,
        162–65
    diminishing influence of,
        107–8
    nation status for, 83–87
Quebecor Media, 250
Queen's visit, 263–64